AF662248

A-Z
ADVERTISING

A-Z ADVERTISING

Alok Satsangi

CENTRUM PRESS
NEW DELHI-110002 (INDIA)

CENTRUM PRESS
H.O.: 4360/4, Ansari Road, Daryaganj,
New Delhi-110 002 (India)
Ph.: 23278000, 23261597

B.O.: No. 1015, Ist Main Road, BSK IIIrd Stage
IIIrd Phase, IIIrd Block,
Bangalore - 560 085 (India)
Tel.: 080-41723429
Visit us at: www.centrumpress.com

A-Z Advertising

© Reserved

First Edition, 2009

ISBN 978-93-80106-00-7

PRINTED IN INDIA

Printed at Salasar Imaging Systems, Delhi-110035 (India)

Contents

Preface

Advertising has very much become a part of our lives. With the market glutted with endless brands of products, the consumer is influenced largely by advertising to survive in the ruthlessly competitive market. Consequently, the profession of advertising has gained much importance and recognition in today's society. More and more students are pursuing advertising courses. there are over 160 ad agencies in our country today, and the number is escalating in geometrical progression. In spite of all these developments, there is not a single book to cater to the needs of our students at home, and they have to rely on foreign author publications. this is what spurred me on to writing this book—the first of its kind in India.

All of the chapters and commentaries show healthy tension between the more theoretical interests and dispositions of the academic community and the more applied, results-oriented interests and dispositions of real-world research. The bottom line, as the real-world participants would say, is that measuring advertising effectiveness is so complicated that, although it is both a valid, important academic topic and a consequential applied problem, neither academic researchers nor industry researchers are likely to make decisive progress without help. Instead, reliable and valid measures of advertising effectiveness are most likely to emerge from constructive criticism and mutually supportive interaction between the two camps.

Author

Chapter 1

International Communication Theory

INTERNATIONAL ADVERTISING THEORY

The purpose of this chapter is to critique current international advertising research for being uninformed about the status of theory in international communication and to suggest that international advertising research must be placed theoretically within the broader context of international communication research. Theoretically informed research should prove both more interesting and more viable to advertising researchers and practitioners. However, it may also prove more challenging because the theoretical perspective may lead to critical questions that suggest significant dilemmas that the industry itself may not care to pursue.

Critical approaches have been suggested by a number of industry and academic researchers as work that is important and useful, though not immediately practicable. My contention is that critical work will in fact prove useful to both academics and practitioners because such work is more analytical, revealing problems of process at the social and cultural levels and at the levels of individual consumers, campaigns, or advertisements. International advertising in particular, linked as it is to political and economic policy decisions, must be analyzed at a theoretically informed level.

INTERNATIONAL ADVERTISING

Outside of academia the importance of international

communication has been clearly linked with policy concerns, as policy analyst Mark Fowler suggested:

International Communications... has become an important expression of the posture of the United States toward the rest of the world, a significant aspect of our foreign policy, and a vital tool in the economic interdependence which is becoming a fact of life for all international policy. Even within academia, advertising is recognized as part of the increasing globalization of the communications industries.

Recent "mega-mergers" among advertising and marketing services companies point up how internationalized Madison Avenue, the symbolic home of advertising, has become.... Increased communication... leads to increased organization and consequently some concentration of control.... Regional and continental media organizations are playing increasingly crucial roles in international news communication.

Hachten's thesis is that free and independent journalism is a key to democratic political practices. But his very brief reference to the increasing concentration of advertising practice is suggestive because it links the growth in international advertising to political-economic and cultural concerns.

Advertising is also acknowledged in the UNESCO MacBride Report on international communication as an important major force in international communication. The MacBride Report was commissioned by UNESCO in an effort to both describe and make recommendations about the current state of mass communication globally, with special reference to transnational communication. The importance of mass media is acknowledged as being especially significant in recently independent nations; as such the report comes down heavily on the side of recommending a "more balanced flow of information, both worldwide and within individual societies". The report shows that much media content is commodified (i.e., packaged and available for sale) and furthermore that advertising supports most mass media whatever its other content. The report continues by enumerating a number of research questions: should ascertain the direct and indirect, intentional and unintentional effects of advertising and could lay the groundwork for new policy decisions, if and as required. How can commercial considerations be harmonized with broad social and cultural goals? How can any negative effects be lessened?

In terms of recommendations, the one area in which the MacBride Report includes advertising specifically is in the area titled "strengthening cultural identity." The specific recommendation is: Introduction of guidelines with respect to advertising content and the values and attitudes it fosters, in accordance with national standards and practices. Such guidelines should be consistent with national development policies and efforts to preserve national identity". The MacBride Report is of concern to advertising researchers for two reasons. First it was authored by a multinational panel and carries a certain amount of prestige among national planners and decision makers. Second, it clearly links international communication generally with international advertising, showing that the research agenda of one cannot be separated from the other. The MacBride Report critiques the disproportionate media and communications wealth of the developed world, and urges a "new international information order" within which international advertising would play a part. The report serves as a common reference point for policy makers who can influence advertising penetration within nations.

The communications industries generally are acknowledged as an area in which the success of Western cultural and economic hegemony continues, in contrast to failures of the more traditional industrial base on the one hand, and the high technology industries on the other. A Canadian academic is quoted in the *The Nation* as claiming "Other people make better cars, better electronics. Our schoolchildren are stupider, and so on. But the one thing the world envies is the miracle of Hollywood. It's very comfortable to focus on something the United States has and everybody wants". International communications scholar Schiller said that "the global push of transnational capital in the information-cultural sphere has been remarkably successful to date". He continued: No activity, national or international, is exempt from the corporate sponsor -not even, apparently, the worldwide programs of the United Nations... corporate sponsorship could be magnificently expanded from Grand Prix and Olympics events to the United Nations itself....

But it is not only U.S. television programming that carries the virus of transational corporate culture. Politics, sports, tourism, language, and business data flows transmit it and reinforce it as well.

Another example of Western (and particularly U.S.) hegemony in the communications industry is the growing attention to media-dominated political campaigns. Political advertising is an acknowledged subfield of advertising research; politicians from other cultures avail themselves of U.S. advertising talent. Thus, advertising is used to communicate about almost every facet of political-economic, social, and cultural life both within the United States and internationally. Although the Canadian academic singled out Hollywood, implying a discussion of the film industry, his comments are equally relevant in terms of U.S./Western advertising. Along with film, journalism, and publishing, advertising comprises the culture industries.

Schiller's comments suggest explicitly that communication of all sorts is effective advertising of a global economic order and a way of life. Thus, it makes little sense to separate advertising research from the broader field of mass communication research. The separation that is maintained through a number of disciplinary and bureaucratic structures is perhaps more related to the establishment of territorial expertise than it is any kind of real delineation between separate fields of practice.

Even more than in the academic literature, advertising trade literature acknowledges that the growth in international advertising is linked to political-economic developments. *Adweek* begins a cover story on *Marketing to the Year 2000: The Chameleon Decade* with the statement that "not since the colonial powers of Europe themselves cast covetous eyes at other continents has a land mass been viewed with such hungry expectation." The article continues with an analysis of what the changes in both Western Europe (EC) and Eastern Europe will mean for both markets and advertising.

Another factor that will increasingly have an impact on international advertising research is the continued interest of the so-called "Second World, " (i.e., the socialist countries) in developing freer market systems. Also of interest are political developments in South Africa in light of Nelson Mandela's release from prison, and the increased likelihood of talks between the apartheid government and the African National Congress, the impact of the Democracy Movement in China, and shifts in governments in Latin America. The fact that political and economic change is so closely linked with advertising issues also indicates that an awareness of the theoretical underpinnings of the research must be carefully articulated.

International advertising research, however, lags behind both the political debates and the advertising industry's awareness. For example, Tse, Lee, Vertinsky, and Wehrung preface their research with the question "does culture matter?". This question identifies the crux of the matter, the main problem around which the theoretical arguments within international communication research have centered. The study identifies four cultural norms by which decision making in marketing can be measured.

Similar kinds of cultural norms are also identified in Frith's American Academy of Advertising paper "Cultural Imperialism or Cultural Empiricism? A Critical Perspective" and in Frith and Frith's "The Stranger at the Gate: Western Advertising and Eastern Cultural and Communication Values." The first article is an empirical, data-based research piece; the second, a critical essay, and the third, a descriptive essay. But although written from different perspectives (positivist/culturalist) and with different goals (industry oriented/critical), all three remain uninformed of the theoretical literature in the area of international mass communication research while attempting to make contributions to an understanding of a major form of international mass communication—advertising.

The cultural norms that all three papers identify derive from Daniel Lerner's concepts regarding the modern and traditional mentalities of cosmopolites (from the West) and peasants (from the East). None of these studies, however, acknowledge Lerner as a source; the authors are apparently unaware that Lerner delineated these concepts in the early 1960s and that his perspective has been all but discredited by international communication scholars and by political-economic realities.

Lerner, writing about modernization in developing countries adopted a system of bipolar oppositions to describe the differences between the modern and the traditional. The concept of bipolar oppositions fit nicely into the development decade's political-economic thrust of growth. Culture does matter; advertising as a consciousness industry is involved in both creating culture and reflecting it. Thus, although international advertising research has an unarticulated theoretical underpinning, that unawareness of the theoretical literature leads to soft or even misleading conclusions. A review of the international advertising research confirms the lack of theoretical grounding. Although interest in international advertising as a legitimate field of inquiry is increasing, responding to the changing world economic order, the field has not turned to international communication research for its theoretical base.

I suggest that international advertising researchers must re-evaluate the usefulness of scientific discourse in understanding international advertising communication. Social-psychological research that is industry driven, will continue to yield insights into some aspects of advertising, but is limited in terms of its application to the international situation.

PARADIGMS OF INTERNATIONAL COMMUNICATION RESEARCH

There are two major, mainstream paradigms within

international communication research literature: the modernization perspective, also called the "dominant paradigm" (within which Lerner's work, mentioned earlier, falls) and the cultural imperialism perspective, also called the "new paradigm." A third perspective, postmodernism, is beginning to be applied to the study of international communication. All three have important implications for international advertising research. Each paradigm suggests its ontology or world view, its epistemology or research questions and levels of analysis, and, by implication, what sorts of answers the paradigm can yield. Thus an awareness of theoretical paradigm or perspective and an understanding of both its uses and limitations provide invaluable information to both the researcher and the "consumer" of the research (i.e., policy makers, social analysts, advertising professionals, "ordinary" consumers).

The "Dominant Paradigm"

Everett Rogers described the first dominant paradigm of international communication, which originated in the late 1950s and early 1960s, as assuming that there is a one-way flow of information from the developed to the developing worlds. International communication was conceived of as a top-down sharing from the dominant world economic powers to the underdeveloped Third World. International communication was perceived as linked to social change, both short and long term, with diffusion of innovations being one of the important models of persuasion. Much of this literature analyzed information campaigns in terms of how both information and adoption of innovations dispersed throughout communities.

To link international communication with social change (and specifically economic development), required an understanding of development in concrete terms as behavioral and psychological, introducing psychological variables (motivation, perception, emotion, attitudes) into the study of economic development along with measures of gross economic data, and operationalizing these criteria quantitatively. As Rogers suggested: "mass communication was... thought to be a very powerful and direct force for development.... a kind of magic multiplier for development..." and communication "effectiveness" could be measured by observing changes in the criteria. The key concepts in this paradigm were *growth, development,* and *modernization.*

It is perhaps not surprising that much of the international advertising research literature implicitly adopts this paradigm, although usually without acknowledging the debt. McQuail, describing the body of literature on diffusion of innovations, said: the model of information diffusion envisaged four stages: information; persuasion; decision or adoption; confirmation. The diffusionist school of thought tends to emphasize organization and planning, linearity of effect, hierarchy (of status and expertise), social structure (thus personal experience), reinforcement and feedback.

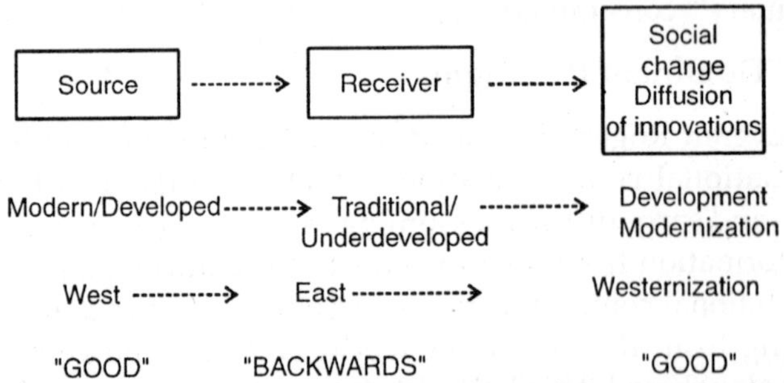

Fig. Dominant Paradigm of International Communication

It seems clear why this paradigm provides an unspoken support to much international advertising research, based as it is on a model of communication that is essentially top-down and persuasive. Also, because this is a perspective that is based on specific notions of economic development (i.e., Western capitalism and the "free market"), it is congenial to the perspective that sees advertising as simply an aspect of marketing, a relatively limited cultural form, which at most "reflects" the larger culture within which advertising is embedded.

The "New Paradigm"

The so-called dominant paradigm of international

communication research, with its focus on gross national product and per capita incomes as measures of economic success, and its emphasis on diffusion of innovations, although appropriate to a strictly market-oriented perspective, offers little insight into "reasons why"; its results are often descriptive in spite of the use of increasingly sophisticated statistical methods. The emergence of a "new paradigm" of international communication research was in part, a direct response to the lack of analytical research. Rogers described the passing of the dominant paradigm, critiquing it as ethnocentric, overly reliant on crude economic measures, unable to articulate structural variables, and generally inappropriate for the newer more complex communications needs of the mid-1970s. In essence, he suggested that culture does matter. He described the new paradigm as redefining "development" in terms of a kind of "self-development" (a cultural awareness). Along with that, the concept of international communication itself is problematized, with an emphasis on the structural and social-system level elements and impediments to communication.

Development within the newer paradigm refers to expand ing choices. Choices suggest alternatives that are then operationalized for research purposes in terms of access via networks of social roles, classes or institutions. Controling that access to choices and promoting the sharing of it according to approved guidelines became the special political concern of development.

Not without reason, the challenges to the dominant paradigm came primarily from Third World researchers and politically committed Western researchers. Thus, the newer paradigm, not tied as the earlier one was to economic growth, seems less appropriate and certainly less hospitable to advertising research. and yet, the critique of the dominant paradigm is a convincing one, especially in its acknowledgment of the importance of culture to an understanding of the issues of international communication. The UNESCO MacBride Report, which is generally sympathetic to the underlying assumptions of the newer paradigm and which is generally supportive of the Third World call for a "new international information order, " also concedes that advertising is an important part of international communication. and furthermore, the notion of development as "choice" is suggestive for advertising researchers whether industry-oriented or critical.

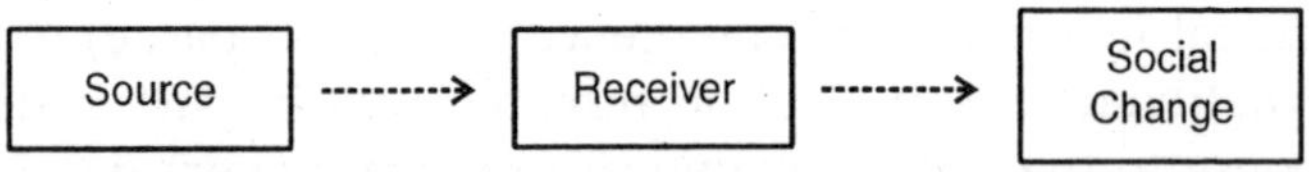

Fig. New Paradigam of International Communication

Other researchers have described the shifting theoretical terrain within international communication research. Critical researcher John Sinclair, in his book on international advertising, described the shift in paradigms:

Contrasting approaches have been noted amongst theorists concerned with the effects of transnationalisation.... "Modernisation" theorists have enthused about the "propag and a" for "a whole modernized way of life" offered by commercial media... while theorists closed to a "cultural imperialism" approach have been more concerned with what they think of as the "cultural homogenization" of the world... and the "export of consumerism...." The "ideological effects" of advertising... are seen to be instrumental in securing monopoly markets for transnational manufacturers of light consumer goods... as well as implementing "a mechanism for political mind control".

Boyd-Barrett, a lecturer at Open University in England, identified three paradigm shifts in international communication research: the missionary approach, which is roughly analogous to the "dominant paradigm"; the pluralist approach, which is roughly analogous to the "new paradigm"; and what he termed the *totalistic* approach, also analogous to the new paradigm, which holds that "there could be no real understanding of the media unless priority was given to an understanding of the fundamental relationship between 'developed' and 'developing' economies, 'the international socio-politico-economic system that *decisively determines* the course of development within the sphere of each nation.".

Boyd-Barrett showed how each of these approaches is aligned with movements in sociological theory, the first with structural functionalism, the second with neo-Weberianism, and the third with neo-Marxism.

BoydBarrett continued by noting that, in terms of theory, the totalistic perspective acknowledges the important role of advertising and marketing within generalized information and mass media activities globally, linking those kinds of industries to developments in related industries such as satellite communication, and the commercialization of innovations in the defence and aerospace industries.

Boyd-Barrett suggested that the totalistic approach opens up or problematizes certain aspects of international communication but he also critiqued the approach for the following reasons.

First, its political position is unquestioningly and perhaps aggressively in line with what he termed the *nationalist-Marxist* alliance (i.e. the movement of "Third Worldism"). Second, it is often a historical and reductionist and third, it takes a simplistic, unidirectional approach to dependency, which assumes that Western media steamroll cultures into subordination.

Thus, although the totalistic approach enlarges the area of concern, and theorizes aspects of the communication process that the other paradigms accept as unproblematic, it does not overcome the limitation of viewing the "rest of the world" (i.e., the "rest" as opposed the the West) as a blank stage upon which the West is the primary actor.

What the new paradigm accomplishes most effectively is the recognition that there is in fact a "transnational" order in both economics and communication, and that any attempt at understanding international communication, including advertising, must theorize both the macro-order and the micro-order.

Boyd-Barrett, unlike many researchers who take a cultural perspective, recognized the "need for an emphasis on micro-analysis of media impacts at small group and individual levels to engage with and to illuminate the present emphasis on macro-analysis of media and multinational structures". But important for advertising research specifically is also the macro-analysis, which often only tangentially addresses advertising issues.

A problem with the new paradigm or what is also termed *critical* research is that the research, as Boyd-Barrett pointed out, is so specifically engaged with its political programme that it fails to question tenets of that programme. Thus, advertising is aligned with "bad" capitalist expansion—and perhaps justifiably—but that perspective, like the dominant paradigm before it, theorizes the world as a dichotomy; the bipolarization, good and bad, is simply reversed.

Postmodernism

The older dominant paradigm of international communication might be characterized as a liberal perspective, with the succeeding newer paradigm characterized as a critical perspective. Both perspectives, liberal and critical, share a specific discourse of mastery, although they locate and theorize power differently.

But to a large extent, both tend to operate in terms of underlying dichotomies, the mastery of the major discourses of the Western world (i.e., male-female, rational-irrational, intellectual-emotional, good-evil, modern-traditional, and so forth).

That explains why critical advertising research such as Frith's remains conflicted; although she takes a more sympathetic approach to other cultures, she merely reverses the dichotomies in terms of their value. Thus, rather than construct emotional or collective as traditional/backward, she sees those as "authentic" values. But the conflict is that the notion of "authenticity" is compromised in an age of almost instant international communication and a world economic order in which interdepency is a political-economic reality.

It is necessary to explore the underlying ontology and epistemology or world view and knowledge system of both perspectives before it is clear as to why each one, useful as they may be in answering some questions, cannot provide the whole picture. The liberal paradigm holds that the "real" world can be known directly through sense perceptions; that is why quantitative methods can be applied, because counting depends on the assumption that what the researcher actually perceives is what he or she wants to measure. This perspective contrasts with that of the interpretive approaches in which it is held that reality is unknown directly and that what may be observed and interpreted are the *effects* of reality, a perspective that suggests historical or textual analysis.

The paradigms also theorize differently on a number of dimensions: the nature of power, the nature of society, the nature of communications media, the nature of the relationship between the media and society, the nature of the relationship between media and change, and the nature of ideology. Within the liberal paradigm, power is understood as diffused and society is composed of groups with competing interests.

The communications media are seen as reflecting reality, or perhaps distorting it for specific purposes. The relationship of the media to the society is that of a corrective where the media has social responsibility to act as a watchdog or fourth estate, a position that includes even advertising. The relationship of the media to social or behavioral change is seen as potentially positive; thus, if advertising is not responsible it must be brought into line used for pro-social purposes. and finally, ideology is understood as beliefs along a political spectrum, but it is not theorized in any special way as a social practice to be controlled.

In contrast, critical cultural studies (post structuralism), the paradigm from which postmodernism emerges, proposes that power is hegemonic. *Hegemony,* a concept developed by the Italian theorist Antonio Gramsci, suggests that an elite shapes the social common sense understanding of reality. Society is composed of a ruling elite who maintain their power with the consent of the many. Media is understood as a defining constellation of institutions, where the hegemony is represented in such as way that it appears natural; thus the nature of the relationship of media to the society is one of reproduction and the legitimation of the status quo. The media can help shape consensus. and ideology is theorized as a reproductive practice; it is not just a system of beliefs or vague consciousness, but a tool in the social jockeying for power.

Given these different understandings and underlying assumptions, it is clear that the research questions, methodologies used, and results derived will differ depending on the paradigm within which the researcher operates. International advertising research has been conducted almost primarily within the liberal perspective. The notable exceptions include the work of Judith Williamson, Gillian Dywer, Raymond Williams, Noreen Janus, and Jean Baudrillard. Of these, most are critical culturalists; Jean Baudrillard is considered a postmodernist. All take a highly critical view toward advertising and apparently are either rejected out of hand or perhaps unread by advertising researchers. Yet their research is highly suggestive, both for criticism and for industry-related needs in the complex international environment.

An alternative perspective to both the liberal and critical approaches is postmodernism. Art critic Hal Foster distinguished between two positions on postmodernism, one which is essentially a neoconservative position (a reaction to the excesses of Modernism), the other derived from a poststructuralist (European responses to Structuralism) position. The postmodernism discussed here is the latter; but it is still necessary to understand the modernism to which it is named and which both positions stand in opposition to.

Modernism is the perspective with which our society has enunciated its dominant values and within which liberal and critical research is conducted. According to Habermas it was the project of the Enlightenment to develop the principles of science, morality, and art "according to their inner logic." "The project of the Enlightenment consisted in [the] effort to develop objective science, universal morality and law, and autonomous art coording to their inner logic... for the purpose of the enrichment of everyday life -that is to say, for the rational organization of everyday social life".

As Habermas, who in fact argued for the recovery of

modernity, shows that this perspective is historically specific; it organizes and directs relations of power and discourse in particular ways that then operate to influence the kinds of questions we ask and the answers at which we arrive.

Postmodernism works to problematize categories and concepts that remain fixed and immutable in Modernism, that is, for both liberal and critical research. It liberates the research from some of the constricting conditions of the scientific discourse, most particularly the condition that a phenomenon is "real" only if it can be measured and that if it cannot be measured it is not real. The need within scientific discourse for operationalizing social phenomenon in quantifiable ways is particularly problematic for international communication research. But more importantly the insistence on qualification exists within a discourse of mastery, suggesting that without the specific understanding of statistical methods, knowledge is inaccessible. Postmodernism is a position that is defined as an oppositional one to modernism, oppositional to both liberal and critical perspectives. Postmodernism, by problematizing the categories of knowledge, by blur ring the distinctions between forms of expression, concerns itself with the interstices between power and knowledge, destructuring the object of analysis and decentering the subject.

Postmodernism is a theoretical perspective or position, a term of historical periodization, and a critical practice. The term is associated with Charles Jencks who used it to describe a school of architecture; its appropriation by both neo-conservatives and neo-Marxists is explained by the need within both positions to help chart out the apparent contradictions of late 20th century life.

"Postmodernism is characterized as a conflict between new and old modes—cultural and economic, the one not entirely autonomous, the other not all determinative... the agenda is to disengage the emergent cultural forms and social relations". In other words, a postmodern perspective can examine advertising at both the cultural and economic levels, simultaneously acknowledging that the spheres exist together. Postmodernism is also a kind of periodization that distinguishes the modern world, the period of industrialization and colonial-imperialism, from the postmodern world of post industrialism and economic consolidation. The postmodern period is one in which class structures and political-economic arrangements are substantially different from the modern period.

As critical practice, postmodernism is associated with semiotics and deconstruction, which locate power as existing within discourses and which attempt to rethink the importance and autonomy of human agency in the face of those structuring discourses that help mold and shape our ability to understand.

In mass communication research a postmodern perspective opens up ways to understand contradictions, for example, to understand how the political and cultural hegemony of the West can exist alongside economic hegemony of Japan and the Pacific Rim. Advertising is one of the prime "products" of a postmodern world, where the production of consumable objects is being increasingly abetted by the production of productions, that is, the production of markets with specific knowledge and needs. Advertising research in an era of multinationalism and the increasing success of monopoly capitalism, and the rhetoric of freedom and democracy, must be able to deal explicitly with profound contradiction, rather than rewrite contradiction as "outlayers" or as unaccounted variance.

INTERNATIONAL MARKETING AND ADVERTISING

Over the past several years there has been an increase in interest in the relationship of values to consumer behaviour. In general, the focus of this interest has been on *personal values* (values that individuals hold that presumably affect their behaviour). Research has shown relationships between values and purchases in particular product classes, as well as factors affecting the choices for a variety of products and services. Personal values have typically been measured by paper and pencil value inventories such as the Rokeach Value Survey or Kahle's LOV Scale. Other approaches to the study of values and their relationships with behaviour have been used, however, including qualitative techniques. It is important to note that this concern with personal values originated, to some extent, from an interest with cross-cultural issues. Personal values were considered to be an important arena with which to compare the consumption of individuals in different cultures. Although the early interest in values was fueled by cross-cultural concerns, research on values and consumer behaviour has moved away from these cultural issues in recent years. Current investigations in this area have tended to focus on personal values and their relationship to consumer behaviour; in general, these studies have dealt with this relationship within a single culture.

The purpose of the present chapter is quite simple, yet fundamental. It is this author's contention that the investigation of values is indeed important in the study of cross-cultural consumer behaviour, however, it is likely that the more fruitful path in this area will be to concentrate on cultural value orientations rather than personal values. Although personal values may be important in understanding variability across individuals within a culture, cultural value orientations will likely be of greater importance in understanding variability in consumer behaviour across cultures.

To understand this distinction more completely, it is useful to discuss the nature of culture, values, and the differences between personal values and cultural value orientations.

THE NATURE OF CULTURE

There have been numerous definitions of culture that have been used by anthropologists, sociologists, and psychologists over the past several decades. Indeed, the definitions of culture were so numerous that Kroeber and Kluckhohn classified the definitions that had been used up to the time of their writing. Although various definitions of culture have emphasized different aspects of the concept, it is clear that several themes have emerged across many of the definitions.

CULTURE IS ADAPTIVE

First, many of the definitions have emphasized that culture is a group's adaptation to the environment. That is, cultures develop as a response to the physical and social environment with which a particular group must deal. Therefore, culture is "human constructed" and develops as a response to specific problems encountered by the group. Cultures differ primarily because different groups are exposed to different physical and social environments. Even if the environments of two groups are relatively similar, the approaches taken to adapting to the environment may be unique in each of the groups.

CULTURE IS SHARED

A second theme is that culture is shared by members of a group. Therefore, on the one hand, culture is not idiosyncratic to an individual and, on the other hand, it is not common to all humankind. Culture is something that members of a group have in common. A useful way of thinking about this is to consider the three levels of mental programming that people possess as suggested by Hofstede. There are some things that are *universal* and therefore shared by everyone. Mental programming at this tier is not dependent on cultural learning; much of this mental activity is innate and /or instinctual. Emotions and the expression of them are examples of mental programming at this universal level.

At the other extreme is the *individual* level of mental programming. This refers to the mental activity that is unique to an individual. Most of what is referred to as a person's personality is at this tier. An individual's personality is unique to him or her in that no two people share exactly the same set of dispositions, traits, and so on. A person may have some things in common with others, but the similarities across individuals are not a function of membership in a particular cultural group. This type of mental programming would include, among other things, how introverted, authoritarian, or emotional a person is. Within a particular cultural group, some individuals may be similar regarding their level of introversion but different from others with regard to that trait. Similarly, the attitudes that a person holds are at this level of mental programming. Some of a person's attitudes may be similar to those of another person, but it is unlikely that any two individuals think exactly alike on all issues. Furthermore, it is unlikely that all members of a common cultural group have a similar point of view regarding a particular attitude domain. In the United States, for example, people differ dramatically on a great number of political attitudes.

The *collective* level of mental programming includes those things that are held by some but not all humans. Furthermore, there is consistency across members of a particular group in terms of what is held in common. Language is an example of this sort of mental programming; most of the things that are considered as part of a group's culture also constitute mental activity at this tier. Therefore, culture is mental programming that is shared among members of a group, yet is different from the programming that is held by members of other groups.

CULTURE IS LEARNED

A third theme that is apparent in many definitions of culture is that it is learned. A member of a cultural group is not born with an understanding of the culture, rather, it is learned through one of two processes. For an individual who is born in the culture, he or she learns the culture through socialization. A person is socialized by parents, peers, the media, and the educational and religious institutions of the culture. Although this socialization process is often explicit, it is generally very subtle. That is, a culture will sometimes make explicit statements about the core cultural beliefs, as when the teachings of the United States stress the belief of freedom. Other cultural teachings may be far more implicitly transmitted. The explicit statements of a culture are often subtly shaded. "Turning the other cheek" when one has been wronged by another is an explicit cultural teaching in the United States, but most people subtly learn that they should not let others exploit them and that a certain amount of looking out for oneself is considered wise.

The alternative process by which culture is learned is through acculturation. Acculturation is the process where an individual entering a culture learns about the new culture. Acculturation is complex because it involves the learning of the new culture by a person who has been socialized most of his or her life in a different culture. Because a person is entering the new culture and has an awareness of this, acculturation is a more active and conscious process than is socialization. When a person enters a new culture, he or she can choose to adopt the new culture or resist it in favour of the culture of birth.

THE SUBJECTIVE CULTURE

A useful construct in the consideration of culture is the notion of *subjective culture,* originally suggested by Osgood and further developed by Triandis, Vassiliou, Vassiliou, Tanaka, and Shanmugam. The subjective culture involves the perceptions of the culture by members of the cultural group. This concept is particularly useful when the data collected by a researcher are the psychological responses of individuals. It should be noted, however, that the aspects of a culture are often subtle and implicit; therefore, the subjective culture of a particular person in a culture may or may not reflect the subtleties of the culture. For example, in the United States it is part of the culture to profess many high ideals, although members of the culture act more pragmatically in many instances. One person's subjective culture may include ideals as well as a subtle understanding how those ideals are not always practiced. Another person's subjective culture may believe that the ideals are indeed held and practiced as stated.

CULTURE, VALUES, AND VALUE ORIENTATIONS

Clyde Kluckhohn, an anthropologist, and Milton Rokeach, a social psychologist, have been particularly important in developing the v1alue construct in their respective disciplines. More recently, Kahle, among others, has been influential in the development of the values concept in the consumer behaviour domain. Values have been considered as an important element in describing individual motivations, as well as a basic element in the description of culture and the differences between cultures.

In this regard, Rokeach's conception of values tends to focus on the personal values of the individual. Kluckhohn defined a value as "a conception, explicit or implicit, distinctive of an individual or characteristic of a group, of the desirable which influences the selection from available modes, means, and ends of actions". Kluckhohn further indicated that values represent what one *should* do in a situation and not necessarily what one may desire to do. Values, therefore, tend to have a positive quality to them: they are generally what is perceived as correct, just, fair, and so on.

It is this prescriptive aspect of values, however, that has caused great difficulty with them as theoretical antecedents of behaviour. There are a great number of influences on the behaviour of individuals in a particular situation. Values as standards of behaviour must compete with other internal motivations of the individual as well as situational demands and constraints. Whether one will act according to his or her values may vary from situation to situation. Furthermore, individuals and /or groups may hold what Kluckhohn referred to as utopian values. These are values to which a person or group may pay lip service, but the person or group rarely acts as these values would indicate. Clearly, the inherent nature of values as ideals or standards is such that their relationship to behaviour is tenuous.

There has been some degree of confusion in the use of the concept of values. This confusion is due in part to the fact that the term *value* has been used in a variety of definitions; these definitions include ones that refer to basic cultural beliefs, some that include both cultural and individual beliefs, and definitions that focus on individual motivations. Therefore, important distinctions between cultural beliefs and individual values have not always been made. It is useful to clarify some of these uses of the values concept.

PERSONAL VALUES

Personal values are values that individuals believe that

they hold as motivating factors in their life. Individuals often conceptualize these values as basic principles in their life and may indeed use the term value to describe these basic motivators. As Kluckhohn indicated, however, values can be implicitly held in the sense that they are at such an abstract level that they are not "clearly and habitually verbalized, " but the ability of a person to potentially verbalize them as motivation is important to be considered as values. The self-concept is a useful construct when considering the role of personal values in the life of an individual; it would generally be expected that personal values will be a fairly central part of a person's sense of self. What individuals value and believe to be the prime motivators in their life are fairly central to the concept they have of the kind of persons they are.

The fact that most values have a positive quality to them is not surprising because most people want to have a positive self-concept and believe they are driven by good motivations. Values need not relate specifically to the self (e.g., an exciting life) to be a part of the self-concept. A person may value a world of beauty and this may be a part of the self-concept in the sense that the person would think "I am the kind of person who values beauty in the world." Personal values, according to Rokeach, tend to relate to desirable end-states (e.g., an exciting life, salvation, a world of beauty) or modes of conduct that help one to achieve these end-states (e.g., ambition, self-control). It is important to note that although values may be a part of a person's self-concept, he or she may or may not act on them because the values are of the utopian sort. One's self-concept and how one actually acts may not always coincide.

THE INDIVIDUAL AND CULTURAL NATURE OF VALUES

Part of the confusion in the use of the values concept rests with the fact that personal values are generally part of the cultural teachings. Most personal values are cultural in the sense that they are learned through the socializing institutions of a society and, hence, can be part of the collective level of mental programming. Kluckhohn argued that all values are at some level a product of the culture in which a person is a member, but it is likely that each person gives a private interpretation to the values that he or she learns from the culture. Personal values, therefore, are cultural and, at the same time, individual. There could be great variability across cultures in the extent to which personal values are consistent across people within a culture. This level of variability may depend on how explicitly the values are taught by the culture and how central they are to a culture.

At one extreme there are the values that are taught explicitly by the culture; these are often the "conceptions of the desirable, " that is, they are what the culture teaches as what one ought to do. These explicitly taught personal values may be closely tied to the basic beliefs of the culture. It would generally be expected that the personal values that a culture teaches in an explicit fashion would show little variation across the individuals in the society in terms of being stated as values. Individuals might, however, vary greatly on how much they act as these values suggest. The belief in these culturally taught values would therefore be a part of the collective level of mental programming.

At the other extreme are personal values that might show a great deal of variation across people in the culture in terms of whether they are expressed as values. This variation might be related to a number of causes. First, the value might be communicated by the culture in a very implicit fashion, thus allowing for a wide latitude in individual interpretation of the value.

Secondly, different socializing agents of the cultures may provide different points of view with regard to certain values. What one particular individual may believe with regard to the value would depend on which socializing force was most powerful in his or her life. For example, the Rokeach value of social recognition may be given different levels of importance by different socializing agents in the culture of the United States. A third reason why some personal values may show variability within a culture is that personal values are often tied to individual motivations and needs. In cultures where there is a fair amount of individual self-determination and heterogeneity among the population, personal values may differ across people because of different needs. These values that show individual differences across people in a culture are a part of the individual level of mental programming because any consistencies across people are not particularly tied to group membership.

Personal values, therefore, are values that are held by individuals. They may vary in the extent to which they are tied to the core teachings of the culture and, hence, vary in the extent to which they are "cultural." The term *cultural values* should be used tc refer to personal values that are very prevalent in a particular culture.

CULTURAL VALUE ORIENTATIONS

Personal values, regardless of the extent they are cultural, should be distinguished from *cultural value orientations,* a different concept with which the term value has been used. A value orientation, according to Kluckhohn, is "a generalized and organized conception, influencing behaviour, of nature, of man's place in it, of man's relation to man, and of the desirable and non-desirable as they may relate to man-environment and interhuman relations". The concern here is in cultural value orientations, although Kluckhohn indicated that value orientations can be at the individual level.

Cultural value orientations form the foundation upon which the culture rests; they are the basic beliefs around which the culture is organized. According to Kluckhohn and Strodtbeck, there are basic problems with which all societies must deal, and cultural value orientations relate to these basic problems. These basic problems, as the definition of value orientations suggests, relates to human relationships with others and with the environment. It has been argued that culture is an adaptation to the environment, so it would seem that cultural value orientations assist the group as a whole in this adaptation process. Therefore, although personal values will often relate to individual motivations, cultural value orientations focus on the needs of the collective.

Cultural value orientations are often such a basic part of the culture that they may not always be identified as a value at the individual level. They are often beliefs that are taken for granted and, therefore, are not necessarily salient to individuals as important guiding beliefs for their own life. Rokeach argued that they should be referred to as basic philosophical orientations rather than values because individuals may not necessarily hold a position on one of them as a desirable state of affairs. For example, the culture of the United States believes in mastery over nature.

It is clear that the culture acts in such a way as to deal with whatever problems nature presents. California is not abandoned as a place to live because of the probability of earthquakes, rather, there is a constant effort to build buildings and so on that can withst and such disturbances. Although the culture as a whole may hold a value orientation of mastery over nature, it is not necessarily true that such an orientation is salient to an individual as his or her value. Mastery over nature is important to the culture as a whole, but not necessarily a part of an individual's self-concept.

CULTURAL VALUE ORIENTATIONS AND INDIVIDUAL BEHAVIOUR

Although cultural value orientations are not necessarily salient to an individual as a guiding belief, these orientations do have influences on individual behaviour and these influences may be strong and pervasive. There are multiple ways in which these values can influence individual behaviour and, in many ways, basic cultural value orientations may have influences on individual consumption behaviour that are stronger and more fundamental than that of personal values. Presumably, personal values affect consumption behaviour to the extent that one's values affect that person's behaviour. To date, however, little research has shown strong and consistent relationships between personal values and behaviour. This lack of relationship is likely related to the nature of personal values. As suggested in many of the definitions of values, values are conceptions of what one should do and, thus, they compete with other dispositions that motivate an individual as well as a variety of situational influences.

Cultural value orientations, on the other hand, may have a far more pervasive influence on individual consumption behaviour. It would seem that cultural value orientations could influence consumption in at least three ways as indicated in Cultural value orientations may be internalized by the individual as his or her personal values, or they may develop in the individual as other types of internal predispositions to behaviour. As previously suggested, many values are learned through the institutions in the culture that socialize the members of the culture.

These values, which are taught through this socialization process, may often be closely related to the core beliefs of the culture. For example, the United States is a very individualistic culture where an emphasis is placed on the individual relative to the group. This cultural orientation may be internalized as personal values such as self-determination and/or independence.

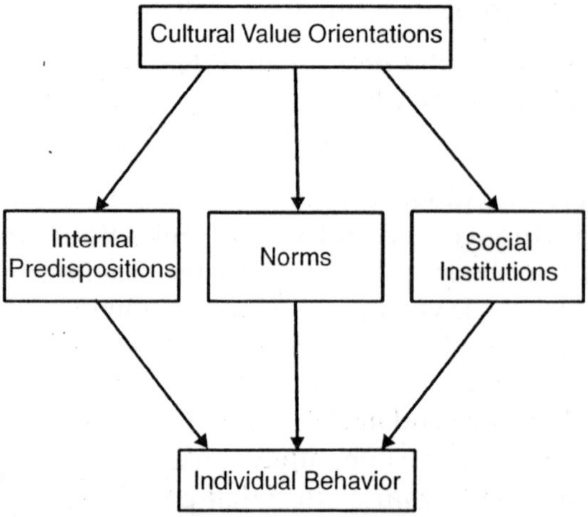

Fig. The Influence of Cultural Value Orientations on Individual Behaviour.

As Triandis indicated, the term used for a person who is individualistic is *idiocentric*. In a similar fashion, the core cultural value orientations may influence other elements of an individual's personality. Therefore, a person may act very individualistically and independently because it is a trait that he or she has acquired, even though this trait is not identified as a personal value by the person.

Whether or not cultural value orientations are internalized by individuals as predispositions, the behaviour of individuals may be affected by these cultural beliefs either through norms or through the nature of social institutions. Norms prescribe the appropriate behaviour in particular situations. As Triandis stated, "Norms are beliefs that certain behaviors are correct, appropriate, or desirable and other behaviors are incorrect, inappropriate, immoral, or undesirable". Norms are a part of the culture and often quite specific to a culture. The core value orientations of a culture can influence the norms that are present in that particular society.

Therefore, norms will likely be consistent with the value orientations of the culture. Because cultural value orientations differ across societies, norms will also vary greatly across cultures. The sanctions against breaking a norm in a society can be quite severe. Therefore, an individual will often consume in a manner prescribed by the norms of the consumption situation in that culture, regardless of what his or her individual beliefs may be. That is, the norms dictate what the appropriate behaviour is in the situation and individuals are obliged to behave accordingly. For example, in the culture of the United States one is expected to tip a waiter or waitress for the service provided at a restaurant. The norm or custom is to tip 15% of the bill for acceptable service. Even though a person may not believe in tipping for service, he or she will often engage in the behaviour because of the strength of the norm.

The social institutions that exist in a culture can profoundly affect individual behaviour, and these institutions can develop in a manner that is -consistent with the cultural value orientations. Simply stated, individuals must consume in the ways prescribed by the institutions in the culture. For example, the distribution system that develops in a culture largely determines the way that a group consumes. Regardless of personal desires to the contrary, in the culture of the United States people must buy most packaged goods through grocery store chains or other large retailers. Most grocery items are prepackaged in specific sizes. In other cultures, the distribution outlets may be quite different and affect consumption accordingly. In France, smaller stores are prevalent and there is less consumption of convenience foods compared to the United States because these small stores do not have the shelf space to stock them. Therefore, in a given culture certain products may be unavailable to consumers because of the nature of the institutions, and individual consumption behaviour is affected accordingly.

CULTURAL VALUE ORIENTATIONS AND CONSUMPTION

Cultural value orientations can have a profound influence on consumer behaviour and aspects of the marketing endeavor. Consequently, a knowledge of the value orientations of a particular culture would seem to be important in the design of marketing and communication programs. In this regard, the investigation of cultural value orientations, rather than personal values, will provide a more fruitful path to understanding the important aspects of a culture. Several examples of cultural value orientations and how they relate to consumption, advertising, and marketing are now presented to illustrate their potential importance.

Individualism-Collectivism

One of the most essential arenas with which a cultural group must deal is humans' relationships with one another. The value orientation dimension of individualism versus collectivism has been discussed by many with regard to the issue of how individuals relate to one another. Individualistic cultures tend to place emphasis on the individual relative to the group, whereas collectivistic cultures tend to subordinate the individual to the group. This is particularly true for goals. In individualistic cultures, individual aspirations are considered as more important than group goals; in collectivistic societies, the group's goals are either more important than individual motivations or the ambitions of individuals are synonymous with group goals. Individualism implies that it is acceptable or indeed expected that an individual can stand out from the group. Individual initiative is rewarded and expected. In collectivistic societies, individuals cooperate with the group; individuals tend to have an identity only as members of the group.

Not surprisingly, a culture's level of individualism affects the relationships of members of the group. In collectivistic cultures, the relationships between members of the group are more nurturant and intimate than such relationships in individualistic cultures.

Furthermore, there is more interdependence of the group members and a concern about the welfare of the group in collectivistic cultures. As Triandis points out, however, this concern may only be among and for group members. Collectivism should not be considered to be synonymous with a general concern for one's fellow humans. Members of a collective may feel nurturance and concern for other members of the collective, yet feel that it is acceptable to exploit those who are not members of the group.

Generally speaking, the more advanced a culture, the more it tends to be individualistic, and it appears that cultures evolve into individualism from more collectivistic pasts. Most research on individualism versus collectivism across cultures consistently shows that the United States is a very individualistic culture.

As Triandis suggested, the major antecedents of individualism are affluence and the complexity of a culture. The United States is a very complex, affluent culture. Other countries that are very individualistic include Great Britain, Australia, Canada, Netherlands, and Italy; all of these cultures are relatively affluent and complex. Collectivistic cultures include Peru, Venezuela, Chile, and Taiwan. Interestingly, Japan seems to be an exception in that it is a culture that is relatively collectivistic, although it is also a relatively affluent and complex society.

Masculinity-Feminity

A second dimension on which cultures vary is masculinity versus femininity; this dimension, like individualism versus collectivism, deals with how people relate to one another. As Hofstede stated, this dimension relates to the extent to which the attributes commonly associated with one sex or the other are considered more popular or favored. Therefore, the dimension is not a question of what is considered to be masculine attributes and feminine attributes, rather it relates to the issue of a society's emphasis.

Hofstede indicated that most research from the social sciences has shown a consistency across cultures as to what is considered masculine and what is feminine. Masculine behaviour is, in general, associated with assertiveness, dominance, achievement, and aggression; feminine behaviour is associated with nurturance, humility, helpfulness, and affiliation. The dimension on which cultures do vary, therefore, is the extent to which these two sets of attributes are dominant within the culture. Therefore, highly masculine cultures tend to consider assertiveness and achievement to be more important than nurturance, whereas highly feminine cultures value nurturance and affiliation.

According to Hofstede, the degree of masculinity of a culture can have a pervasive effect on the society. Masculinity correlates positively with need for achievement. Highly masculine countries also tend to display more differences in the sexes; these countries will tend to have fewer women in professional and technical jobs than highly feminine countries. Interest ingly, masculine countries tend to have higher traffic speeds and more traffic deaths, higher job stress, and more industrial conflict compared with more feminine societies. Countries that are very high in masculinity, according to Hofstede, include Japan, Austria, Italy, Switzerland, and Mexico. Societies that are low on masculinity include Sweden, Norway, Denmark, and Chile. The United States is relatively masculine, although it is surpassed on this dimension by several other industrial countries, including Germany, Great Britain, and Japan.

At the level of individuals, the masculinity versus femininity dimension has been investigated by Bem. Individuals can be classified as masculine, feminine, and rogynous, or undifferentiated, depending on whether they favour male personality characteristics, female characteristics, a mixture of both male and female (and rogenous), or neither (the undifferentiated). There are presumably individual differences across people within a society with regard to the dominance of the characteristics, even though the culture as a whole may be more masculine or feminine.

It would be expected that a society's position with regard to masculinity and femininity would influence their consumption patterns. One arena where this dimension has been suggested to influence consumption is family decision making. It is reasoned that males may be more dominant in family decisions in the Hispanic subculture, whereas females are more dominant in the African American subculture. It is suggested that this relates to the matriarchal nature of the Black subculture and the patriarchal nature of the Hispanic subculture. Although the discussion of Robertson et al. related to subcultures within the United States, similar patterns may emerge when countries of different cultures and family structures are investigated. For example, Mexico would likely be similar to the Hispanic subculture of the United States with regard to family decision making.

Time Orientation

Cultures can differ in their perception of time. Some cultures have a past orientation where there is great respect for tradition and doing things the way they have always been done. Other cultures regard the present as most important. As Kluckhohn and Strodtbeck stated: "They pay little attention to what has happened in the Past and regard the Future as both vague and unpredictable. Planning for the Future or hoping that the Future will be better than either the Present or the Past simply is not their way of life". Still other cultures are future oriented. These cultures may respect the past and live in the present, but there is a premium placed on the future and they change to meet the future. According to Kluckhohn and Strodtbeck, the United States is a very future oriented society. It is a culture that is generally looking to the future as being better than the present. Typically, members of the culture plan for the future and look forward to it. It seems that this future orientation is apparent in the advertising in the United States and the consumption behaviour of individuals in the culture. Although advertisements may occasionally provide a feeling of nostalgia, it is often the case that consumption is oriented with the future and change in mind.

Furthermore, the importance of fast food in the culture of the United States is related to this future orientation. Many feel a need to eat quickly so that they can get on with the day. The time orientation may be very different in other cultures and it is likely that much of the future oriented advertising of the culture in the United States would be cónfusing and misunderstood in other countries. In contrasting the advertising of the United States with that of Japan, Mueller found that Japanese advertising had a greater tendency to reflect tradition. Her research did not, however, show differences between these two cultures on appeals to modernity.

Humans' Relationship with Nature

Yet another value orientation that has implications for advertising and consumer behaviour is how a cultural group believes that they relate with the world around them. It is the belief of some societies that humans can not control the forces of nature and that they are powerless to change the course of natural events. This subjugationto-nature stance is typical of less advanced cultures. A different stance held by some cultures is that humans live in harmony with nature. As Kluckhohn and Strodtbeck indicated, this point of view sees no separation of humans with nature or the supernatural. One is simply an extension of the others. A third point of view, typically held by more advanced societies, is that humans can master nature. For these cultures it is not enough that the events of nature are understood and planned for; it is believed that steps can be taken to change them toward more favorable outcomes for the group. As Kluckhohn and Strodtbeck stated:

Natural forces of all kinds are to be overcome and put to the use of human beings. Rivers everywhere are spanned by bridges; mountains have roads put through and around them; new lakes are built, sometimes in the heart of deserts; old lakes get partially filled in when additional land is needed for building sites, roads, or airports; the belief in man-made medical care for the control of illness and the lengthening of life is strong to an extreme.

Triandis suggested that the value orientation of mastery over nature versus subjugation to nature can be represented at the level of individuals as a feeling of internal versus external locus of control. Individuals who have an internal locus of control feel that they control their lives to a great degree and can shape their future. Alternatively, those who have an external locus of control feel that they have little control over the events in their lives and can not change the course of events affecting them. These individuals feel powerless to forces beyond their control.

A society's belief about their relationship with nature will have a fundamental effect on the types of products that are available and the way that these are marketed. The culture of the United States, for example, is a culture where mastery over nature is held as a core belief. This belief is apparent in a variety of products and services.

Vehicles are available to transverse virtually every type of terrain. The equipment of these vehicles such as snow tires, windshield wipers, and so on allow driving in any kind of road condition and weather. In a different domain, all sorts of products are available to the home dweller for use in the lawn and garden such as weed killer, pest spray, and fertilizer. For the most part there is a product available that will assist with any problem encountered on a person's land. In yet another arena, a variety of medications can be purchased to relieve most ailments that a person can have.

The promotion and advertising of products in the United States tends to reflect this mastery over nature orientation. Belk and Bryce found that U. S. print advertising was more likely to stress actively changing the environment than adapting to it, compared to advertising in Japan. Examples of advertising stressing such mastery can easily come to mind. Advertisements for cold and flu remedies often emphasize the ability of the medications to keep you going when you have such an ailment, effectively mastering the situation. Numerous advertisements for automobiles show how particular vehicles can get you through the most adverse weather conditions.

Activity Orientation

Kluckhohn and Strodtbeck identified three possible orientations that a society can have with regard to activity. Two of these, *being and doing,* are the traditional stances that have been identified by philosophers; they added a third stance with regard to activity: being-in-becoming. As the name suggests, a doing orientation indicates a culture value placed on acting and doing. A being orientation, on the other hand, suggests that a premium is placed on experiencing life deeply, an orientation toward reflection about life and one's actions. The doing versus being distinction is, simply stated, a distinction between acting and reflecting. The being-in-becoming orientation suggests an evolutionary process that an individual is to go through in his or her life. That is, one should evolve into a better individual and reach a higher level of self-understanding.

According to Triandis, the activity orientation that a culture has can have a pervasive effect on the activity of individuals. Individuals in doing cultures score higher on scales of aggression, autonomy, dominance, and achievement compared with people in societies with a being orientation. Also, people in doing societies typically have shorter reaction times than people in being countries and, if asked to estimate a minute of time, those in a doing culture will underestimate whereas those in being cultures will overestimate.

At the level of the individual, the doing versus being distinction might relate to the individual difference variable of private self-consciousness. Individuals who have a high level of private self-consciousness tend to examine their motives and reflect about themselves a lot, whereas those who are low in private self-consciousness tend not to engage in self-reflection. Although self-consciousness is an individual difference variable that probably exists in all cultures, it is likely that the cultural stance on the doing versus being orientation relates to the prevalence of this trait.

It would be expected that a culture's orientation with regard to activity would be reflected in the themes used in advertising. The United States, for example, is a very doing oriented culture, and a doing theme has generally been more prevalent in the advertising than a being theme. Advertisements in the United States typically show people as active rather than reflective, although this would obviously relate to product category, as certain products would relate more to one theme than another. In a study of three Chinese cultures by Tse, Belk, and Zhou, the level of being themes versus doing themes was consistent with the differences in activity orientations of these three cultures.

GENERAL RESEARCH ISSUES AND IMPLICATIONS

The intent of this section is not to provide an elaborate discussion of cross-cultural methodology, rather, broad issues regarding the investigation of value orientations across cultures is the focus. The thorough investigation of cultural value orientations is essential when considering marketing and advertising in other cultures. To date, however, our knowledge of the variation in cultures is mostly anecdotal.

Several key points have been made with regard to cultural value orientations that bear on the method of assessing them. First, because cultural value orientations are basic beliefs of the culture, they are often very abstract. These basic beliefs are usually implicitly and subtlety communicated to cultural members through socialization. Therefore, these beliefs may be known by the members of a society, but group members may not easily be able to explain or discuss the ideas. Secondly, it was noted that value orientations differ from personal values in that value orientations are not necessarily held by the individuals as personal values. Value orientations are important to the culture as a whole, but not necessarily salient to individuals as guiding principles. Value orientations may be internalized by individuals as personal values, but they may also affect behaviour through other forms of predispositions such as traits, behavioral tendencies, habits, and so on.

Several examples of value orientations as individual predispositions are given in the previous section (e.g., internal-external locus of control, private self-consciousness). Furthermore, value orientations may not be internalized by individuals at all; these core beliefs may affect behaviour through norms or social institutions. Third, because personal values are often utopian ideals of the culture, these values may be widely held by individuals but not routinely acted upon. These utopian values may or may not accurately reflect core cultural value orientations.

This suggests that the investigation of personal values may or may not provide a researcher with insights about the value orientations of a culture. In some cases, personal values may simply not be relevant to the core beliefs of a culture. Other approaches to the study of value orientations will likely be necessary. Moreover, because of the complex nature of value orientations, it is probable that a multimethod approach to their investigation is warranted. As Spates observed,

This is dictated by the subjective nature of values and the different social settings in which they emerge. Single techniques - even grounded ones -cannot provide complete portraits. For example, an analysis of a community newspaper may show values A and B to be dominant while an interview with community members may indicate X and Y are preferred group values. While a multi technique approach is expensive and time-consuming, the discrepancies created by past data make it a prerequisite for adequate value work of the future.

One of the approaches that can certainly be a part of this multi technique approach is the study of the individuals in a culture. Two possibilities for studying individuals would be to: (a) investigate the subjective culture of individuals and (b) study individual predispositions that are likely to relate to particular value orientations of the culture. As mentioned, the subjective culture is the way that individuals perceive their culture. Therefore, the investigation of the subjective culture in a society is a matter of individuals reporting about aspects of their social environment. In a sense, this method is treating the respondents as informants about the culture; it is the informant's insights about what is generally true of members of his or her group that are important, rather than the informant's own point of view.

In this approach, not only are the individual beliefs of the respondents studied, but also their perceptions of norms, role relationships, and antecedents and consequences of behaviors. For example, through interview and survey techniques, respondents can relate the normative influences in a culture and can do so regardless of whether individual respondents are motivated to comply with such norms. The report of such norms can provide the researcher with an insight to the value orientations in a particular culture.

It has also been suggested that cultural value orientations can be internalized by individuals as beliefs, personal values, traits, and so on. One approach to understanding the basic beliefs of a culture would be to survey the beliefs and predispositions of individuals in the culture. Given the abstract nature of value orientations, it would be difficult to directly ask individuals to describe them. Kluckhohn and Strodtbeck did, however, advocate a relatively straightforward approach to tapping value orientations.

Through an interview situation, they posed a variety of life situations to respondents who were forced to choose among the alternatives; each of the alternatives represented one of the stances that could be taken with regard to a particular value orientation dimension. For example, one of their life situations dealt with how three different farmers planted crops and took care of them, which pertained to the value dimension of humans' relationship with nature. One farmer's behaviour exemplified harmony with nature, another's exemplified subjugation with nature, the third description expressed mastery over nature. Respondents were asked which approach they felt was best, which was the next best, and which would most people (in their culture) think was the best. Consistency in the responses of many individuals in a culture would provide a sense of the cultural orientation toward its relationship with nature.

These life situations would need to be tailored to the particular culture studied (the cultures that Kluckhohn and Strodtbeck investigated were all rural cultures where farming was a way of life), but if designed correctly, this approach could provide relatively direct information about the value orientations of a group.

In a similar vein, Triandis, Leung, Villareal, and Clark developed a scale to measure individualism and collectivism at the individual level; their scale has been tested in both China and the United States. The measurement of individuals on the idiocentric-allocentric dimension should provide some indication of the degree to which a culture tends toward individualism or collectivism. Although there would be variability within a culture, it would generally be expected that a greater percentage of individuals in an individualistic culture would respond to the scale in an idiocentric fashion compared with individuals in a collectivistic culture.

Other dispositional states could be used as surrogate measures of the value orientations of a culture. It would be expected that if a value orientation is relatively strong in a culture, this could lead to a prevalence of certain personality types in that culture. As mentioned, Rotter's construct of locus of control probably relates to the value orientation dimension of humans' relationship with nature. If a culture has a high percentage of individuals who have an internal locus of control, this should indicate that the culture has a belief in mastery over nature. Similarly, private self-consciousness may prove to be useful as a surrogate measure for being versus doing; to date, however, this individual difference measure's relationship to the activity orientation has not been investigated.

The content analysis of the media in a society has often been considered as a method of understanding a culture.

Cultural values have been investigated via the study of the fiction of a culture and biographies. In a cross national study, Wayne analyzed magazine pictures in the Soviet Union and the United States for an indication of values in these two cultures. Virtually all advanced societies have a variety of media that can be content analyzed for value orientation themes.

Advertising can be a significant source of information about a culture and the value orientations of a society. The examples mentioned in the discussion of specific value orientation dimensions have indicated this to be true. Several cautions should be addressed, however, with regard to the current advertising of a culture as an indication of value orientations. First, the culture as presented in advertising may be a distortion of reality, as suggested by Belk and Pollay. After reviewing the available evidence, they concluded that advertising tends to reflect an image of the good life rather than the mundane reality of many people's lives.

Although it is unclear whether a picture of a society's value orientations are distorted by their advertising, it is possible that advertising may provide an inaccurate picture of the core beliefs of a culture. Secondly, it should be emphasized that the advertising for products in a particular country may have been the work of a marketer in a different culture. Many products are marketed internationally, and the advertising may be handled by an advertising agency of the country where the product is produced. Therefore, the advertising may reflect a different culture's conception of the value orientations of the culture where the advertising is being seen or read.

The accuracy of that conception is a matter of how well the particular marketer has investigated the culture. Third, as Belk and Pollay noted, advertising can either change lifestyles or reflect current lifestyles. Particularly in developing societies, the advertising may not reflect the current value orientations but the orientations of a society that the culture is progressing toward. As cultures progress, they tend to become more individualistic, believe more in mastery over nature, become more future oriented, and so on. Therefore, current advertising may reflect the evolving value orientations of the culture. Finally, advertising may reflect value orientations that are consistent with the nature of the product, regardless of the orientations of the culture. For example, a product that helps a person get something accomplished may stress a doing orientation, as this is consistent with the nature of the product.

Other approaches to the investigation of a culture have been suggested, including observation, physical trace measures, and archival research. As previously emphasized, the understanding of a culture's core beliefs will require a multimethod approach so that the subtleties of the beliefs are understood.

PRACTICAL IMPLICATIONS

International marketing is a task of monumental difficulty. Cultures differ on a variety of dimensions that will affect the marketing effort, including wealth and its distribution, levels of literacy, and linguistic heterogeneity. These factors are important to consider in the early stages of deciding whether a product should be marketed in a particular country. For example, the wealth of a country and how the wealth is distributed among its population may determine whether marketing a particular product is viable at all in that country.

If it is determined that a product should be marketed in a country, then an understanding of the cultural value orientations of that society is necessary. The value orientations of a culture may affect the way a product is packaged, positioned, promoted, and distributed. The understanding of the core beliefs are particularly important with regard to the positioning and promotion of a product. For example, fast food restaurants are particularly important in a doing oriented culture but the speed at which one gets their food may be unimportant in a being oriented culture. In a being culture, the experience of dining in a restaurant may be more important. A fast food restaurant would make little sense in a culture that values the experience of eating. Knowledge of the activity orientation would be useful in the considerations of how to position the restaurant chain. Marketers have likely advanced beyond the obvious cross-cultural blunders caused by language differences and custom. More subtle blunders are still possible and mistakes that relate to implicitly held beliefs may not be so easy to discern. Through a multimethod research process, the core value orientations of a culture can be investigated such that a product or service can be marketed in the most advantageous way in a particular society.

Chapter 2

Consumer Understanding and Advertising Strategy

Two major obstacles exist to the proliferation of laddering as a management tool. First, the sheer magnitude of tedious work an analyst must perform to complete an analysis adds excessive costs to any study. Second, many who are familiar with the technique still have difficulty bridging from data to strategy to executional design and implications. This chapter addresses both of those issues by describing a newly available software support tool to make the data analysis a more reasonable task and by discussing the issue of strategy development and implementation. An example within the product category of dog food data is used.

An important issue for both industry and academic consumer researchers is the development of an understanding of how consumers derive personally relevant meaning about products. This meaning is the basis consumers use to shape their decision criteria among competitive products and services. The process by which pragmatic analysis of qualitative data on consumer meaning can be achieved and how this analysis can be used to enhance creative copy development. All too often, the results of qualitative research could have been written before the research was performed, either because the final results are merely the a priori opinion of the researcher involved or because the results are so obvious that the research need never have been performed.

The intent here is to suggest a methodological process that will alleviate both of these problems when gathering information on consumer meaning. Numerous academic studies have addressed this fundamental issue of meaning from the traditional product-attribute perspective. Under the attribute perspective, product meaning is the observable physical characteristics of the product. This limiting perspective ignores any type of personal meanings of the product attributes.

Recognizing this deficiency, product meaning has been expanded beyond merely attributes to include benefits those attributes symbolize to the consumer. This orientation concentrates primarily on the direct results the product delivers to the consumer through product purchase or consumption. More recently, the definition of product meanings has been expanded yet again to include higher levels of abstraction, namely, personal values.

The ever-broadening focus on understanding the consumer meanings that underlie the decision-making process, from attribute to benefit to personal-value perspectives, is primarily driven by the competitive forces in the marketplace. That is, the dramatic increase in the number of competing brands in most product categories forces marketers to look for positionings that are more directly relevant to the decision-making criteria of the consumer. Clearly, understanding the personally relevant meanings that consumers hold for a product, and the new positioning strategies that may stem from these meanings, is invaluable to marketing strategists.

Means-end theory presents an appealing framework to more comprehensively represent the consumer meanings that underlie product-positioning research. Rather than focus on a particular level of meanings, the means-end framework incorporates all levels into a conceptual model that additionally focuses on the associations (or derived meanings) between the levels. The associations between concepts offer an explanation of how consumers interpret a product attribute as symbolizing associated benefits. Consumers translate product attributes into the benefits they produce, and benefits are ultimately translated into the consumer's driving value orientation.

For example, a dog food may have an attribute of being "dry and crunchy." To a dog owner, "dry and crunchy" means the dog food will help deliver the consequences (benefits) of "cleaner teeth" and "healthier dog." In turn, these consequences help the dog owner to fulfill a personal value, to feel a sense of "responsibility as a good owner." Put simply, the product, as defined by its discriminating perceptual attributes, is the *means* that satisfies the more personal *ends*, represented by values.

Importantly, the means-end framework adds a much richer understanding of how consumers derive meaning from products. Within this framework, meanings reflect the linear pattern of concepts and associations across levels of meaning, which, taken together, serve to explain the underlying reasons why the consumer considers a given attribute to be salient. The cognitive perspective of means-end theory can be seen to incorporate attribute, consequence, and value research paradigms into a framework encompassing all three models. It is the associational aspect of the means-end model that provides a unique perspective on consumers' personally relevant meaning.

Recently, several aspects of means-end theory are receiving increased attention. Several articles address research methodology. Others have addressed the application to positioning strategy design. Still others apply means-end theory as a conceptual framework for the strategic assessment of advertising. This attention resulted in the broader realization that significant potential lies in using this consumer-based, strategically oriented research framework.

However, three major practical problems emerge:

- The significant time and cost of gathering individual in-depth, means-end (laddering) data;
- The time and effort required to perform the content analysis of the qualitative responses (steps in the ladders) and the quantitative summaries of the dominant pathways;
- The lack of any detailed framework or system to translate strategic options as represented in the

summary Hierarchical Value Map into a working format for the agency creative staff.

LADDERING DATA ISSUES

Data Collection

Several researchers recently addressed the first of these problems: the issue of data collection. Gengler used an interactive computer programme to assess strengths of associations between concepts. The concepts were derived a priori in focus groups. Vallette-Florence and Rapacchi used a card-sorting task to group concepts that were related. Both of these techniques relied heavily on a priori definition of concepts to be associated and are in that respect inferior to the open-ended format of laddering interviews.

However, both techniques are quicker and easier to administer than laddering interviews. The main issue is whether or not researchers feel their consumers are homogeneous and predictable enough to use a predetermined set of concepts. Walker and Olson used a paper- and -pencil technique of data collection. In their technique, a questionnaire was administered to a group of individuals simultaneously.

This technique shows promise but precludes the insightful probing characteristic to laddering. In sum, a number of researchers are attempting to find more cost-effective and efficient methods of data collection, but each of these has potential shortcomings when compared with the laddering technique advocated by Reynolds and Gutman. Indeed, it is difficult to justify any small savings in time or money when compared with the enormous cost of inaccurate or incomplete results.

Analysis of Laddering Data

The second problem offers a better place to increase the efficiency of conducting a means-end study: streamlining and improving the process of analysis. Analysis of laddering data is a cumbersome task requiring several days of effort by highly skilled analysts for even a medium-sized study. The basic analysis steps can be summarized as Reynolds and Gutman, 1988, for a detailed description of these tasks):

- Breaking the raw, conversational data into separate phrases. These phrases are the basic elements on which subsequent analysis is based. This involves reviewing the verbatim notes or tapes of the discussion probes for the elements that best represent the concepts expressed by each individual subject.
- Content analysis of the elements selected in Step 1.
- Summation of associations between the content codes, resulting in a quantitative assessment of all paired relationships, termed *implications*.
- Construction of a diagram to meaningfully represent the main implications, termed an HVM.

Translation of means-End Results into Strategy and Creative Copy

The third problem involves the lack of any detailed framework to translate strategic options from a laddering study into a working format for the agency creative staff. Although the issue of divining strategy from results is often discussed, the focus generally concentrates on definition of the strategy and ignores the issue of translating that strategy into creative, executional concepts for advertisements.

Discussing advertising strategy, Little stated: "Good strategy requires imagination and style and always will. At the same time, strategy emerges best from a foundation of reliable facts and sound analysis". Integration of creativity and means-end study results to develop a strategy and design creative executions is an art. To become accomplished at any art requires the development of technique. A key issue, then, is the outlining of techniques which can aid creative staff in developing executions from strategies.

STAGES OF COMPUTER ANALYSIS OF MEANS-END DATA

Analysis of the responses gathered through laddering interviews involves several steps. To illustrate this process, data gathered on consumer choices of food for their canines is used as an example. This data set contains responses from 67 laddering interviews, with one to four ladders produced from each subject. The discussion of analysis is presented in terms of the stages the analyst must go through, the important considerations at each stage, and how these stages can be facilitated using Gengler and Reynolds' decision-support tool, LADDER MAP.

Stage A: Specifying Elements of a means-end Chain

First of all, the conversational nature of the raw data from laddering forces the analyst to separate the ladder responses of each individual into chunks of meaning. These chunks correspond to the distinct levels of product meaning identified by the analyst within the ladder. Two important decisions must be made by the analyst at this stage.

First, because the interviews are open-ended and conversational in nature, response not germane to the topic must be eliminated. Secondly, specifying what composes a chunk of meaning is extremely important because these units are the basis of all further stages of analysis.

For example, an extract from a typical laddering interview may go something like "I prefer brand J (of dog food) because it is dry and crunchy and it cleans my dog's teeth when she eats it." In this statement, the subject is actually stating two different chunks of means-end information, specifically, the attribute "dry and crunchy" and the consequence "cleans my dog's teeth."

The LADDERMAP software is designed to assist in this stage. An interactive data entry feature is provided. Under this feature, analysts can enter multiple ladders per interview subject and up to ten "chunks" of meaning per ladder. As ladders are entered for each respondent, the analyst is prompted for the first stage of content analysis that is classifying each "chunk" as either an attribute, a consequence, or a value. This classification underlies the theoretical basis of the analysis and aids the analyst in discerning what are and are not relevant "chunks" to include from the verbatim responses.

Stage B: Content Analysis of means-end Data

Next, the "chunks" of meaning must be content analyzed in order to aggregate and generalize across subjects. This process involves two steps. The first step is to define a dictionary of content codes into which classifications can be made. This involves a preliminary review of the data and the development of a comprehensive (and exhaustive) set of categories into which to classify all of the chunks.

The second step is the actual assignment of each verbatim to these codes. In a well-defined product category, in which analysts typically have strong insights into consumers' perceptions and motivations, many of the category codes may be defined a priori. More often, however, in laddering data analysis the steps of code definition and classification process are interwoven and the codes essentially evolve during the classification.

To facilitate this highly labour-intensive and recursive task, which inherently requires intensive human judgment and decision-making, the software allows interactive coding in an easy-to-use format. Actual content from the interviews is shown on the screen, grouped under the codes it has been assigned to. An example of the screen, where verbatim responses have been coded under the categories of "Flavour" and "Taste." If, upon inspection, it is found that some concepts are assigned incorrectly, they can be easily corrected and assigned to the proper content code. Also, if the initial coding scheme is very specific, many content codes may have relatively few actual concepts assigned to each. For example, the codes of "Flavour" and "Taste" above could be combined under flavour.

Similar codes can then be easily grouped hierarchically under a larger code, making reassignment an easy task. For example all of the items under "Taste" are easily moved under the major heading of "Flavour" by simply assigning "Taste" under "Flavour" in the coding scheme. This enables the analysts to split, combine, or redefine categories quickly and easily on-line. The content analysis task is truly the heart of laddering analysis. It is the step where qualitative data (the raw, verbatim responses from the laddering interviews) are converted into nominal codes that can be quantified. Because codes can be easily combined hierarchically within each other when using the software, we recommend a large number of very specific codes when first analyzing the data and gradually combining and grouping similar meanings until a manageable number of approximately 50 remain.

However, if you are performing analysis by hand, we recommend attempting to reduce the number of codes to approximately 50 immediately. Although this may result in a slightly higher misclassification, the combination of categories by hand would be restrictively difficult and tedious, besides being error prone. The lexical listing reports from the software, which report what verbatim responses are categorized under each content code, can be referenced at any future point to see what exactly was collapsed into the final content codes. Any further analysis of the data is only as good as the content analysis. Hence, this task should not be underrated in importance.

Stage C: Defining Connections between Content Codes

Once the laddering data is classified into codes, it can be quantitatively analyzed to produce a diagrammatic representation of the meaning structure. The end product of a laddering data analysis is a graphical representation of means-end structures aggregated across all subjects, the HVM. An HVM consists of the different content codes derived from content analysis arranged on a map and connected with lines.

These lines show the common pathways of meanings, representing how product attributes are related to personal values. The main goal of analysis is the construction of the HVM, which is the framework for assessing strategic positionings in the marketplace. This involves two stages: determining what connections should be represented on the HVM, or directed graph, and constructing the HVM in a fashion that is easily readable.

Reynolds and Gutman presented a straightforward decision rule for determining what associations should be illustrated in an HVM. Each association is compared with a cutoff level. If an association has a strength greater than or equal to that value, then the association or connecting linkage is illustrated on the HVM. The LADDERMAP software implements this decision rule in its HVM construction algorithm.

The algorithm consists of three steps. First, we construct an aggregate implication matrix, which contains the sums of all of the instances where concepts were linked in the laddering interviews. These associations can be counted in two ways – only the direct associations are included, or all the direct plus indirect associations are counted. To illustrate what direct and indirect associations mean, consider a means-end chain of A '! B '! C. Here, we have direct association from A to B and from B to C and an indirect association from A to C.

The sum of direct and indirect associations is an indicator of the strength of a given association. Often, multiple ladders will be gathered from each individual in the course of an interview. The number of ladders elicited from each individual respondent is usually dependent on the respondent's depth of knowledge or involvement in the product category. Also, a respondent may name an association between two concepts several times in different ladders elicited. In this case the association is only counted once per respondent when constructing the implication matrix in order to prevent bias in the aggregate results.

After the implication matrix is constructed, a cutoff value is selected by the analyst to determine which connections should be represented on the HVM. To assist the analyst in making this decision, a bar chart is provided on screen by the software to show how much variance would be explained by different levels of cutoff values. Typically, this cutoff value is compared against the aggregate of direct plus indirect associations in each cell of the implication matrix.

A binary matrix is formed that contains a "1" in each cell for which the corresponding element of the implication matrix is greater than or equal to the cutoff value and a "0" otherwise. These binary flags indicate which associations or connecting linkages should be illustrated on an HVM. However, in the interest of constructing a meaningful uncluttered HVM, not all of the marked associations are actually drawn as individual lines. Some of the connections indicated in the binary matrix are considered redundant and, therefore, do not need to be illustrated.

If, for instance, the matrix indicates X → Y, X → Z, and Y → Z, then the direct connection X → Z is redundant because it is captured in the X → Y and Y → Z relationships. Although some may argue that this conceals the X Z connection, the map would quickly degenerate into an unreadable state if all redundant connections were included. After all of the redundant, "pass through" relations are eliminated, the binary matrix can then be used to draw the final HVM.

The process of summing the implication matrix and determining the connections to be made is a relatively simple task and takes only a few seconds on a microcomputer, whereas it is an extremely long and laborious task by hand. This allows the analyst to go back and make content-analysis-coding changes and subsequent alternate analysis without concern because the quantitative steps can be reproduced rapidly and effortlessly.

Furthermore, automation of the task allows the analyst more flexibility and control over the process. This allows for experimentation with different levels of cutoff values and different coding strategies. Interestingly, the total number of 1s accounted for in the HVM that is reported can be considered a measure of the representativeness of the solution. This percentage index serves as a useful summary measure that should be reported in all laddering research.

Stage D: Drawing the Hierarchical Value Map

After the data is analyzed to determine exactly which associations should be illustrated as connections on the HVM, the final stage of producing an HVM must be performed. Two requirements are imposed on the analyst at this stage. First, the finished HVM must represent a significant number of the associations derived from the raw laddering data. From experience in conducting over 100 studies, the minimum threshold value should never be less than 70% with an average number typically in the 75% to 85% range. To represent any smaller percentage can cause valuable insights to be lost. Second, and perhaps more importantly in many business environments, the final HVM must be easily interpretable by management if it is to be a viable tool. Again, this stage involves qualitative judgments made by a skilled analyst to produce an HVM that is both accurate and aesthetically pleasing, hence a tradeoff between validity and parsimony.

The algorithm discussed in Stage C only determines what connections should be made but does not actually indicate where nodes should be placed to draw an intelligible HVM. Gengler and Reynolds presented a heuristic-based algorithm and interactive editing software that can aid analysts in drawing an HVM derived from the binary matrix. This facility allows the analyst to quickly and easily view several HVMs based on different cutoff points and different coding judgments. Because an aesthetic component of readability affects the interpretability of the HVM, the software provides several interactive capabilities to adjust the map and enhance its readability, such as moving nodes about, cutting and redrawing lines, or renaming nodes to be more representative of the data. In sum, the construction of an HVM from raw laddering data involves several stages of both quantifiable and nonquantifiable analysis. The major task of bridging from qualitative to quantitative analysis lies in content analysis of the subjects' verbatim responses. Inherently, this is a human judgment task but can be greatly facilitated by the use of interactive computer software. Furthermore, the use of software at this stage facilitates the subsequent quantitative stages of analysis, in particular, summarizing the frequency of the codes by subgroups within the total sample.

Although this final stage can be automated to a great degree by the LADDERMAP software, this is not a task that can be entirely put through a black box to produce useful results. Analyst judgment and decision-making at all stages of the process is a critical component of the analysis.

CONSUMER COMMUNICATIONS

Culture often manifests itself in political decisions and consumer decisions. These decisions are driven by the individual values that members of the culture hold. Studying political and value structures often provide more efficient and accurate windows to culture than studies of peripheral habits.

Most of the major countries of Western Europe have been moving toward economic cooperation for several decades via what has been known as the Common Market, the European Economic Community, or more recently simply the European Community (EC). The chosen 12 current EC participants are listed in Table, which in addition provides the population and Gross National Product (GNP) of each listed country. Table also shows the relations among the EC, the military North Atlantic Treaty Organization, and the European Free Trade Association.

Several neutral countries have not participated in the EC, such as Austria and Switzerland, as well as the northern-most countries of Finland, Sweden, Norway, and Iceland. Austria and Turkey would explicitly like to join the EC, and the EFTA, at worst, has cooperated with the EC. At best, some anticipate unification of the EC and EFTA. Other NATO countries, such as the United States, will most likely not become EC members any time soon, raising questions about the continuing significance of NATO. Some have advocated completely Coupling the EC from the United States to form an anti-Stalinist, anti-capitalist type of socialism.

The EC is gradually moving toward functioning as a super country. The EC has as permanent governmental structures the Council of Ministers, the European Parliament, a Commission, and a Court of Justice. The current structures began functioning on July 1, 1967, although the groundwork dates back to 1951. The countries want to coordinate social developments, to integrate Economies, and eventually to bring about political union. Sixty African, Caribbean, and Pacific nations are affiliated with the EC, and it has had free trade agreements with the EFTA since 1973. The world-wide significance of a unified EC is evident from the figures in Table.

Clearly the unified EC will play in the same league as Japan and the United States.

Table. Selected EC Countries' Population, Gross National Product, and Membership Status in Major European Economic and Military Alliances

Country	POP	GNP	EC	NATO	EFTA
Belgium	9.9	$ 111	Yes	Yes	No
Denmark	5.1	101	Yes	Yes	No
France	55.8	724	Yes	Yes	No
W.Germany (BRD)	60.2	898	Yes	Yes	No
Greece	10.0	37	Yes	Yes	No
Ireland	3.7	29	Yes	No	No
Italy	57.4	368	Yes	Yes	No
Luxembourg	.4	6	Yes	Yes	No
The Netherlands	14.7	190	Yes	Yes	No
Portugal	10.2	29	Yes	Yes	Yes
Spain	39.8	188	Yes	Yes	No
United-Kingdom	56.6	504	Yes	Yes	No
EC TOTAL	323.8	3185			
Iceland	.3	3	No	Yes	Yes
Norway	4.2	64	No	Yes	Yes
Austria	7.6	95	No	No	Yes
Finland	4.9	97	No	No	Associate
Sweden	8.4	109	No	No	Yes
Switzerland	6.5	171	No	No	Yes
Canada	23.3	367	No	Yes	No
Turkey	55.4	52	No	Yes	No
US	247.5	4500	No	Yes	No
E.Germany (DDR)	16.7	367	No	No	No
Japan	123.2	1900	No	No	No
U.S.S.R.	287.0	2300	No	No	No

In June, 1985, the Commission of the EC issued a White Paper, "Completing the Internal Market", which proposed 279 changes to increase Economic union. Of the 279 proposals, the council has adopted most, although some of the proposals are currently in various states of ratification, and many of the remaining proposals are among the most controversial. The target was to complete ratification of these changes by the end of 1992, at which time sales and value-added taxes, product specifications, transportation regulations, monetary units and tariffs became equal for all participating nations.

Goods, money, workers, and services pass internal EC borders freely. The EC will experience greater internal competition and will be better positioned to compete in and even lead the globalizing Economy. The EC will maintain its social commitments evidenced in the last line of Table, which may both help and hurt its Economic fate. Recently the leaders of the 12 nations called for political union by 1992 as well.

Table. Relative Sizes in 1987 of Western Economic Powers

Dimension	EC	Japan	U. S.
Population (mil)	323	122	244
GDP (tril ECUs)	3.669	2.058	3.869
World's exports	20%	12%	14%
Social cost as per cent of GDP	25%	18%	16%

Note: Adapted from Beatson, and Emerson et al.

These changes may have profound effects on how Europeans conduct business, although no one is exactly sure what all of those effects will be. Estimates range from a 0.35 to a 4 per cent increase in output simply from improved efficiency. North American pessimists see the changes as leading to the blockading of "Fortress Europe," creating a nearly impenetrable economic union of former trading partners who will establish prot Ctionist barriers to outsider participation. The Table data regarding the importance of European exports would argue against a Fortress Europe mentality because exports are too important in EC countries, and most relevant communiques from the EC headquarters dismiss this consequence of integration, too.

Optimists see the 1992 changes as simplifying and stand ardizing western European business practices, as eliminating long-outdated local traditions and restrictions, and as launching an enormous opportunity toward more efficient marketing. For the most part, European big business and large North American multinational corporations have provided the push toward 1992. These forces from the political right have cooperated with forces from the political left, who want greater international understanding and tolerance, to work toward a goal grounded in realism but idealistic enough to shape dreams. Modern communications have homogenized European culture to some extent, paving the way for left and right to travel together toward increased cooperation. The road, however, still has potholes and steep hills.

As with all predictions about the future, we can only look at where the present is heading and guess where it might arrive. Anyone who claims to know the future for sure is either God or not honest, and we have more aspirations toward honesty than deification. With the rapid changes in Europe that are taking place apart from the development of the EC, we must view economic unification as only one force for change out of many. Numerous forces other than the "1992 changes" will also alter Europe. Certainly the reunification of East and West Germany is modifying the nature of the continent, as are the rapid other changes in Eastern Europe set in motion by the Soviet Union's admission that the Cold War is over and by its economic and political difficulties. Western Europeans trust the Soviets and the East much more now than 10 years ago, with the correlated decline in reliance on the United States for economic and military security.

We should not underestimate the significance of transportation and information technology changes in the reshaping of Europe, either. On the other hand, cultural, political, geographic, and linguistic barriers did not all suddenly evaporate on January 1, 1993. Some of the targeted economic changes were not even in place, and others will not respond to new policies as anticipated. But let us at this point assume for the sake of edification that the targeted economic changes are indeed occurring as planned.

THE NEW ECONOMY OF THE EC

The White Paper proposed the planned changes clearly

enough. Let us look at each of the broad classes of targeted changes more carefully.

FISCAL BARRIERS ENDED

For example, excise taxes and value-added taxes are not to be levied anew each time a product passes another border. Tariffs and quotas had presumably already been removed, although a few still remain, for example in agricultural and steel products. These internal tariffs ended. Direct state control of interest rates and lending quotas ended Government subsidies of industry receded and usually ceased. Subsidies from the governments are being heavily discouraged by the EC Commissioner for Competition. The EC has ordered over $1 billion in subsidy paybacks in 26 cases since 1981. More will certainly follow.

Technical Barriers Are Being Removed

Divergent technical norms for goods and services essentially ended. Health and safety standards in the work place are synchronized. Foreign companies are allowed to establish subsidiaries more easily, and foreign company bids do not receive discriminatory treatment in government procurement. Countries within the EC are able to bid freely on government procurement, and outside countries can win procurement bids if they can provide at least a 3 per cent saving over EC competitors. Trademarks, patent, and intellectual property rights now extend throughout the EC Protection of intellectual properties involves many issues, not just traditional trademark, copyright, and patent issues. For example, who controls computer data documents, screen displays, and software? A proposed copyright law in the EC would give more control over software interfaces to the companies who write them, thus giving a boost to large computer manufacturers and creating more difficulty for small software companies Consider an example of how technology change will be an inevitable part of the new Europe. Currently, Europeans cannot use "beepers" to page one another across national borders. The United States has at present eight times as many beepers as the ec. In December 1992, a common paging system became available, allowing increased paging and presumably increasing sales greatly. This change is not a revolutionary one, but it exemplifies how technology transfer has increased with stand ardization of technical specifications and how it will increase access to people Regulations did not disappear in 1992, they only became more uniform.

Tobacco ads, for example, are generally banned on European television, but in print they may take many forms. In an effort to integrate the laws, all tobacco advertising of any type may be banned. The European Parliament passed legislation, yet to be ratified, banning print, broadcast, and event sponsorship advertising of tobacco products.

Physical Frontier Barriers Have Been Removed

Vehicles now do not have to stop for customs inspection at each border, for example. Because excise taxes and technical specification differences ended, the prior justifications for strangling the transportation industry in red tape disappeared. Laws against backhauling, which prevent truckers from returning with full loads, ended, for example. Currently trucks cross the United States at an average of 64 kph, whereas prior to 1992 they crossed the EC at an average of 12 kph, in spite of very liberal speed limits on, for example, the German Autobahnen. These changes should speed up transportation considerably. Increased competition in air transportation should result from reduction of regulations and subsidies.

Calingaert suggested that several changes are especially important for North Americans, and we must monitor how these changes are occurring.

The terms and conditions of participation for foreign service providers have major implications both for American companies operating in Europe currently and for companies desiring to operate there in the future. The vital financial and information technology services warrant special attention. Quraeshi and Lyqmani suggested that protectionism, openness of directives, and the view of reciprocity top the list of US concerns Synchronizing regulations and standards changed them, but it is too early to tell how exclusionary new regulations and standards will be. North Americans should monitor testing and certification regulations, and we should also focus on how local content rules are fashioned Public procurement laws allow foreign competitors to bid on public projects, reducing the number of local sweetheart deals.

This fact may be especially important in construction, communication, and power equipment sales. These fields are ones in which the United States excels, but it is too soon to tell whether the new laws will include open competition only for other EC countries or for all countries. Bids from non-EC countries will have to be at least 3 per cent lower than EC bids to win contracts. Most of the other changes, according to Calingaert, have a more general influence on North Americans, Japanese, and Europeans alike: common legal framework, capital liberalization, border controls, freedom of movement, and tax harmonization influence everyone more or less equally.

These Changes Are Increasing Internal Competition

Thereby, they will reduce prices while increasing efficiency. If each country currently has two or three major suppliers, removal of internal market barriers could suddenly create 20 or 30 competitors. The current pace of European mergers and acquisitions, however, suggests that three or four major competitors may more often be the norm. In the grocery business, for example, many European tastes are becoming more homogeneous, thus leading to border-jumping by many brands before 1992. As with supermarkets in the United States, European retailers are tempted to stock only the top brands. The same type of oligopoly may emerge in the EC's currently-fragmented airline industry.

Related laws that are not part of the White Paper also influence European trade, especially the rules of origin and local content. Rules of origin give a product its nationality, which in turn determines EC tariffs. Local content regulations define whether a product is an EC product, based on the value of EC inputs relative to its total value. Local (e.g., European) content laws become especially complex in the information and entertainment industries. An example of a recent localcontent law that influences communication is the rule that at least 50 per cent of all EC television programming, except news, sports, and game shows, must be of EC origin "where practicable". Currently 70 per cent of all nondocumentary shows, films, serials, and soap operas are imported, and over half of those imports come from the United States.

Because the United States has a larger homogeneous audience and allows far more commercials, it can produce exportable entertainment more efficiently than Europe. The new ruling is increasing joint ventures between United States and EC entertainment companies, and it may also necessitate EC-wide government subsidies on the entertainment industry. Some perceive these rules as politically, but not legally, binding.

CORPORATE STRATEGY IN THE NEW EUROPE

Strategically, many international companies are planning to manufacturer (or to ally themselves with a manufacturer) in western Europe, in case local content and origin laws exclude countries outside of the chosen 12. Mergers and acquisitions top the priority list of many corporations. Japan has doubled its investment in Europe in the past 2 years. American investments in the EC have risen sharply in recent years, as have European investments in America.

Strategic alliances are also becoming more commonplace, such as the "intensive cooperation" between Daimler Benz, West Germany's largest company, and Mitzubishi, Japan's top manufacturing and trading conglomerate. Buyouts, mergers, acquisitions, franchising, joint ventures, and redirecting investments all are dominating international activity aimed at strengthening European companies. The new companies that emerge in Europe will be bigger, stronger, and more international.

Companies will need to adapt their strategies to the new environment. Friberg suggested that the four most basic challenges will be to reduce overcapacity, build scale, recognize international competition, and work to homogenize local tastes a goal especially relevant to advertising. The objective will be to operate as efficiently as possible in a much larger, mass market. European business leaders are becoming more democratic, pragmatic, global, entrepreneurial, creative, and aggressive as they adapt to this new environment.

U.S. companies have traditionally tried to treat Europe as a single market; hence, North Americans may have an advantage in this regard. On the other hand, Americans have been slow to conceptualize the implications of changes in Europe. Perhaps because many U.S. companies are already satisfied with their successes in Europe, or perhaps because the United States is less internationally oriented than other countries, the major changes have not yet influenced behaviour as much for U.S. companies as for Japanese and EC companies.

One exception to the lack of U.S. savvy is the recognition that pan-European market niches will be more viable in the future. Pan-European marketing will soon be the norm for most large and middle-sized companies. Strategies will be developed and niches identified with the entire EC in mind. Retailer integration across national boundaries will certainly occur as well.

Different types of companies will necessarily respond differently to the changes because different structural characteristics will imply different outcomes. Magee, for example, suggested quite different strategies for established multinationals, corporations with one European subsidiary, businesses that export to Europe, and business with no interest in Europe.

No one can predict all of the consequences of the changes taking place, but the changes will reverberate throughout society. Labour worries that manufacturing's new capital investments will seek locations with low wages and benefits. For example, wages and benefits are nearly double in former West Germany what they are in Spain. Unrest and frustration could result if this trend does indeed emerge.

To provide one example of an American company in its quest to adapt, consider General Motors (GM). GM Europe was established in Zurich in 1986 to coordinate all of GM's European subsidiaries. GM developed a mid-sized car with suspension rugged enough to hand le German Autobahnen and smooth enough to please the French.

Options allow the austere Northern Europeans and the flashy Southern Europeans to obtain what they want. Without all details of technical standards, GM has had to take some risks, such as assuming catalytic converters will be required on all EC cars. GM has tried to integrate its advertising, too, with Lowe International planning its United Kingdom and West German launch, and with McCann-Erickson, Zurich adapting its campaign for other European countries.

ADVERTISING IN THE EC AFTER 1992

Unification Benefits

Fewer but larger companies will be willing and able to spend larger amounts of advertising money in attempts to create mass markets. This should create a positive environment for advertising. Companies will pursue niches that transcend national boundaries more aggressively. For example, lifestyles transcend borders. German and British yuppies are more alike than yuppies and blue collar workers within either country. "Businessmen all over the EC have similar lifestyles". Advertisers will reach for lifestyle niches more than political niches. Another potential consequence of EC changes will be an increase in pan-European advertising, and evidence corroborates this as a trend. "Many advertisers are consolidating spending by brand or product category with a single agency and launching products with a pan-European rollout. More than $1 billion in pan-European advertising has been awarded to agencies since 1988". The direction of EC rulings should increase the ease of cross-frontier advertising.

Pan-European advertising will benefit from removal of technical specification barriers because one product will be available for all ECcountries. Thus, preparation of catalogues and product descriptions will not change (except for translations) from country to country. Likewise, uniform legal requirements will end the need for legal opinions about controversial activities from each country. Recent relaxing of laws on television advertising in Europe has boosted advertising expenditure growth in Europe to double what it is in the United States. The Interpublic Group may be the best-positioned American company to cash in on this change because it already earns 35% of its profits in Europe. Murdoch is also well-positioned for internationalization of media markets.

Unification Challenges

Although advertisers hope to develop pan-European ads, the task will not be easy. This goal will partly suffer from the lack of pan-European media outlets. One forecast is that by 1995, only 10% to 20% of media will be pan-European. Reed International plans to expand its international efforts in Europe. Maxwell Communication circulates a newspaper called *The European,* which is a weekend newspaper designed to inform Europeans about what is going on in Europe. It anticipated an initial circulation of 350, 000 in Europe, and it eventually hopes to reach a world-wide audience.

Media that already have outlets in several EC countries, such as the Reader's Digest, promote this virtue to potential advertisers. A recent Reader's Digest ad from the *New York Times* Magazine with the headline *"Ready for 1992"* noted that Reader's Digest already has 15 European editions. It claims to be the number one magazine in Europe. The copy provided an important clue to its plans: "As Europe's internal barriers disappear, Reader's Digest will continue tailoring each edition to serve readers' native cultural and language differences. Our editors—who live and work in the countries they serve—speak their readers' language, know their customs and are intimately familiar with their interests and concerns."

Not everyone sees a trend toward pan-European advertising, however. Beatson believed that cultural characteristics, although blurring, are nevertheless strong enough to require a predominance of local advertising. Language and culture will inhibit truly international ads, as will the current lack of truly international brands and the lack of truly international product usage.

Language certainly remains a barrier. Although English—often American English—is widely used, most countries want to preserve their own linguistic heritage. Machine translations will increase in popularity over the years, but the quality of these translations still falls short for many formal purposes. Of the 70 machine translation systems available today, the best translate only roughly. Some specialized tasks can be performed with about 95% accuracy, but we can expect EC electronic companies will focus considerable effort on improving translation machines.

Another solution to the language problem is the visual or nonverbal advertisement. Graphic visual depiction often expresses a concept without words. Music can also aid in nonverbal communication, even if message recipients share no language. Cultural tastes vary from country to country. For example, the *Benny Hill Show* has achieved popularity in the United Kingdom, the Netherlands, and Scandinavia, but it has not been particularly appreciated by German, Swiss, or Belgian viewers.

Unification will not end unique national characteristics. Product usage often differs from country to country. For example, laundry habits and washing machines differ from Northern to Southern Europe. The cost of energy varies widely from one country to another, leading to product and demand differences. Identical ads are pointless if products or services are unavailable, unattractive, or impractical in certain places. Agencies face the difficult task of eliciting employee cooperation in any attempt at pan-European advertising. European advertising executives often subscribe to the "Not Invented Here Syndrome", which implies that agency officials object to creative strategies and executions imposed on them from elsewhere. International cooperation must occur at the individual employee level as well as the governmental level.

Technology

Technology change will influence advertising. The

technologies especially important for pan-European advertising are information technologies. Communication among businesses is easier with computers and fax machines. Television is benefiting from satellite and cable systems, although penetration has not come as rapidly in Europe, perhaps because of local regulations. The United States currently has about double the telephone usage of the EC. In the EC, voice telephony currently accounts for 85% to 90% of transmissions, with up to 10% derived from facsimile and up to 5% from telex.

It is expected that within 20 years the transmission of data will exceed voice transmission in the EC. The imminent introduction of Integrated Services Digital Networks (ISDNs) will greatly improve EC communications. In fact, the EC has been slow to modernize in anticipation of the 1992 technical synchrony. When specifications are established and implemented, the EC could well race toward the most modern telecommunication system in the world, leapfrogging over the Asians. Europe currently has state-run telecommunication monopolies, similar to but more controlled than the United States prior to the divestiture of AT and T. Increased competitiveness and multiple players seem almost certain to loom over the horizon in the near future.

Television technology will change in Europe, just as it has changed in the United States. Already in the United Kingdom we are witnessing an intense battle over satellite. British Satellite Broadcasting (BSB) is launching a 5-channel system to compete with incompatible technology with Rupert Murdoch's 4-channel Sky Television. Sky costs subscribers $30 per month plus $17 for premium movies. BSB costs consumers $26 per month. Sky spent $45 million advertising itself last year, and it received considerable favorable publicity in other Murdoch-owned media. BSB plans to spend $164 million on advertising in the next 3 years. After its first year, Sky is losing $3 million per week in spite of having 1.1 million subscribers. There is a question regarding whether both Sky and BSB can survive. Cable TV may also become a competitive factor, although for now experts apparently believe that the cost of laying cable, which must all be underground in Britain, will limit cable's growth. The penetration of both cable and satellite varies widely from country to country. Many U.S. companies, such as baby-bell U.S. WEST, have aggressively pursued cable opportunities in Europe. In Ireland TV3 launched a new competitor for Irish entertainment. A new radio network will also lure ad revenue from the current competitors there.

Scandinavia has been the last outpost of commercial-free television, but a 2-year-old satellite channel, TV3, has been broadcasting to affluent Scandinavia from London, in order to circumvent Scandinavian laws. In February, it was viewed by 33.4 per cent of TV homes in Sweden, 37.3 per cent of TV homes in Denmark, and 36.2 per cent of TV homes in Norway. It has met with significant success, perhaps breaking even by 1991. It has had the political effect of relaxing Scandinavian laws on advertising, in order to prevent further defection of advertising revenue.

On Sept. 15, 1990, Nordisk TV4 began cable casting in Sweden. It allows 6 minutes of ads per hour. Norway allowed radio advertising in 1989 for the first time since 1945, and it will likely soon have a commercial television channel. Most Norwegians can receive Swedish broadcasts; hence developments in Sweden influence Norway. In Denmark TV2 will likely increase its advertising from the current limit of 15 minutes per day.

Because Spain and Portugal only recently joined the EC, advertising there has been growing rapidly. In 1989 Spain's advertising increased by 24 per cent after inflation, and it increased by 12.7 per cent in Portugal, compared to 2.8 Per cent in the BRD. More open television will change advertising in Spain, too. One channel started to broadcast in December 1989, and two more are expected soon.

Research

Pan-European marketing research has become easier. A.C. Nielsen Co., for example, has traditionally allowed subsidiaries in each country to set up unique methodologies because international research was too difficult. For example, lemon-flavored Perrier could be classified as a mineral water in France but a soft drink in Italy. Bottle sizes might vary. In one country sales are in francs, in the other lira. Now it is possible to have integrated European databases.

VALUES AND ADVERTISING IN THE GLOBAL ECONOMY

Table. Social Values in Several Countries

Value	France	BRD	Denmark	Norway	U.S.	U.S.S.R.	Japan
Self-fulfillment	30.9%	4.8%	7.1%	7.7%	6.5%	8.8%	36.7%
Sense of belonging	1.7	28.6	13.0	33.4	5.1	23.9	2.3
Security	6.3	24.1	6.3	10.0	16.5	5.7	10.9
Self respect	7.4	12.9	29.7	16.6	23.0	10.1	4.7
Warm relationships with others	17.7	7.9	11.3	13.4	19.9	23.3	27.6
Fun and enjoyment in life/excitement	16.6	10.1	16.8	3.6	7.2	9.7	7.5
Being well respected	4.0	6.1	5.0	8.4	5.9	8.5	2.1
Sense of accomplishment	15.4	5.4	10.9	6.8	15.9	10.1	8.3
Total	100.0%	100.0%	100.0%	100.0%	100.0%	100.0%	100.0%
N	175	1008	239	457	997	321	387

We know that relating products to values is one of the more effective means of advertising. Personal values have consistently shown a clear and noteworthy relation to consumer and other behaviour. In order to discover the extent to which values differ and therefore imply different approaches to advertising, we need to ask how values differ from country to country.

All of the difficulties of international survey data characterize these results, including linguistic issues such as translation and connotative meanings, methodological issues such as the differences in divergent types of surveys, and sampling issues such as how one obtains adequate and comparable samples in different countries. It is even possible that the values from which one chooses are indeed different in, for example, Denmark and Japan; hence, one should offer different lists from which to choose values in different countries. In short, these data are more suggestive than definitive, more heuristic than conclusive.

Nevertheless, the data do have a certain face validity and are instructive inasmuch as they have any external validity. Contrary to what one might expect, the respect values are weak in Japan, but self-fulfillment is quite strong. Self-fulfillment is a value humanists have introduced to the West from the East; hence, its prevalence in Japan is not too surprizing. Germans turn out not to be puritanical workaholics, inasmuch as they emphasize fun and enjoyment in life more and accomplishment less than other countries.

The supposedly stoic Danes also value fun more than the norm. The French, as well as the Americans, place far more emphasis on fulfillment and accomplishment than the Germans. The image of the obsessed Nazi probably tells less about contemporary Germany than the image of the Bavarian beer hall patron. Grunert and Scherhorn attributed German concern about security to Germany's location on the eastern edge of Western Europe. The next survey of German values will present a fascinating test of that hypothesis because, presumably, concern about Eastern Europe as a threat to security has diminished greatly in the recent past. The U.S.S.R. and Japan have been characterized as ruthless in U.S. media, but the data show warm relationships with others to have great appeal in these two countries.

One need look no further than the first two columns to see the difficulties facing the EC. EC partners France and

Germany have at least a 5% difference in all values except the relatively unimportant being well respected. Sense of belonging and security are the most important values in Germany, together comprising the values of over half the population. These two values are endorsed by only 9% of the French sample. Nearly half of the French endorse either self-fulfillment or warm relationships with others as most important, a far cry from the 12.7% of Germans who endorse this value.

These differences among countries, even limiting the scope to EC countries, are much greater than we have observed within the U.S. regions. They suggested a tremendous amount of diversity and a great need to tolerate diversity. The tolerance will be necessary for the community to hold together. Germans and French, for example, will need to respect their diversity as much as, say, the other British people tolerate the Welsh or the other Spanish people tolerate the Catalans. Much of the splintering in Eastern Europe is resulting from groups who do not want to participate in a community whose activities in the past have shown little respect for their unique contributions.

These value differences also suggest that merely removing regulations will not immediately increase the ease of communications among all Europeans. Value-based advertisements will still be splintered throughout Europe, even if legal complexities do not require diversity. Sales presentations still need to consider unique local values. For example, appeals to sense of belonging will still primarily be targeted at Germany and Norway rather than France and Denmark.

OTHER SOURCES OF CHANGE

Consider some of the things about Europe that have not changed: language, preferences, habits, culture, climate, incomes, and many other variables that influence consumer desire for certain products. The difficulties in achieving the 1992 goals run deep in the fabric of Europe. "The social, cultural, and even linguistic repercussions may pose more of a threat than real economic issues". The changes are all on the supply side, yet market acceptance will, in the end, rule.

In spite of the stated goals and the very real progress toward political unification, Europe still seems quite a distance from true coordination, in the United States sense. Most people in the United States probably have a greater loyalty to the United States than to their own particular state, but we are probably several generations away from a Europe in which, for example, French consider themselves to be more European than French.

Europe is facing many demographic trends similar to the trends in North America. For example, the average age is increasing. Women are participating in the work force to a greater extent. European trends in marriage mirror North American trends. These changes are independent of economic regulation.

Changes to the East require monitoring. Eastern Europeans may provide new markets with pent-up demand, and they will provide low-cost labour. Many countries in Eastern Europe expect to move rapidly from a planned economy to a market economy. The next decade in Eastern Europe May resemble the decade after World War II in NATO countries. The infrastructure will have to be rebuilt, from telephones to pollution control devices and consumers will want many of the products they have been denied. Yet pent up demand associated with decades of political suppression could undermine Eastern Europe's economic progress. Ironically, Western European countries that have allowed independence are seeking unity while Eastern European countries that have experienced forced unity have sought fragmentation.

With German reunification now a reality, many wonder whether Germany will be too dominant in the EC. France and the United Kingdom have roughly the same population as the BRD, but the BRD already had more economic power than the other two major EC powers. With the DDR attached, the German economy is roughly double the size of France's. Redefining business, political, and military relations will provide a fascinating series of stories from Eastern and Western Europe over the next decade. The German value for sense of belonging seems especially pertinent here. If Germans see themselves as belonging to the EC, they may emphasize continental cooperation.

Consider, for example, the German beer industry, one of our favorites. In 1516 Germany began observing the *Reinheitsgebot,* requiring that beer be manufactured only of pure ingredients. In 1987 the ECoverturned that law, allowing all manner of beverages to be called beer and to be sold in Germany. As the world's leading beer-drinking nation on a per capita basis, Germany would seem a prime candidate for foreign brewer penetration. Germans, however, prefer pure, German beer. In spite of the now-open market, German habits have not substantially changed.

German beer brands, of which there are nearly 4000, comm and nearly genetic brand loyalty in the domestic market, are perceived as having high quality, control channels of distribution tightly, and quite frankly are unlikely to suffer from competition with foreign brands that are considered inferior by consumers. In fact no foreign brewer has obtained significant market share in Germany since the EC removed the "barriers." The point is that ultimately consumer lifestyles and tastes will direct economic outcomes more than policy. Policy only allows options, it does not insure what choices are made.

CONSUMER SEGMENTATION

Segmentation divides a heterogeneous marketplace into smaller and more manageable homogenous components. These smaller market segments can be targeted with more personally relevant positioning strategies that have greater appeal to individuals within the group. In theory, marketers can tailor a unique marketing mix to each segment that can be optimally effective in persuading consumers in the segment to choose their brand or increase brand usage.

Thus, the potential benefits of efficient segmentation are substantial, particularly given the fragmented media market that exists today. Evidence of this is given by the emergence of micromarketing practices that target individuals with customized selling propositions through direct mail, direct solicitation, or cable programming.

To provide efficient segments, differing segmentation classifications have been developed, including demographic characteristics of the consumer, benefits sought by the consumer, and behavioral measures of the consumer. Segmentation by demographics is very popular and quite easy to do.

But broad demographic segments and most other unidimensional segmentation schemes provide only a piece of the segmentation puzzle. In most cases, the unidimensional classification schemes have to be combined with other segmentation variables in order to market to what appears to be a more homogenous target.

Lifestyles and psychographics can provide these additional variables and are segmentation forms that more closely reflect the way people live and why they buy.

Lifestyle segmentation, for example, would group together those people who are suburbanites or those who are "generation X, " whereas psychographic segmentation is based on consumer psychological profiles that presumably define their consumption behaviour.

Many segmentation approaches, however, are limited in their ability to provide actionable guidance to managers, because segments are ill defined or they exist more in the data than the reality of the marketplace. In extreme cases, segmentation becomes an end unto itself rather than a marketing tool.

Segmentation efforts further suffer from a lack of causal relations between the defining characteristics of a segment and the behaviors of interest. Also, it can be difficult to accurately classify a consumer into a segment without knowing details about the individual, including demographic, psychographic or behavioral characteristics. These are some of the fundamental reasons why attempts at broad-scale segmentation often fail to provide managers with useful information that leads to better, let alone optimal marketing solutions.

Indeed, inappropriate customer classification can mislead managers into unnecessarily limiting their target market. A segment defined by both behavioral and demographic variables will exclude potential customers who might qualify on behavioral variables alone.

Likewise, some segmentation schemes might include low-probability prospects in the same group as high-probability prospects. For example, segmentation based only on psychographic variables or personal characteristics might include both users and nonusers of a category. Further study of such segments, without identifying more refined subgroups, would tend to hide potentially critical differences, such as the barriers that keep people out of the category or the brand franchise.

But are these potential results serious problems for marketing management? One can think about segmentation error the same way one thinks about statistical effort. Type I segmentation errors result in people being excluded from the market segment in which they should have been included. Type II segmentation errors result when people are included in the segment who should have been excluded.

What are the downsides of Type I or Type II segmentation errors? How large do these errors have to be before they matter, and which error is more serious? The answers depend on the costs of communication to groups of prospects and the probability of making a sale to these prospects. In most marketplace situations, both types of error are inefficient and waste limited marketing resources. Clearly, the ability to target consumer groups with the most appropriate strategic message offers both a significant challenge and an opportunity to marketing management.

A methodology of segmentation based on understanding the consumer's choice process. This approach has the potential to reduce these two sources of segmentation error. The methodology is based on our belief that effective segmentation is a result of differentiating a heterogeneous population based on the decision-making criteria used to select a product, as well as by the dimensions of consumer behaviour of greatest interest to the marketing manager.

Therefore, we believe that segmentation schemes should include both attitude and behaviour variables to allow management to efficiently target customers with appropriate communications. A second challenge facing the marketer is delivering the most appropriate message to the target group, which we discuss as well.

Segmentation is disaggregative in its effect in that it tends to bring about recognition of several demand schedules where only one was recognized before.... Market segmentation... consists of viewing a heterogeneous market (one characterized by divergent demand) as a number of smaller homogenous markets in response to differing product preferences among important market segments. Segmentation reflects the desires of consumers for more precise satisfaction of their varying wants. Said another way, disaggregation shows that the relation between price and quantity, the demand schedule, will be quite different based on individual needs and wants. This is good news for marketers because disaggregation may identify high-value-high-profit needs and wants that are unobservable in pooled data. Smith has since been acknowledged as the forefather of segmentation.

However, demand may not always be the most appropriate basis for segmentation, particularly if the underlying reasons for demand are not consistent across members of the segment. Further dividing segments based on these underlying reasons for purchase may provide additional insight and guidance concerning the types of marketing activities or communication appeals that might work best for each segment.

Winter provided a definition of cost-benefit segmentation that is perhaps more useful for selecting marketing activities and developing communications. He wrote:

Market segmentation is the recognition that groups or subsegments differ with respect to properties which suggest that different marketing mixes might be used to appeal to the different groups. These subsegments may then be aggregated if the reduction in cost exceeds the reduction in benefits (revenues). This aggregation is based on the fact that both subsegments respond most to the same marketing mix.

Winter further pointed out the problems with most segmentation analysis: weak relations between demographic characteristics of a segment and behaviour, no causal base, and a lack of actionability. For example, what does one do with a segment identified as "Our primary target market for frozen pie crusts consists of females 35–60 with a high school education living in the Midwest and Southeast, making $20, 000–$35, 000 per year and with 3.2 children who no longer live at home but who visit two times per month?".

Winter offered a procedure of segmentation trees that is based on understanding specific consumer needs to overcome some of these problems. The segmentation tree approach accounts for two key factors. First, the situation may dictate the segment into which the consumer falls. Second, segments based on needs rather than behaviour help select the marketing mix strategy that will be most effective. Thus, marketing activities aimed at subsegments identified by a tree approach are likely to be less wasteful of marketing resources. The problem remains, however, to identify the "optimum" tree.

At this point, managerial goals must enter the process. What will management do with the segments? There are two primary applications of segmentation. One is to identify markets for new or potential products. This might be useful in the product development and design stages, as well as for new product introductions into the market. More often, the goal of segmentation is to identify or refine markets for existing products and then sell to them. Segmentation for this purpose would assist the development of the marketing mix.

Distribution, pricing, and communication strategy might all be of issue. Our focus is communication strategy because of the fundamental difficulties in developing and implementing targeted communications such as direct mail, television or print advertising, and sales promotions. Segments for communication strategy must then reflect homogeneity of the characteristics, ideas, or concepts concerning the product or service that are included in the marketing communications.

THE THEORETICAL BASIS FOR A COGNITIVE SEGMENTATION APPROACH

Marketing communications, in general, are meant to alter or reinforce beliefs and attitudes, which in turn alter or reinforce behaviour (i.e., communications are meant to be persuasive). Petty and Cacioppo provided a model that recognizes persuasion as a process of multiple determinants. In their Elaboration Likelihood Model, there are two routes to persuasion.

The central route requires cognitive effort and results in relatively stable and enduring attitudes that tend to predict behaviour. The peripheral route involves little or no cognitive effort and results in unstable attitudes that are less predictive of behaviour. A persuasive result or attitude or belief change, then, is a result of one or both of these routes. Logically, segmentation for communication strategy should be based on the key elements that lead to persuasion. Often, central-route persuasion is desirable because this route leads to more enduring attitudes and associated behaviour.

Means-end theory describes consumer decision-making as a cognitive process involving different levels of associations. These levels combine in memory to provide the consumer with the personal motivation to choose and use a product or service. Thus, means-end theory describes a cognitive process that corresponds to central-route persuasion.

In means-end theory, the product is defined by tangible attributes at the most concrete level. In contrast, very abstract, personal goals or values that motivate behaviour define the consumer. The consequences of product attributes that help consumers satisfy or achieve their goals represent the cognitive link between the external product or service and the internal personal value orientation of the person. These consequences can be physical in nature, such as "quenches my thirst" or psychological, such as "I feel refreshed."

People have multiple values or goal orientations, and they

place differing emphases on the respective orientations that exist for them. Values, then, might serve as an initial basis for segmentation because they represent the motivations for behaviour. Unlike the popular Values and Life Styles approach, however, means-end theory recognizes that a person strives to satisfy different values across different consumption occasions that further differ across product classes.

Said another way, means-end theory recognizes that people interpret their world in different ways depending on the product and context of consumption. For example, a professional photographer might consider a deer stand ing in a meadow for a graphic project in order to fulfill a value termed *financial security*, whereas a zoologist might study the deer's behaviour as a way to achieve success. The converse may also be true — namely, the photographer could be driven by success, whereas the zoologist is driven by security. Therefore, using values as the only criterion for segmentation is not enough.

People learn to associate certain chains of ideas that connect a product or service with self. Summaries of these means-end chains, called *Hierarchical Value Maps*, provide graphical representations of the perceptual marketplace. Each pathway on the map represents a dominant perceptual orientation among consumers.

Importantly, each pathway includes both the value orientation of the consumer, as well as the personal interpretations of how the product or service fits with the consumer's self-goal and values. The pathways are based on experiential or media learning or on cognitive reasoning. In either case, the pathways are always context specific for the respondent. Reasoning occurs within situations from the real world or with equal validity, in "minds-eye" frames. Segmentation based on these perceptual orientations yields segments that will differ in response to marketing messages because the consumers' decision hierarchy served as the basis for identifying the segments. The following case example demonstrates this segmentation process, from problem identification to segmentation based on consumer decision-making to the process of developing communicative tactics for each segment.

THE CHEMLAWN CASE

ChemLawn Services Corporation of Columbus, Ohio was the first company to offer lawn-care services on a national basis. This new service was met with widespread acceptance, while ChemLawn's only competition included the "do-it-yourself" market and local "mom and pop" operations. From 1975 until 1986, consumer acceptance remained high while disposable incomes grew.

During this period, several national companies entered the market, and additional local companies were formed to compete directly with ChemLawn. By the late 1980s, ChemLawn' s period of rapid growth and expansion had ended due to the combined forces of increased competition, ChemLawn's high level of penetration in many markets, decreasing levels of disposable income, and increased consumer concerns about environmental safety.

Nevertheless, ChemLawn remained the U.S. leader in lawn-care services, with an approximate 30% share of all revenues in the industry, compared with less than 10% for its nearest competitor. Growth throughout the lawn-care services market also came to an end in the late 1980s. The number of lawn-care service customers peaked in 1986 then began to decline with the onset of hard economic times.

Customer turnover in the industry rose to 32% per year. Competition, already intense due to the number of players in the industry, became fierce. Most major competitors adopted price as their competitive platforms with a focus on recruiting new customers to deal with the increasing turnover problem. At the same time, widespread publicity over industry practices and materials led to increased consumer concerns about health and the environment. Do-it-yourself product manufacturers, taking advantage of these concerns and the economic downturn, greatly improved their marketing efforts. In an attempt to counter these negative trends, ChemLawn increased its service offerings and expanded into new markets, but neither of these strategies proved effective in slowing ChemLawn's customer-base erosion.

In fact, ChemLawn's annual customer turnover rate approached 42%, considerably more than the industry average. Also during this time, all national lawn-care service companies, save one, continued to lose market share to small regional and local companies.

There were two possible explanations for this. One, the smaller companies had lower cost and overhead structures and thus could charge a lower price. This belief, though, assumed that the industry had become mature, with no real difference among service providers or the quality of their service. In such a scenario, the only solution would be to cut costs. An alternative view was that the national providers had not been effective at differentiating their services from the regional and local companies and were out of touch with how these differences might appeal to particular market segments. This suggested an urgent need to understand segments of the market. If changes in their positioning were then made based on an adequate market segmentation, ChemLawn could adapt effectively to market circumstances it could not control, thereby exercising comm and of its own fate.

Laddering Interviews and Analysis

The first step in developing a positioning for ChemLawn consisted of 80 in-depth consumer interviews across a representative sample of ChemLawn service users, competitive service users, and do-it-yourselfers. The interviews, using the laddering technique, identified five motivational value orientation groups. Laddering is a one-on-one interview process that uncovers the personally motivating reasons and feelings associated with the functional and physical aspects of the product or service that serve as stated initial reasons for choice.

Laddering also uncovers the barriers to choice when it focuses on the reasons for rejecting an alternative. Examples of both benefit and barrier ladders for lawn-care services. Although each customer respondent typically has multiple ladders or perceptual pathways associated with the different physical features (attributes) of the product or service, individuals' dominant reason for choice can be represented by primary pathways. These dominant reasons also are called the individual's *perceptual orientation*.

The laddering data was used to develop an "HVM of the lawn-care services industry, which included multiple segments based on how the customer related the tangible service aspects to their personal motivating value or goal orientation. Analysis of the laddering interview data in the HVM revealed six distinct customer segments representing six primary decision-making orientations:

- Environmentalist,
- Parent,
- Justifier,
- Busy Guy,
- Perfection Seeker, and
- Green Thumb.

Individual consumers typically had characteristics and beliefs from more than one of these categories, but their primary motivations were associated with one of these dominant pathway. Thus, they could be classified into one of these groups.

An example of how to translate the laddering data into a descriptive segment is shown for the Justifier segment. Based on the primary decision-making ladder associated with this group and additional quantitative analysis, we developed an understanding of the group's buying behaviour. The Justifier was not satisfied with a quality product; he or she had to justify its purchase through the judgment that it was a good value.

Thus, the Justifier was price sensitive but also recognized the worth of value-added attributes. Justifiers were unique in the market because of their emphasis on cost-benefit relationships for the purchase decision. This made them a hard sell but potentially a good target group. They did not make snap-buying decisions, but once convinced of the value of the product or service, they did not change their minds unless they perceived a change in value.

In addition to grouping consumers based on attitudinal and motivational factors, segmentation must be able to contrast beliefs between people with and without desired purchase or consumption behaviors. From a managerial perspective, marketing activities must affect behaviour — in particular, purchase and consumption behaviors.

One of the best ways to deal with this issue is to contrast the perceptual orientations of groups with the relevant purchase or consumption behaviour. In the case of ChemLawn, the critical behaviour of interest was based on the consumer's relationship to ChemLawn. For example, the behaviour of interest among ChemLawn's current customers was to "continue to employ ChemLawn."

The desired behaviour among customers of other national providers of lawn-care service was to "switch to ChemLawn." The key behaviors for do-it-yourselfers were first "consider employing a service" and then "begin using ChemLawn." Finally, the relevant behaviors for nonusers of lawn-care products were to "start using fertilizers or lawn chemicals, " (and then "employ a service" and "begin using ChemLawn.")

Clearly, the primary emphasis in this analysis was to understand the consumer types in ChemLawn's current customer base to better meet their needs and reduce turnover. The secondary focus was on the do-it-yourselfers because the do-it-yourselfers represented substantial industry growth and seemed easier to recruit than customers of other services and non-users.

Market Survey

To provide estimates of the relative sizes of the segments and additional qualitative and quantitative information focusing on the perceptual differences between the segments, we conducted a survey of 539 lawn-care service users including both customers of professional service providers and do-it-yourselfers. In the survey, each respondent was given brief descriptions of all six customer segment profiles described previously. Respondents were to order the profiles with respect to how well each one described them. The top two profiles were used as a basis of questioning to determine which consumer group was most representative.

Each respondent was then classified into one of the six groups, and estimated segment sizes were determined. In addition, each respondent evaluated each of the service providers and the do-it-yourself option, on the elements identified by the laddering research. Respondents rated both the importances of the elements and associations between elements and lawn-care alternatives. These evaluations would be used later to help identify the key elements to include in communications to each segment.

The survey confirmed that ChemLawn dominated its competitors in the current customer market for lawn care; however, they had been less than effective in addressing their customers' personal needs. Even more apparent was the combined size of the do-it-yourself market, which at five times the size of the current base of lawn-care customers, represented considerable growth potential.

Based on this analysis, ChemLawn had an opportunity to target critical customer segments to maintain their current base – Busyguys, Justifiers, and Perfection Seekers. ChemLawn also could target other segments to grow both their share and the category – Parents, Green Thumbs, and Environmentalists. Of course, some share growth could come from attracting customers of other lawn-care services, but category growth would come primarily from attracting new customers from the do-it-yourself segments.

DEVELOPING STRATEGIC COMMUNICATIONS

The segmentation approach described previously identified the key perceptual pathways and motivational orientations that could form the basis of a positioning strategy for each of the target segments. Before communications could be developed, however, we must identify the *leverageable elements* in these pathways. Leverageable elements are those concepts in the HVM rated as important by both current customers and do-it-yourselfers, and seen by current customers as substantially positive for ChemLawn but not so by do-it-yourselfers. This suggests that if do-it-yourselfers could be taught the positive characteristics that customers already knew about ChemLawn, their likelihood of choosing ChemLawn should be increased. By comparing the strategic elements within each the three perceptual segments that comprised the majority of do-it-yourselfers with the key elements for the three segments that were the majority of ChemLawn's current customer base, we identified the leverageable elements that would become the focus of communications.

The next question to be answered was how to design the appeal to reach each segment. The first step was to translate the leverageable functional and psychosocial consequences into simplified, benefit-oriented concepts that could then be used in marketing ChemLawn's products. With the Justifier segment, for example, the primary marketing concepts that would reinforce or stimulate purchase were Reliable and Value. Although these represented the most salient motivators, other elements identified in the perceptual orientation diagram for this group may well have played secondary roles in the decision process. The Benefit Concepts also had to be supported by ChemLawn's tangible service features or attributes in order for a Justifier to switch to or continue with ChemLawn.

Barrier elements were identified in the research as well. For example, safety concerns prevented the parent do-it-yourselfers from selecting a professional provider. Therefore, in the final development of marketing messages, both benefit concepts and barrier concepts had to be determined. Message development is a powerful use of the decision-making ladder. Successful messages are both personally relevant and believable to the target segment because they are directed at the most important needs of the prospective customer as supported by (linked to) product and service attributes.

An example of a message that would communicate "Reliable" to the Justifier segment follows. Although the words used here do not represent the actual phrases of final copy, they were the keystone messages or ideas on which actual copy would be based. ChemLawn provides proven, professional service through its highly trained and experienced team of Landscape Specialists. ChemLawn's experienced team of Landscape Specialists are trained to recognize and diagnose the needs and problems of your landscape and to offer reasonable and immediate solution options.

A healthier, more beautiful landscape is easier to achieve with ChemLawn's team of highly trained Landscape Specialists. With years of experience, these specialists use only the best landscape care products, proven effective through extensive research and development in ChemLawn's own research facility.

The next step was to identify delivery strategies for the key messages for each segment. For example, the Justifier consumers use cost-benefit relationships in their purchase decisions. They are price sensitive but recognize the worth of value-added attributes. They do not make snap decisions, and therefore are not a candidate for short-term trial. Justifiers use information to analytically support or refute their decisions and need a lot of critical information before making a purchase.

Television, radio, and newspapers are unlikely to be effective because of the information requirements of the Justifier. Direct-mail pieces showing a lush, beautiful lawn would likewise miss the mark because the Justifier needs to hear that his or her investment will be returned in value. Two steps may convince the Justifier of ChemLawn services. [1] The first was a lengthy, direct mail piece laden with information that strongly portrayed the critical Reliable and Value messages. The second was a face-to-face visit from a ChemLawn representative when the sale would actually be made. Other tactics, could also be used.

The delivery strategies, or tactics, created for the Justifier segment were also valid for other segments. For example, the direct-mail piece was also appropriate for the Partner segment, and a modification was appropriate for the Perfection-Seeker, Busyguy, and Yardwork-Hater segments. A communication matrix based on an understanding of the delivery tactics that would work best for each segment was developed as a managerial tool for allocating resources and conducting cost-benefit analyses for each segment.

Identifying these people in the real world was the final challenge that remained. Here, demographic characteristics or a self-selecting questionnaire could have been used. Several sophisticated demographic and psychographic tools could identify the most effective ways of reaching these specific market segments as well. This case review is but a single example of the utility of information derived from means-end based consumer research. Other strategic marketing and communication issues also can be addressed using the resulting deep understanding of market segments.

Chapter 3

Advertising is Image Management

The advertising function may be equated, at least in part, to the creation and management of product imagery; that is, the set of meanings and associations that serve to differentiate a product or service from its competition. Obviously, the authors are not the first ones to come upon this way of looking at advertising. One might refer back to Ogilvy's *Confessions of an Advertising Man* for a recommendation that brand image should be the basis for developing sound advertising strategies.

The *raison d'etre* for this point of view has not changed since it was first put into practice — the majority of product classes are comprised of products that do not differ from each other in any significant way. Therefore, advertising functions to enhance physical attributes and their relative importance with respect to how the consumer sees himself or herself, essentially providing psychological benefits through the image-creation process.

The contributions the means-end chain research model (the linking of attributes to consequences to personal values) can make to creating images for products and services. First, definitions of image and approaches for studying image are reviewed. After a review of the means-end chain model, research implementation techniques are discussed.

Then an illustrative example is provided that demonstrates how the research findings can be directly translated into the specification of "image" advertising, through the detailing of a consumer-research-based strategic framework.

DEFINITIONS OF IMAGE

In order to move beyond the basic posture that brand images add value to products, one must consider defining and operationalizing image. Obviously, this is necessitated due to the fact that the way image is defined determines the manner in which research to understand image is designed, executed, and, ultimately, translated to the creative process. To illustrate, consider the various ways in which image has been translated into an operational framework:

- General characteristics, feelings, or impressions
- Perceptions of products
- Beliefs and attitudes
- Brand personality
- Linkages between characteristics and feelings/ emotions

Let us consider each of these in turn as the basis of defining image.

General Characteristics

Does this term simply mean descriptive phrases such as "decaffeinated coffee" or "cold water detergent?" Or, are the feelings and impressions that are derived from thinking about a product what image is all about? For example, if one mentions Johnson's baby powder, is image the warm feeling you get when you think of the loving, caring relationship between a baby and his or her mother?

If so, the closely tied link between a product and these emotional feelings would appear to be a good beginning toward defining image. This also suggests that general characteristics of a product are a bit too concrete or descriptive of the physical nature of the product itself to be useful in defining the more personalized emotion-laden components of image.

Perceptions of Products

Obviously, this is a very general way of defining an image. In this context your perception of a product represents your image of that product. This conceptualization seems too broad to be of much use in defining image, although it represents the basis for multidimensional scaling's contribution to advertising strategy development. Focus groups, although more qualitative in approach, also stem from this point of view, yielding as it were respondents' general opinions or perceptions of a product or other stimulus object.

Beliefs and Attitudes

Although this perspective is somewhat more specific than perceptions, attitude leans heavily on evaluation, whereas beliefs lead us to think about standard measurement paradigms and models that are thought to reflect image. Beliefs themselves can be defined in a number of ways suggesting a considerable latitude in actually defining how image should be thought of.

The attitude- and -belief orientation of defining image has led to the use of multi attribute attitude models that focus on attributes that are assumed to underlie preference, which in turn act as a surrogate for choice behaviour. Boyd, Ray, and Strong based their advertising strategy formulation procedure on such an attitudinal framework. This approach, of course, necessitates determining which choice criteria are used to evaluate brands, thereby allowing these characteristics to be changed (added to, subtracted from, increasing or decreasing the importance of). In general, approaches such as these restrict image to consisting of product characteristics, one primary reason being the inability of paper- and -pencil procedures to effectively deal with more personal orientations.

Brand Personality

The notion of personifying the brand with characteristics we use to describe individuals certainly does suggest personal bonds of greater meaning than beliefs about product attributes. Yet, without a more general framework to know how these characteristics derive their meaning, we do not know the relation of these characteristics to those of the product or the product's degree of differentiation with respect to its competitors. Kover presented some interesting strategic applications in this area, essentially working backward by establishing the typologies of consumers by the assumed personality of a mix of brands across categories. Unfortunately, the strong emphasis on interpretation in this case, as well as making sure to look at the appropriate product classes, does not make this as methodologically rigorous an approach as one might desire.

Linkages Between Characteristics and Feelings and Emotions

This definition seems to combine some of the best features of the prior definitions while including the notion of the connections between perceptions. Thus, when you think about a product, some feature of it typically comes to mind. This feature itself brings something else to mind, which in turn brings yet another thought to mind. For example, take a moment and consider Perrier. What comes to mind? Now use your initial response as the stimulus. What does that bring to mind? The reader following this demonstration should be going through a sequential process of elicitation, tracing the network of associations in memory.

As is apparent, the linking of concepts undoubtedly has descriptors in it that in no way relate directly to Perrier. What has happened is that concepts imply other concepts, producing an implication network reflecting memory linkages which the authors put forth as the fundamental component of image. These views are not dissimilar from two major theories of memory, levels of processing and spreading activation. The distinction that does serve to distinguish the authors' view from the traditional memory theories is the focus on the episodic nature of the network, elements that derive their meaning in terms of their connection to self, thus serving to modify self. This connecting of key elements that define the product to those that modify self affords a translation of the meaning of the product to personally-relevant descriptors that provide the basis for image.

In defining image as stored meanings that an individual has in memory, and by relating these stored meanings to a memory network, one can suggest some research directions that go beyond those suggested by earlier definitions. Two aspects of this definition are of importance at this point. First, what is called up, or stored in memory — the content — provides the meanings we attribute most basically to image (this is the perception viewpoint). Second, the organization or connections that represent the relationships, or what causes particular classifications or meanings to be called up or linked to one another, is the structural component. As is readily apparent, if we can determine the network of personally-relevant connections associated with a particular product class, we can conduct meaningful research on image that will contribute to creating more effective advertising strategies, and, ultimately, product positionings.

Basically, then, we need to understand types of cognitive representations consumers have with respect to products. Once the network corresponding to the product class can be isolated, what remains is to determine the relation of the component parts to the product of interest. That is, to what differentiating characteristics it is related, and more importantly, what linkages can be made to the personal lives of consumers to best maximize the product's perceptual position or image.

A MEANS-END CHAIN ORIENTATION FOR DEFINING IMAGE

A means-end chain is defined as the connection between product attributes, consumer consequences, and personal values. Attributes are features or aspects of products or services. Consequences accrue to people from consuming products or services. They may be desirable (benefits) or undesirable. Values, or end states, are important beliefs people hold about themselves and about their feelings concerning others' beliefs about them. It is values that determine the relative desirability of consequences.

Embodied in the means-end chain model is the concept of levels of abstraction. Put simply, *levels* refer to a way of categorizing the contents of associations about a product class that extend from physical aspects of a product to personal values. To amplify, one way to operationalize levels is to think in terms of subcategories of attributes, consequences.

Physical characteristics are defined as being measurable in physical units, such as colour or miles per gallon. The abstracted properties represent attribute designations that are more subjective in nature, like "smells nice" or "strong flavour." Functional consequences are exemplified by such outcomes as "saves money" or "don't have to wash your hair every day." Such consequences are instrumental to our achieving psychosocial consequences such as having more friends, having fun, or being more attractive to others. The instrumental-values level reflects an external orientation relating to how we are perceived by others ("makes me feel more important" or "makes me feel accepted"). The terminal or internal-values level relates to how one views oneself (self esteem or security).

Again, the key point to be made is that some system of categorization by level is required so that aspects of the product can systematically be related to important aspects of self. Conceptualizing the contents of associations in this manner aids us in probing into the nature of the hierarchical structure of the contents of consumers' associations about brands within a product class.

To recap, the levels of abstraction conceptualization represents a meaningful way of organizing the contents of memory about a particular product (i.e., its network of associations or image). What needs to be known, then, is how these components or levels are linked to one another to form an associational network representing image. In this context "attributes'! consequences'! values" linkages, or means-end chains, are the fundamental units of analysis in understanding image. Such structures provide useful research concepts for understanding consumer orientations with respect to image, thus providing the framework for developing image positionings.

APPROACHES FOR STUDYING IMAGE

Standard approaches in practice today for gaining insight

into both the content and organization of product images, serving essentially as extensions of the theoretical formulations detailed previously, are focus groups, standard attitude and usage survey methods, and perceptual-mapping techniques. Some brief comments about these approaches have been made earlier in connection with the various definitions of image. Let us look a little more closely at them in the context of the definition of image developed in the previous discussion.

Focus groups revolve around understanding consumers' own words in a basically unstructured format, except for a directional outline, thereby permitting basic orientations and feelings to emerge. This satisfies the need to uncover contents of image. The failure of the standard content analysis to reveal, in a systematic manner, the organization or mental networking that is representative of the links between the various concepts elicited, is the major drawback of the use of this approach for studying images.

That is, by simply labeling the various concepts elicited, the researcher has no real information with respect to his or her interrelationships, nor any structure to provide a basis for critical analysis. Secondarily, the group environment also has to be questioned with respect to how freely (and accurately) respondents will discuss higher value levels, which obviously represent the personal level at which image is seen to operate.

Issues relating specifically to the use of attitude models have been dealt with in detail elsewhere. The problems with these models, with respect to studying image, centre on the fact of their use of a predetermined set of items that are not guaranteed of either being important to respondents, or even of being expressed in terms meaningful to the respondents. Additionally, the classification of items generally lacks delineation as to the level of abstraction (attribute, consequence, or value) of the items.

Moreover, the linkages between items are not dealt with directly; rather they are inferred by analysis based on assumptions that are typically unrealistic, reflecting the compositional (structure of the attitude model used.An alternative methodology that addresses both the problems of predetermined items and the prespecified analytical framework, multidimensional scaling, involves the direct scaling of dissimilarity judgments obtained from an individual into a multidimensional space that denotes the relative differences between products.

The underlying rationale is that these spatial distances reflect the true differentiation, reflecting the image differences of one's perceptions with respect to a particular product class. In this context, the primary problem with the scaling approach stems from the inferential process that the researcher must go through in interpreting the resulting space. Although analytic methods do help give insight to this problem, the lack of a model reflecting the relational linkages tends to make the interpretation highly subjective.

Implementing the Means-End Chain Model for Studying Image

If we are to have a better way of uncovering what goes on in people's minds, given the theoretical issues detailed previously, the following would seem to be required. First, the analytic frame of reference would be at the individual level; that is, we have to understand the individual before we can understand the group or the mass of consumers. Second, the technique should draw on the consumer's own language. Basically, it seems unreasonable to ask consumers to translate our concepts to their way of thinking; and, if they are using their own concepts it certainly behooves us to find out what they are.

Third, the analysis should permit content classification by some version of the levels of abstraction notion so that the contents of image can be divided into meaningful groupings. and, fourth, linkages between levels, attributes, consequences, and values need to be directly recovered, rather than inferred, so that we can understand the defining structure of image, not merely its contents. Translating all this into research needs results in four basic issues:

- How to tap into an individual's network of meanings?

- How to explore this structure in terms of content or levels of abstraction and determine the linkages between these levels?
- How to identify the common framework across respondents that can be used to summarize the data reflecting perceptual orientations across brands?
- How to translate these perceptual orientations into advertising strategy?

The remainder of this section presents a total methodological perspective that addresses all of the above research issues.

The Repertory Grid has been used successfully to elicit distinctions consumers make among products. The Repertory Grid begins with a triadic sorting task in which the respondent is given three products and asked to think of some overall way of thinking about the three products in which two of them can be considered the same but yet different from the third. The intent here is to uncover the basic distinctions an individual uses to classify products. The respondent is asked to specify both poles of the distinction he or she is making as well as to which pole each of the three products belongs.

With respect to Repertory Grid applications to consumer products, it has been pointed out that distinctions given by consumers to the triadic sorting task tend to be at the attribute level. To get at higher levels of abstraction and to determine the connections between the lower and higher levels, a series of directed probes is necessary. This technique, called *laddering,* entails using the preferred pole of the initial triadic distinction and then sequentially probing into why that distinction is important to the respondent. By taking the preferred pole at each level, a series of linkages connecting attributes to consequences and then to personal values is thereby uncovered.

Although these techniques are not complex, they do offer interesting analytical possibilities as well as some interesting qualitative data. The summary of this type of data has been dealt with elsewhere. Basically, a simple counting procedure between adjacent elements yields a hierarchical map constructed from the pairwise connections between elements above a specified criterion level. This results in a map connecting the key elements. Each distinct pathway is interpreted as a possible perceptual orientation.

Thus, "tapping into" the consumer network of meanings is accomplished by the triadic sorting task, with the laddering task serving to provide the higher level interpretations of the more concrete attribute distinctions. Laddering, then, satisfies the content requirement as well as the structural by uncovering the linkages or connections between the content elements. The hierarchical analysis yielding the latent pathways or dominant orientations across respondents results from a joint analysis of the frequency of connections between common content elements. Remaining, then, is the translation of the research framework into an advertising framework.

TRANSLATING IMAGE RESEARCH TO STRATEGIC POSITIONINGS

To utilize the attribute→ consequence→value connections for creating brand images with advertising, the components of advertising strategy have to be coordinated with the levels of the means-end chain. The Means-End Conceptualization of the Components of Advertising strategy, the MECCAs Model accomplished this purpose. MECCAs translates advertising strategy into five specific characteristics that correspond to the levels of abstraction conceptualization. The characteristics of Driving Force, Consumer Benefit, and Message Elements stem directly from values, consequences, and attributes, respectively. The Executional Framework relates to the plot, scenario, or tone for the advertising, with the specification for advertising tone coming from an overall understanding of the way of perceiving the product class as indicated by particular means-end chains.

With all these elements in mind, it is still necessary to specify just how the values-level focus for the advertising will be activated. That is how the executional components of Message Elements, Consumer Benefit, and the Executional Framework can be positioned as personally relevant to the consumer, activating or "tapping into" a personal value. This is accomplished through the concept of the Leverage Point.

The MECCAs model, then, allows for the creation of advertising that identifies important aspects of self and relates these to important consequences associated with product use, and, in turn, with key product attributes that produce these consequences. The specification of the tone and scenario for the advertising allows for the presentation of all these elements in a consistent fashion. The resulting complete strategy statements provide creative people and management with a document that provides the level of understanding necessary to focus creative energy on creating image-building advertising.

ILLUSTRATIVE EXAMPLE

Airlines are used to demonstrate the application of these research techniques for developing strategic opportunities that can be translated by the consumer into personal identifications, which represent image. Airlines were chosen because they have obvious people and equipment components that provide opportunities for image development. Further, it is easy to construct a research format using triads consisting of sets of three airlines, or one's last three flying experiences, which could yield discriminating distinctions such as: wide bodies versus regular aircraft; pleasant interiors versus unpleasant interiors; or more deals on fares versus less deals on fares.

Although these descriptors would undoubtedly be an integral part of a typical attitude and usage survey, they offer a rather limited perspective as to the higher levels of consequences and personal values that mediate these perceptions. As is apparent given the initial focus of this discussion of image, this type of input is limiting when the intent of the research is to give direction to both marketing strategists and creatives.

As mentioned previously, laddering can be initiated by ascertaining the preferred poles for each distinction and following up with a "Why?" question about why that pole is preferred. Let us say that "wide bodies, " "pleasant interiors,

" and "more deals" are the preferred poles of these distinctions. Probing the first distinction might produce the consequence-level distinctions.

Stepping up the laddering the result of asking the "Why?" question to "wide bodies" that yielded "more physical comfort" that when probed further led to "get more done, " and that derived its personal relevance from the need to "accomplish more." The perspective gained here is the apparent translation of the aircraft type into a perception that the additional seating provides an environment that more easily facilitates getting work done on the plane. This is meaningful due to the competitive and demand ing work and travel schedule the business person is required to deal with.

It is important to note that not all of the distinctions at the various levels are represented by bipolar opposites. This is the case in particular at the higher levels, where by having the respondent detail the negative or potential negative pole, substantial insight is often gained with respect to the true meaning the respondent is trying to express. Similarly, by understanding the even more personalized meaning of accomplishment – in this case, a desire to feel better about oneself through success – although not stated explicitly, gives additional information about the orientation of the respondent.

Probing the second distinction resulted in the "pleasant interiors" to "relax" linkage that was then linked to the "in-control" distinction, which was considered important in terms of satisfying a need for "security." Thus, the diagrammatic view of laddering can be analogized to a "ladder of abstraction" that follows the means-end chain, moving from attributes that are considered as part of the product/service to the personalized meaning or interpretation with respect to how the individual sees or would like to see himself or herself.

The third distinction, "more deals, " when probed further, leads to the distinction, "save money." This latter distinction then leads to "feel prudent, " which is important to the respondent for reasons of manifesting "security". Of note here is the fact that the same term as above was used by the respondent, yet a different meaning was intended. The obvious fact that the specific nuances such as this must be incorporated in the analysis of the elicited distinctions is apparent.

As is readily apparent, the interpretations of even rather straightforward descriptive attributes, when moved to these higher level personalized meanings, can be quite revealing. The obvious caveat, of a highly trained interviewer, to make sure the nuances are accurately denoted as well as to insure the meaningfulness of the responses at the various levels, and a rigidly formatted content analysis, certainly need to be pointed out. Thus, the same concerns of any qualitative analysis hold true for this type of in-depth interviewing. A major advantage of this approach, however, is that the representation of elements across levels of abstraction permits a solid structural framework with which to initiate the content analysis. By simply classifying all mentioned distinctions into the appropriate breakdowns downs across and within the basic levels, the analysis is greatly expedited.

Codes representing all mentioned descriptors are applied to the original data thereby permitting a nominal summarization of each level for each respondent. The issue, then, is the nature of the patterns represented in this data.

HIERARCHICAL-VALUE-STRUCTURE MAPS

A type of market-structure analysis, termed a *value-structure map*, intrinsically hierarchical in nature, can be constructed from the series of linkage ladders across respondents. Thus, the individual means-end chains referred to previously can also be used to create an aggregate map of these relations. All attribute, consequence, and value distinctions are cast as the rows and columns of a square matrix. The frequency with which each element leads to or implies each other element is represented by the cell frequencies of such a (dominance) matrix. The relationships between key elements, as summarized by the frequencies, serve as the basis for constructing the value-structure map.

A hypothetical hierarchical-value-structure map for the airline category. Note that many of the ladders are interconnected, and at the high levels, the merging of the lower level distinctions into the same value occurs. One way to examine such a map is to trace the paths from the bottom of the map to the top. As can be seen, there are a number of ways of moving from the attribute level to the consequence level and then to the values level. These paths represent common perceptual orientations, essentially perceptual segments.

"Advanced seat reservation, " "aircraft type, " and "first-class cabin" all lead to "more space, " which in turn leads to "physical comfort." "Physical comfort" is an important node (also reached through "no distractions") leading to "status, " "getting more done, " and "reducing tension." These consequences are the gateways to higher order consequences and values-level considerations.

"Reduce tension" is itself also an important node in the hierarchical-value-structure map; "save time" and "dependable" lead into it. It represents a crossover point for the lower level attributes of "ground service" and "on-time performance" to reach up to the values of "accomplishment" and "self esteem." On the right side of the map, the functional benefits of "able to plan" and "prudent" lead eventually to "security." On the far right side of the map, "food quality" leads to "enjoyment, " but not to any higher-order values. This demonstrates the fact that perceptions underlying preferences do not always tie into higher values.

The box contains the notation of "personal interaction." This interpretive addition to the map points up a nuance that might represent something respondents did not explicitly say, yet which was implicit in much of what they did say. It suggests that personal interaction is a key factor in translating "physical comfort" into "relaxing environment, " leading to feelings of being "in-control, " and eventually to "security." The suggestion here is that the flier gives up control when he or she makes a commitment to fly.

These feelings of being locked in an artificial environment can be dealt with through the medium of personal interaction. Though certainly subjective as compared to the construction of the value-structure map, such insightful qualitative analysis as would be typical in a focus-group analysis does bring substantial richness to the interpretation of the key linkages and pathways.

WOMEN'S USE OF LANGUAGE AND LANGUAGE'S USE OF WOMEN

Men and women occupy separate cultural spheres as well as separate biological ones. Cultural differences between the sexes occur in all known societies and are made manifest in language, the shaper of human reality. Shulamith Firestone in *The Dialectic of Sex* argued that "the sex role system divides human experience; men and women live in these different halves of reality; and culture reflects this".

Marketing and advertising researchers have studied several cultural domains in reference to women: stereotypes of women in advertising, feminine themes and values, and pictorial depictions of gender roles. The focus is ordinarily on visual images and depictions of typical characters, settings, and occupational roles. Most advertising studies rely on content analysis and count denotative elements in the visual imagery to assess depictions of women. Although some research efforts have incorporated more connota tive message elements, these are characteristically conducted outside of the advertising discipline.

Even advertising studies of "latent" content, requiring not simply observation of what is "manifest" in the visuals but also interpretation of what the images mean, do not ordinarily focus on language. Although feminist critics since Robin Lakoff have identified a dichotomy between male and female language, the impact of genderization on the language used in advertising messages has not yet been widely studied. Yet research on advertising verbals is necessary, for language is the vehicle through which culture is transmitted.

The perspective of feminist language-based criticism—the discipline that focuses on women's experience as a proper subject for study in its own right. It draws specifically on feminist literary criticism to examine advertising's words in order to clarify how women use language and how language uses women. The purpose is to adapt another methodology from a different discipline to enrich our understanding of the nature of role portrayals. Literary criticism can contribute to advertising research by rendering women's language visible. In so doing, it may assist advertisers to design persuasive appeals with greater verisimilitude to position or reposition products more effectively to men's and women's markets.

Some cultural differences between men and women that give rise to three qualities characteristic of women's language: propriety, hesitancy, and verbal excess. It next describes the influence of sex-specific language on advertising dialogue and male/female role portrayals. Last, it discusses two contributions that awareness of women's language can make to better advertising. First is the creation of realistic scenarios for dramatic advertisements, those in which characters speak. Second is the development of copy language for product positioning where male and female characters speak and/or are spoken about. Advertising as one kind of creative text and relies primarily on feminist literary criticism as the interpretive filter. It is limited to the verbal parts of advertising, and thus excludes elements such as pictures, scenery, or music. Additionally, it does not deal with other cultural factors such as age, race, or social class likely to interact with sex.

LANGUAGE AND WOMEN'S CULTURE

Examination of women's language as a special and separate entity begins with an overview of the pervasiveness of male norms in a patriarchal society. The gender asymmetry that characterizes male- dominant society went unquestioned for millenia. It was not until the 1960s that feminist critics brought to light the hidden assumptions of male-centered culture in which *female* is defined by negative reference to *male* as the human norm.

For most of human history—read by feminists as "his story"—women internalized civilization's reigning patriarchal biases and accepted the cultural constructs defining masculinity and femininity. Although debate continues as to whether men and women are different, and if so, why, consensual beliefs about the stereotypical personality traits that characterize and differentiate the average man and woman have remained consistent for nearly 20 years.

Stereotypical maleness and femaleness are built into the patriarchal culture and expressed in the language of both art and life. Language is now widely viewed as basic to the constitution of social life, a dynamic social phenomenon, rather than a stable neutral medium of communication. Feminist theorists pointed out that language categorizes and structures one's concept of oneself, others, and society, and they amassed evidence indicating the male bias encoded in our linguistic conventions. For example, the nouns "man" or "mankind" are used to define all human beings, and the pronouns "he" and "his" often refer to ostensibly gender-neutral nouns such as God, inventor, author, poet—and the advertiser as well.

Lacan stated that women's relationship to language must be seen in terms of the traditional cultural construction of language "around the male term. or the privileging of that term". The gender identification created and maintained in language was based on the male as a normative model of the self, and the female as a deviant "Other, " first identified in Simone de Beauvoir's land mark book, *The Second Sex*. Since that time, feminist critics have brought to light the almost unthinking acceptance of male norms and female opposites hidden beneath the surface.

By the 1960s, feminist researchers had begun to uncover the extent to which male-dominance is so rooted in our terminology that it is accepted as "normal" language. Feminism—also called "women's studies"—has taken as its domain the study of women's "place" in many disciplines. Its foundation is acceptance of women's role as cultural "other": the largely invisible subculture unexamined for centuries.

Feminism was the first organized school of criticism to recognize the presence of women, the kinship among them, and the differences between *this sub rosa* group and that of the male mainstream. Feminist criticism always examines cultural factors, for to understand a woman's point of view, a critic must take into account the social, legal, and economic status of women in society. In order to do justice to the female point of view, feminist criticism in America began by investigating the concept of an appropriate cultural "place" for each sex. Linguists and literary critics set out to expose the hitherto unquestioned assumptions embedded in language as a result of "place". American society, like most others, has traditionally assigned a different place—an appropriate sphere of activity -to men and to women. Women historically assumed the role of homemaker and men that of provider. In at least one consumer behaviour text, sex-linked traits are treated as subcultural differences, and the argument is made that since sex roles are culturally determined, gender as a subcultural category is appropriate.

Interestingly, this consumer-oriented definition of subculture as a "distinct cultural group which exists as an identifiable segment within a larger, more complex society" parallels the feminist view of women's culture. In this view, women exist as an identifiable segment within the larger more complex male society that dominates American life.

In post-Industrial Revolution America, the distinction in place became more rigid. By the mid-19th century, the new manufacturing economy and its attendant prosperity led to a more sharply schismatic differentiation between male and female roles than had existed in the past. When men and women both worked at home-a common pattern in society based on an agrarian economy their experiences were centered in the same sphere, although role differences existed.

Once men left the home, however, and went into the work place, their paths diverged: man's place became the factory, later generalized into the "workplace, " and woman's became the home. Victorian society solidified the separation, and idealized the woman enshrined within her home as a "lady": pure, dedicated to her husband and children, and untouched by the rough and tumble of the external world. This pedestalization was commonplace in American thought in the 19th century, evident in literature and language as well as in social life. The nature of women's language was, for the most part, circumscribed by the limitations associated with her place in society.

THREE CHARACTERISTICS OF WOMAN'S LANGUAGE

Feminist critics beginning with Lakoff have set out to specify the impact of place on "woman's language, " that distinctively feminine style of speaking and writing. They have focused on sentence structure, diction (word choice), organizational flow, and characteristic images to ascertain how women select and combine words in everyday life.

This usage is related to the covert messages that culture sends about women's place. Women's speech reflects cultural imperatives calling for niceness, politeness, ladylike expression, and concern for the feelings of others. Women's style is described by Firestone as "personal, subjective, emotional, descriptive" in contrast to men's "vigorous, spare, hard-hitting, objective" expression.

Women externalize society's message to be "nice" in their speech, just as men externalize society's permission to be "rough": male talk can be powerful, hard, and intellectual as a result of man's place from childhood on—the ball field, the army, the factory. But women are expected to speak more softly. Three characteristics that mark women's language as special are its propriety, hesitancy, and verbal excess.

Propriety

Propriety in word choice (diction) and grammar reinforces the dual sexual standard. First and foremost, women are expected to talk "like ladies." This entails avoiding obscene words, curses, and angry expletives. Sexual or scatological terms are taboo for women, whereas men who curse are considered "one of the guys."

One reason why obscenity is off-limits for women is that words like "fuck" are expressions of anger historically associated with male hostility. When a woman uses an expletive like this or any other, she expresses a degree of rage that threatens the social order, for women are expected to soothe angry words, not hurl them.

Powerful Anglo-Saxon curse words are deemed unladylike, and when women do use curses in literature, they are labeled as either rebels (intellectual bluestockings, defiant temptresses) or outcasts (whores, addicts, illiterates).

In addition to sanitized diction, women are also expected to use hypercorrect grammar and any polite forms of address that the language possesses. The expectation of perfect correctness harks back to women's role as the keeper of the cultural flame: whereas men went off to work and war to protect society, women stayed home to preserve its cherished values for transmission to future generations.

Women have traditionally been regarded as guardians of the language, primarily as mothers teaching their children informally, but also in more formal occupational roles as elementary school teachers and librarians. Women were thus conventionally cast as conservators of language deemed proper in reference to dictional choice and grammatical structure.

Hesitancy

Women's language also avoids the taint of impropriety by displaying hesitancy or tentativeness. This hesitancy is expressed in two ways: a tendency to make assertions using tag-question form, and a reliance on "hedge" or filler words. Women are likely to state things tentatively either by appending a question to a declarative sentence or by turning a statement into a question. For example, a simple declarative sentence reads: "It's a nice day."

This is made tentative by a tacked-on question: "It's a nice day, isn't it?" or by the interrogative, "Isn't it a nice day?" Women are thought to avoid commitment to a point of view that declarative statements imply in order to avoid potential conflict with those who might disagree. Conflict, like anger, is unladylike, and women who declare themselves in no uncertain terms are considered at best, unfeminine, and at worst, aggressive "pushy bitches."

A second way to express uncertainty is to circumlocute, and women tend to use filler and hedge words that undercut ideas so that they may be stated, but not sufficiently strongly to provoke disagreement. Empty adjectives, long stripped of substantive meaning, such as "divine, charming, cute" are all-purpose descriptors attached to nearly any noun. Additionally, meaningless filler expressions such as "well, " "you know, " "sort of, " or "like" punctuate women's sentences. The avoidance of assertive language is entertainingly demonstrated in a short parody by Veronica Geng, reporting a conversation overheard in a restaurant:

Valerie: "Their sole am and ine sounds nice."

Man: "I would quarrel with that, Valerie, I'm afraid. Though you are free to disagree. I'd like nothing more than to hear you disagree. Show some spine, Valerie, for a change."

Valerie: *"Well, to be honest—maybe I'm way out of line* on this one, but I'm *pretty* positive that *I probably* don't want the sole, *I almost* think."

Man: "Among aware, intelligent people there will always be some difference of opinion. You should have the sole Valerie, even if it is wrong choice. Nobody's keeping score."

Valerie: *"Well,* your willingness to discuss this has *meant a lot.* I *really* appreciate it. *I guess I'll just* have the gravy."

Verbal Excess

Related to women's use of tentative expressions and filler words is the last characteristic: a tendency to verbal excess. One kind of excess is sheer verbosity: constructions that use more words than necessary to express a thought. This, of course, inevitably accompanies reliance on filler phrases, and is a means of softening direct assertions by circumlocution, or beating around the bush. Another kind of excess is hyperbole or overstatement. Language is hyperbolic when frequent underlining or italicizing of words and expressions occurs, when unremarkable comments end with exclamation points, and when emphatic words are sprinkled throughout.

Although advertising in general is often condemned for puffery, it is important to note that some forms of overstatement are more characteristic of women's usage patterns than of men's. For example, women's language often attaches words describing excessive emotions to mundane things. McLuhan was one of the first to point out that technology provided the "ever intenser thrills" that characterized advertising depictions of the "mechanical bride's" sexuality. This particular kind of excess is still with us, for a 1989 advertisement for Alberto Culver's Bold Hold hair spray says: "Go ahead... give your hair a thrill!" Here, a hype-word, italics, and an exclamation point are used all at once. Despite the changes that have occurred in the last generation, then, women's language is still deeply etched with ingrained cultural patterns that lend legitimacy to hesitancy and hyperbole.

ADVERTISING AND WOMEN'S LANGUAGE

An understanding of women's language is necessary for the creation of realistic scenarios in dramatic advertisements—those in which the characters speak to an audience or to each other. These mini-dramas often use everyday speech, and verisimilitude is enhanced when the characters sound "right." One example of a slice-of-life print drama using realistic dialogue is Talbot's announcement of the 1989 opening of its main New York store.

Exhibit A: Talbot's Advertisement.

[WOM 1] "Look at that brick building... I've never noticed it before. What do you think it's going to be?"

[WOM 2] "I think..."

[WOM 1] "It's so classic... like this blazer of mine. I've had it for so long. It's starting to wear out. Where do you think I can find a new one?"

Tag-line: A new tradition in classic women's clothing is coming soon to 525 Madison Avenue.

The ad reveals several characteristics of women's language in spoken dialogue. WOM 1 asks naive and self-doubting questions (what is that building? where can I get a new blazer?) and twice repeats the intensive "so, " another typical hedge word. Neither WOM 1 nor WOM 2 completes a thought, for the elliptical periods ("...") indicate a trailing off of ideas expressed by a long pause. WOM 1 is garrulous—she allows WOM 2 only two words before resuming speech—and her train of thought appears disconnected. She moves from contemplation of a new building to a metaphorical comparison of the building to her blazer, based on the common dimension of "classic." The characters' questions and incomplete thoughts demonstrate the mildly tentative and inoffensive women's language that lends verisimilitude to advertising as well as to literary dialogue. This newspaper ad relies on words alone to delineate the characters by letting them speak in a language recognizable by other women, the sex-linked target market for a new women's clothing store.

It is essential for advertisers who seek to create convincing dramatic scenarios to put suitable language into a character's mouth. Verisimilitude requires sensitivity to differences between appropriate language for men and women. An example of typically male language is found in a Perry Ellis ad for men's cologne, the first instance of a speaker using "fuck" in a nationwide print ad (although the word was not spelled out in full). When women do use obscenity, their curses are milder and less sexually explicit.

For example, A Paco Rabanne cologne for men ad features an unseen woman talking on the telephone to a scantily dressed man. She describes her fantasy of him "wearing that Paco Rabanne cologne—and damned little else." *Damned* is not a very strong expletive, and is categorized as a profanity rather than a reference to scatological or sexual activity. The word suggests that the woman is a sexually frank "liberated" partner, whereas something stronger might imply that she is a whore. Advertisers who are sensitive to women's language can strike a note of authenticity in dramas, even those where visual images are not present.

Language and Cultural Roles

Women both use and are used by language, for cultural roles, values, and constraints can be read in language that describes and defines women whether or not they speak directly. Feminist critics point out differences between the way male and female characters are read, for most readers (men and women) interpret the male experience as dominant and the female experience as peripheral or subordinate. It is important to understand that these norms are almost automatically called into play when people come into contact with male and female characters in a text. Literature—like advertising—is a textual mirror that reveals the realities of the men's and women's lives. Some advertising critics feel that it is a "distorted" mirror, and feminist theoreticians often adopt a prescriptive agenda for ameliorating what they judge to be predominantly negative stereotypes of women.

A contribution of feminist literary criticism to decoding how language uses women has been the revelation of the existence of sex-linked readings by pointing out the underlying "masculinist" assumptions. The methodological process at the heart of feminist theory is the simple act of reversing the sex roles of characters to highlight underlying norms.

Feminists suggest that one way to test the assumptions that we take to be the "natural" order of things is imaginatively to reverse the positions of commonly paired binary opposites such as man and woman. This enables us to see that what we take for natural is socially conditioned. These societal norms are invoked when people "read" about male and female characters. Goffman summed up the method as follows: "by imagining the sexes switched and imagining the appearance of what results, one can jar oneself into awareness of stereotypes".

Stereotyping pervades literary images of women. Women characters are described in positive terms when they behave appropriately *as women* -when they embody socially approved feminine traits such as kindness, tactfulness, patience, and selflessness. If women embody masculine traits such as aggressiveness, independence, or leadership, they may be judged negatively and stereotyped as "bitch, " "ball-buster, " and so forth. Feminist critics point out that masculine traits are ordinarily culturally rewarded to a greater extent than feminine traits, but only when men display them.

Cultural changes in sex roles in the past 20 years have been associated with the change in woman's place from home to work site. Nevertheless, despite the 1970s call for and rogyny and rereadings of cultural texts based on a man's or a woman's conformance to generally valued human traits (autonomy, unselfishness, humaneness), a traditional traitdichotomy still differentiates the sexes. Even *Ms.* magazine, despite an explicit commitment to nonstereotypic portrayals of women, presents substantial levels of "sexism" in the course of its 18 year history. With few exceptions, the and rogynous or nonsexist ideal did not become popular reality, and men and women characters are still likely to be read differently.

Reading Women in Advertising

Culturally held beliefs about the sexes can also be read in ads, for as McLuhan pointed out: "ad agencies express for the collective society that which dreams and uncensored behaviour do in individuals. They give spatial form to hidden impulses, and when analyzed, make possible bringing into reasonable order a great deal that could not otherwise be observed or discussed". Because advertisements present advertisers' views of how men and women can be profitably pictured, they are likely to show the culturally approved version of maleness/ femaleness.

Advertisers often devise male/female characters as spokespersons when it is necessary to position or reposition a product on the basis of sex. Marketers now feel that a wide range of products can be targeted to both sexes. Although the Advertising to Women ad agency, for example, positioned itself in the 1970s as an agency for "women's products, " its philosophy shifted in the 1980s: "We feel that you can take almost every product that's traditionally marketed to men and now market it to women".

Products that were formerly marketed to men have been repositioned for women, just as products once marketed to women only have been repositioned for men. The question that arises is, should there be one ad with one spokesperson to appeal to both sexes, or separate ads, one with a male spokesperson and one with a female spokesperson? Strategic decisions as to the superiority of single versus dual approaches can be made more knowledgably if more can be learned about how audiences read the men and women who speak for products and services. The ads can be read as illustrations of prevailing mid- 1980s norms for masculinity and femininity. Traits related to instrumentality, dominance, and assertiveness are believed to be more characteristic of men, and those related to expressiveness, warmth, and concern for other people are believed to be more characteristic of women.

Jere's language reveals aggressiveness, competitiveness, and self-confidence, whereas Saly's reveals nurturance, cooperativeness, and reliance on the strength of ML masculine rivalry, which has long been identified as a popular advertising theme. Competition for financial success was especially prevalent in the money-oriented 1980s. However, women's progress in the male workplace caused profound changes in the financial services market. Once women embarked on lifelong careers and gained sufficient education to compete for lucrative positions, they began earning salaries that made them a tempting target for financial vendors. ML's marketing strategy, which formerly targeted financial planning to men, now repositioned the services bundle to attract women.

The Saly ads appear to be designed to appeal to women by depicting a female financial consultant who displays traditionally feminine traits such as caring, commitment, and patience. Men and women are thought to differ in their interpretation of the desirability of particular behaviors: women judge communality as more desirable than do men, whereas men judge self-assertive acts as more socially desirable. Jere and Saly appear to conform to the stereotypical cultural norms that expect women to be modest and self-effacing and men to be heroic and nonconformist. Although women as financial advisers may now be a commonplace modern role, the language they use relies on traditional concepts of how women are expected to sound.

This may relate to financial industry wisdom, suggesting that women are not as confident in financial management as men and rely more on their advisers. Proprietary research found that women were more likely to respond unfavorably to "hard sell" than to offers of advice and assistance, for they want someone with whom they can "talk about financial services". Saly personifies the "personal, subjective, emotional, descriptive" style that women are said to prefer. Thus, the reading of Saly as feminine and Jere as masculine appears to be part of ML's positioning strategy in using a female spokesperson for the new women's market and retaining a male spokesperson for the men's segment.

However, even though male and female consumers read text through the filter of sex-specific concerns, much additional research on stereotyping is necessary. Several questions arise in reference to the creation of effective product appeals in an age of evolving target markets and to the role of advertising as an agent for social change. The question of advertising effectiveness requires more informed understanding of whether women ought to be set apart as a distinct market segment in situations where this does not seem warranted by specific relationships between gender and product.

This requires further examination, for at present it is unclear whether women do indeed respond more favorably to a woman financial adviser than to a man. It is at least arguable that women may read authoritativeness in a male character as preferable, for women may not yet be conditioned to accept their own self-sufficiency. Recent research in social psychology using reader response theory suggests that when readers are faced with a narrator, they have been culturally conditioned to expect the narrator to be male. This is based on previous reading experience and on general cultural beliefs.

The issue of cultural conditioning leads to the need for more careful examination of whether (or how) advertising perpetuates/changes sex-role stereotypes. Despite objectively similar roles that can be adopted by men and women nowadays, stereotypes about sex-linked appropriate behaviors in language persevere and are embodied in advertisements. Even though women have entered the work force and educational institutions in record numbers in the past decades, old habits built into the traditional cultural heritage die hard. The construct of appropriate role behaviors may be changing more slowly than the actual sociocultural changes in role performance. The habit of language -the vehicle for transmitting the beliefs and values that make culture—is one of the most significant definers of sexual identity. Advertisers can benefit from greater sensitivity to the way women use language and are used by it to create messages that talk to the contemporary consumer in a language she understand s. However, since advertising seems less an agent of social change than a reflection of the cultural context, its language concretizes societal norms.

Nevertheless, both norms and language change over the course of time, and advertisers must keep pace with the ongoing culture to create effective appeals. As Goffman said, By and large, advertisers do not create the ritualized expressions they employ; they seem to draw upon the same corpus of displays, the same ritual idiom, that is the resource of all of us who participate in social situations, and to the same end: the rendering of glimpsed action readable. If anything, advertisers conventionalize our conventions, stylize what is already a stylization.

PRODUCT-BRAND ASSESSMENT

Evaluation of a product or brand is another important marketing question for which the results of laddering research may be of use. It is advantageous to allow respondents to use their own frame of reference when providing their evaluations of a brand rather than some researcher-supplied attributes that may not be the subject's own. For many product categories or subclasses of categories, respondents are much more likely to make preference judgments at the consequence and values levels than at the attribute level.

A statistical approach, Cognitive Differentiation Analysis (CDA), was developed to enable researchers to determine the level of abstraction (attribute, consequence, or value) at which preference judgments are being made by consumers. This approach provides indices indicating the discrimination power of each of the descriptors with respect to a set of pairwise discrimination between stimuli.

To collect data for this type of analysis, respondents are asked to sort or rate pairwise combinations of brands in the relevant product class according to their respective preference distance. Respondents are also asked to provide information on the extent to which the brands possess or satisfy the elements at each level of abstraction in their ladders. One appealing feature of this analytical method is that it only requires ordinal data — no interval scale properties are necessary. This information not only allows a determination of the levels within a respondent's ladder at which preference is determined, but the overall index of the ladder allows the researcher to determine each respondent's optimal ladder. Results from CDA analyses have shown that people are not particularly good at recognizing their own most discriminating way of evaluating the brands within a product class, nor do they recognize the level of abstraction at which their judgments are being made. This suggests that researchers ought to be suspicious of self-report rating systems inherent in many attitude models and consumer surveys.

The output from laddering, coupled with the unique analytical procedures it allows, provides researchers with a better understanding of the basis on which consumers make distinctions between competing brands. Further, it provides a basis for developing a product space that is truly aligned with preference, as such spatial maps may be obtained using different levels of abstraction as a frame of reference.

Too often product-planning decisions are based on discrimination differences and not preference differences. Consumers, given the means-end framework, are assumed to have multiple orientations that are triggered by a given occasional context (i.e., combination of situation and actors). Thus, if the means-end perspective is valid, preference would in most cases be multidimensional in nature. Therefore, the laddering approach provides a unique opportunity to understand the product class in the consumer's own context. This would seem to provide a good start for making decisions about products and brands.

ASSESSING ADVERTISING

Another important use for the results obtained through

laddering research is to uncover respondents' evaluations of advertising. Advertising is viewed differently when perceived in the context of different levels of abstraction (attribute, consequence, and value). To accomplish this, after laddering, when respondents are sensitized to the complete range of their internal feelings about a product class, they are shown a series of ads and asked to rate them on the extent to which the ad communicates at each level and to provide some comment on why it does or does not communicate at that level.

Analysis of these comments leads to the construction of a series of statements reflecting their content. To further broaden the coverage of these statements, a model depicting an advertising research paradigm can be used. This model indicates the components of an ad in relation to levels of involvement the consumer may have with the ad. Fifty to sixty statements can be developed covering the advertising's message elements, executional frameworks, perceptions of the advertisers' strategy and involvement with the ad, involvement of the ad with the respondent's personal life, and the extent to which the ad taps into values at a personal level.

These statements can then be used to assess the relative communication at the various levels. This can be accomplished, after a sensitizing laddering procedure, by showing ads and asking "if the following statement applies" to each respective ad. This process can be operationalized by a game-board approach where a triangle is provided to the respondent with each vertex representing a separate ad.

The use of three ads is suggested as an attempt to avoid the respondent from becoming too much of an advertising expert. As each statement is read the respondent can record the applicability to one ad (recording the statement code at the respective vertex), or two ads (recording on the connecting line), or all three (recording in the middle of the triangle). If the statement does not apply to any of the three ads, a "not applicable" response alternative is also provided.

The resulting percentage endorsement of each statement for each advertisement provides a good indication of how the ad is viewed and the level at which the ad communicates. That is, some ads may communicate well at the attribute level but not at the consequence or values level. Conversely, other ads may communicate well at the values level but be weak at the attribute level. An effective ad in this context is defined as one that communicates across all levels, linking attributes to benefits and to personal values which often drive consumer decision-making.

DEVELOPING ADVERTISING STRATEGY

Perhaps the major benefit of laddering is the insight it provides to advertising strategists. A definition of advertising communications that will permit advertising strategies to be developed from the HVM is briefly discussed.

The levels of abstraction framework, which underlie the formation of means-end chains, provide a basis for coordinating the results of laddering to advertising strategy development. That is, the perceptual constructs depicted in the HVM can be used as the basis for developing a strategy that will appeal to consumers with that particular orientation toward the product class.

The Means-Ends Conceptualization of Components of Advertising Strategy (MECCAS) in terms of five broad characteristics that correspond to the levels of abstraction conceptualization. "Driving force, " "consumer benefit, " and "message elements" are directly coordinated to the values, consequences, and attributes levels of the means-end model. The executional framework relates to the scenario for the advertisement — the "vehicle" by which the value orientation is to be communicated.

The specification of this tone for the advertisement is a critical aspect of strategy specification. It comes from an overall understanding of the way of perceiving the product class as indicated by a particular means-end path. As is apparent with this specification, added guidance can be given to creatives without infringing on their creativity.

The remaining and key aspect of advertising strategy specification is the concept of "leverage point." Having all the other elements in mind, it is finally necessary to specify the manner by which the values-level focus will be activated for the advertisement, that is, how the values consider ations in the advertisement are connected to the specific features of the advertisement.

Nonetheless, the advantages of being able to specify advertising strategy for all relevant parties—management, creatives, and researchers—can be reviewed. The strategy statement itself becomes a concrete way of specifying advertising strategy alternatives. These alternatives are linked to the chains that underlie them, and thus a direct connection exists between the strategy and the perceptual orientation of the consumer.

Furthermore, the MECCAS model coupled with the results from the HVM facilitate the development of several (truly different) strategies for comparison and review. Lastly, when a strategy has been selected for execution, the MECCAS model provides for a better common understanding of what the final product should be. This obviously leads to the use of the MECCAS specification as the basis for evaluating the effectiveness of the advertisement.

Chapter 4

The a-b-e Model in Advertising

Probably the most important purpose of advertising is to promote the benefit or benefits of the advertiser's brand. However, the term *benefit* is used rather generally in advertising to refer to several points of promotional focus that include *attributes* (what the product has), *benefits* per se (what the buyer wants), and *emotions* (what the buyer feels). According to this a-b-e distinction, attributes, the first potential focal point, are relatively objective properties of the product or service. Benefits, the second potential focal point, are subjective reinforces, often, but not necessarily, resulting from an attribute. Emotions, the third potential focal point, are the affective experience of the reinforcement itself. Often called the end-benefit, emotions may derive from a benefit or, we note, may be a free-stand ing emotional association with the brand. For a brand of coffee, for instance, good-quality coffee beans are an attribute, good tasting is the benefit, and gustatory enjoyment is the emotional consequence. For a bank, for instance, numerous ATM machines are an attribute, fast service is the benefit, and relief from one of life's hassles by being able to allot a predictably short time to banking transactions is the emotional consequence.

Which point or points of benefits to focus on in an ad is an unsolved and somewhat randomly approached problem in advertising. Should the ad focus on the attribute point, or on the benefit point, or on the emotional point? Relatedly, should the ad attempt to establish paths (implied causal sequences) between points, such as attribute-to-benefit or benefit-to-emotion? No model to date has comprehensively addressed these questions — not even the means-end model that is the theme of this volume. We propose an a-b-e (attribute-benefit-emotion) model that we believe to be an improvement on the means-end model and that is designed to answer the question of which point to focus on in ads. First, we consider the obvious but infrequently asked question of whether benefits (of either the a, b, or e type) are necessary in ads. Second, we introduce the a-b-e model and examine what we believe to be its advantages over the well-known means-end model. In the third, fourth, and fifth sections, we postulate the conditions for attribute focus, benefit focus and emotion focus, respectively — including relevant paths that end with one of these points as the focus. Finally, we review what remains to be done to develop the a-b-e model further.

BENEFITS ARE NECESSARY IN ADS

Brand awareness and brand attitude, in Rossiter and Percy's theory, are regarded as the two universal communication objectives that every ad must address. Whereas brand attitude usually is triggered by the presence of benefits in ads, it can also be cued by the brand name alone. There are a number of cases in which "benefit-less" ads are employed. We should examine these carefully because they logically pose the question of whether "no benefit" should be one of the points in our model.

Resnik-Stern Content Analyses

A number of content analyses initiated or influenced by the original Resnik and Stern study and summarized in Stern and Resnik have attempted to measure the proportion of advertisements in various media that contain *information,* defined as "cues... to assist a typical buyer in making an intelligent choice". From the studies cited by or conducted by Resnik and Stern, it appears that about 90% of business publication ads, 80% of consumer magazine ads, but only 51% of major network TV commercials contain information. The informational cues permitted by Resnik and Stern are, understand ably, focused on physical attributes of the product or service. For instance, in 1986 network TV commercials, Resnik and Stern found the following incidences of types of informational cues:

Components or contents	— 22%;
New ideas	— 15%;
Price or value	— 9%;
Performance	— 8.5%;
Special offers	— 7%;
Nutrition	— 7%;
Usage demonstrations	— 6%;
Packaging or shape	— 4%;
Availability	— 3.5%;
Quality	— 3%;
Guarantees or warranties	— 33%;
Taste	— 1%; and
Safety	— 0%,

Although this last type was found in earlier content analyses. These types of information cues would be characteristic of what Rossiter and Percy called the informational advertising style.

Resnik and Stern explicitly excluded image ads or the transformational style of advertising in Rossiter and Percy's terminology. Although excluding them from their studies, however, they admitted that image ads may be informative for consumers seeking to satisfy psychological or social motives. Image advertisements often contain benefits that are not directly attribute-derived and emotional cues that can guide the buyer's choice. Thus, it would not be correct to conclude from the Resnik-Stern content analyses that approximately half of TV commercials are benefit-less. Rather, most ads, including TV commercials, would include one or more benefits in the broad sense of attributes or benefits or emotions.

Brand -Awareness-Only Ads

Advertisements that contain nothing more than the brand name or visual brand logo can positively influence choice and purchase behaviour — a fact that has long been established.

This is because, in order for choice to occur and indeed for brand attitude to be operational, the prospective buyer must first be aware of the brand. This can be expressed by the conditional equation:

P (Choice)= P (Preference | Aware) = p (Brand attitude | Brand awareness)

Thus, choice of a particular brand can increase simply by raising its awareness even with attitude held constant. For instance, on a 0 to 1 scale, where 1 represents maximum favorability or maximum strength, a buyer might have equal attitudes, 0.7 and 0.7, toward Heineken and Beck's beer brands. However, if Heineken can raise its brand awareness to 0.8 while Beck's stays at, say, 0.6, then the relative choice probabilities in the conditional model are 0.56 for Heineken and 0.42 for Beck's. Thus, Heineken will be more likely to be chosen on the next purchase occasion. Moran has called this brand awareness effect *salience.* We would add that the type of awareness heightened by advertising must be correct in terms of brand recognition or brand recall according to the buyer's choice process.

For a new brand, it would be most unlikely that advertising would be initiated with only brand awareness content and no brand attitude (and therefore no benefit) content. Whereas it is known that repeated exposure to a name or logo alone can increase attitude via the mere exposure effect, this effect is relatively weak, and it would be inadvisable for advertisers to try it when launching a new brand.

For an established brand, however, benefit-less advertising is a different matter. In a very interesting analysis, Fraser Hite, Hite, and Minor recommended the use, when certain conditions hold, of what they somewhat pejoratively call *dissipative ads* — ads that mention the brand name only or the brand name and price in the case of retail advertising. The conditions for recommending the use of a dissipative ad are, firstly, that the brand is an established one and, secondly, that there is a reasonably large segment of consumers who wish to reduce their search and brand comparison time and are willing to pay a slight premium for doing so. It has been estimated that consumers are willing to overpay, on average, by about 12% for brand -name items that *Consumer Reports* or other objective rating sources have shown to be no different in performance quality from lesser-name brands. Comparative brand performance quality is often practically unascertainable by consumers. Because *Consumer Reports* tests brands side-by-side, differences are often found; however, consumers test products in a sequential fashion during normal usage, and their indirect comparisons are often insufficient to detect differences between brands.

However, we would emphasize that there is still a need for brand attitude content (benefit) in the brand's prior advertising, even if its later, mature-status advertising can be reduced to what is essentially a brand awareness advertisement. Only later it is likely that the brand name or logo alone is a sufficient cue for the prospective buyer to mentally supply a previously-established favorable attitude (perhaps via a cognitive response or simply by an automatically elicited affective response) without a direct brand attitude or benefit cue having to be present in the ad.

We should also mention the related case of sponsorship, whereby billboards or posters at sporting events or other public venues contain simply the brand name or logo. In Rossiter and Percy, we note the example of LaCoste ads at tennis tournaments. The likelihood here is that either the target audience supplies a previously established favorable attitude or that the context in which the ad is shown, for instance a prestigious tennis event, supplies the favorable emotional cue that forms a brand attitude during exposure.

ADS FOR SOCIALLY NEGATIVE ESTABLISHED PRODUCTS

There is one other circumstance in which no benefit would be recommended from the advertiser's stand point. This is for socially negative, but established products. The reason for avoiding benefits is to prevent counter-arguing, by both social critics and the target audience, who already know the benefits of the brand. For instance, the single word *Marlboro* is now virtually sufficient for its advertising. The Marlboro cowboy is being rendered in abstract or phased out. Whether the attitude will stay positive, over the long run and with new consumers, is doubtful, however, although we observe that the Marlboro brand attitude is well supported by interpersonal influence among younger smokers.

Overall, we see that there are rare circumstances in which truly benefit-less ads are used. Where benefits are not used, there are supplementary explanations as to why the brand attitude objective is nevertheless likely to be met. Certain types of sponsorships are the only circumstance in which benefit-less ads may have to be used. Established but socially negative products are one circumstance in which benefit-less ads should be used. Retail (re-) advertising of well-known brands is a circumstance where benefit-less ads can be used. These circumstances could justify our formulating an a-b-e model. However, we concentrate on the far more prevalent circumstances of the explicit use of benefits in ads, for which we propose the a-b-e model.

THE A-B-E MODEL OF BENEFIT FOCUS

ATTRIBUTES, BENEFITS, AND EMOTIONS

As we commented at the outset, advertisers use the term *benefit* in a rather general way. More specifically, a benefit is any potential negative or positive reinforcer. This is in line with Rossiter and Percy's definition of brand attitude as representing overall delivery (a super-belief about the brand) on a negatively originated or positively originated purchase or usage motivation. A *reinforcer* is any stimulus that tends to increase a response. It could be a positive reinforcer, as in the good-tasting coffee example, or a negative reinforcer, as in the bank's reduced waiting-time example. For benefits in ads, the reinforced response is brand attitude. Occasionally, the advertiser may wish to decrease an attitude and may include *disbenefits* or punishers, as in public service campaigns.

For the a-b-e model, however, we must distinguish more sharply between attributes, benefits, and emotions. Table 8.1

provides definitions of these terms, as we use them. An *attribute* is what the product has — physical features, for a product, or objective characteristics, for a service, such as delivery time. A *benefit* is what the buyer wants — subjective relief or subjective reward. An *emotion* is what the buyer feels — sometimes before or after a benefit and at other times, independently. In this framework, if a benefit is what the buyer wants, then a *motive* is why the buyer wants it — that is, to satisfy a currently relevant motivation.

All ads display or imply benefits in one form or another — as attributes, benefits, or emotions. At the micropositioning level, the advertiser has to decide whether to focus primarily on the attribute (a), or on the benefit (b), or on the emotion (e). Of course, combinations of these focal points are possible and are theoretically specified in our model.

THE A-B-E MODEL OF BENEFIT FOCUS

An a-b-e model of the alternative points of focus in an advertisement. The graphic model is adapted from the work of consultant Gayle Moberg. We have extended her model, notably by including negative as well as positive emotions and supplied its functional properties. In the a-b-e framework shown in the figure, it can be seen that there are no less than 3 focal points and 3 focal paths that can be used in advertising:

- Attribute focus (e.g., a thick potato chip): a
- Benefit focus from an attribute (e.g., better chip taste because it's thick): a(b)
- Benefit focus (e.g., better tasting, no reason given): b
- Benefit focus from an emotion (e.g., dissatisfied with taste of thin chips; solution is better taste of thick chips): e'' (b)
- Emotion focus from a benefit (e.g., fun because of better taste): b(e^+)
- Pure emotion focus (e.g., simply "fun"): e'' or e^+

Whereas other paths are possible, such as a to e, or a to b to e, the paths listed above are the most likely (and theoretically most important) ones. A second example — for Healthy Choice — is shown in the figure to illustrate (the potential focal points and paths. In presenting our a-b-e model, we concentrate on whether the primary focus should be on attributes, or on benefits, or on emotions (or on their associated paths). Before doing so, however, we point out differences between the a-b-e model and the means-end a-c-v model.

COMPARISON TO THE MEANS-END MODEL

The a-b-e model is superficially similar to the means-end model proposed by Gutman and Reynolds and Gutman. In their model, Reynolds and Gutman distinguish attributes, consequences, and values a-c-v, which form ladders or benefit chains. The a-c-v model and the in-ad application of it, called *MECCAS*. Because the (means-end model is used so widely, it deserves detailed comment.

The a-c-v and *MECCAS* models, in our view, have three significant problems: definitional, methodological, and overall conceptualization. We briefly point out these problems below and indicate how our model may improve on these earlier models.

Definition Problems. The first term in the a-c-v model is *attributes* (operationalized as message elements in the MECCAS model), which is the same as in our model. However, attributes are sometimes inappropriately operationalized in the MECCAS model in that consequences are included in the identification of message elements. For example, in Reynolds and Rochon's example of a ladder for Miller Lite, they give "less calories" and "great taste" as message elements. The former is clearly an attribute and the latter a consequence (a benefit, in our terminology). The a-c-v and MECCAS models, we omitted consequences from the definition of message elements.

The second term in the a-c-v model — *consequences* (or consumer benefits in MECCAS) — has two main problems. One is the very word "consequences, " which implies that these are always the result of an attribute. This is an unnecessary implication, as we discuss under the conceptual criticisms following. Secondly, when translating consequences as consumer benefits in the MECCAS model, Reynolds and

Craddock drew a questionable distinction between (positive) "benefits" and "avoidance of negative consequences" when clearly *both* are benefits to the consumer. Indeed, in the example Reynolds and Craddock gave for Federal Express, they listed "less worry" and "avoid looking bad" as consumer benefits and thus obviously deny their own definitional distinction.

The third term in the a-c-v model, *values*, and the driving force in the MECCAS model, also is problematic. Values are inferred as the latent end-goal of the advertising and are tapped into manifestly in the ad via the leverage point. The assumption that all advertising, indeed all consumer choices, must be motivated by values is far too broad. Many if not most consumer choices become purely habitual, even zero-order stochastic. In Howard's theory, for instance, values are involved only at the first (extensive problem solving) stage of consumer learning.

Similarly, questionable is the assumption that the consumer's self-concept (because all values are self-values) is inevitably engaged in consumer choice and should be addressed in advertising. To quote Reynolds and Rochon: "The central principle of the means-end approach is the interpretation process between the brand and 'self' ". Psychologists from James onward would dispute the notion that the self is always implicated, consciously or unconsciously, in behaviour.

People's personal values are sometimes directly or indirectly engaged, particularly when values are the source of importance weights (or emotional weights) for benefits. But importance weights can also come from purely mechanical learning, such as the negative importance of flatness in a beer, which, we would maintain, has nothing to do with values. To make values the necessary end point of the model limits its validity.

Lastly, we note the questionable worth of Rokeach's distinction between instrumental and terminal values, which is sometimes invoked in an extended version of the theoretical means-end chain. We observe that all of Rokeach's instrumental values are adjectives, such as "ambitious, " "responsible"; whereas all of the terminal values are nouns (or noun-phrases), such as "wisdom, " "a comfortable life." This, we contend, produces a methodological confounding in the measurements of values. We doubt that Rokeach's distinction would hold up empirically if we were to exchange the parts of speech used to measure instrumental and terminal values — for example, changing "responsible" to "a responsible life, "or changing "a comfortable life" to "comfortable."

Thus, the instrumental or terminal distinction seems tenuous at best. In fact, Feather has shown that the Rokeach values can be translated directly into Osgood, Suci, and Tannenbaum's emotional dimensions of evaluation, potency, and activity. Cacioppo, Petty, and Geen go one step further and show that potency and activity can be adequately scaled in terms of the single evaluative dimension. This suggests that the functional aspect of values is an emotional response.

In our a-b-e model, we use the term "emotions" rather than values. These seem somewhat closer to the leverage point in the MECCAS application in that we, too, see emotions as manifest elements in ads that tap into something latent — namely motives rather than values. Motives are much more generally operative than values, and a good case can be made that they underlie *all* purchase (and usage) acts, noting that we include our normal depletion motive to explain the repetitive behaviour of brand loyals.

Methodological Problems. A first methodological problem with a-c-v laddering stems from the assumption that consumers are aware of, and can validly report, all three levels of their linkages. If all three levels — attributes, consequences, and values — are always operative, then why, in the empirical studies of laddering, do the self-reported incidences consistently decline across these levels? Not only is this observed empirically, but the a priori target levels of a, c, and v in the MECCAS applications always show declining percentages for a, c, and v in a ladder.

A second methodological problem is that the a-c-v ladders

typically are aggregated across consumers. For instance, consumer 1 may exhibit the ladder a_1-c_1-v_1, consumer 2 produces the ladder a_1-c_2-v_2, and consumer 3 has a ladder a2-c1-v2. In aggregate, the common ladder is a1-c1-v2 because each of these terms appears twice; however no individual consumer actually exhibits this ladder.

Of course, it could be argued that the aggregate ladders are merely hypothetical. Recently, Gutman appeared to be making this argument (which other ladder modelers have not) when he selected prototype ladders, presented them to consumers, and had them rate the extent to which they agree "that's me." This methodology implicitly recognizes that ads do not have to reflect existing ladders but may indeed present new ones, as in positioning a new brand or deliberately repositioning an old brand.

The aggregation methodology also tends to lengthen the ladders artificially (in that few individuals exhibit long ladders). This is based on the unsupported theoretical claim that longer chains are better for advertising development. The aggregation procedure is one way of ensuring that all three levels, a, c and v, are represented, which they may not be in the individuals' ladders. But this is spurious, surely. Currim and Schneider's analysis of shoppers' protocols, for instance, suggested that individual chains are typically only one or two levels. There is no evidence that consumers naturally pass through all levels either when encoding ads or when making brand choices as a result.

Related to the aggregation methodology is the necessity that many of the links between a's, c's and v's are imputed rather than natural. Reynolds and Gengler improved on imputation by asking consumers to (subsequently) rate the likelihood or strength of a connection ("little, " "somewhat, " "totally, " which were then given the arbitrary multipliers 5%, 35%, and 75%). Reynolds and Rochon, however, simply multiplied the aggregate incidences of any two levels together to infer the existence and the strength of the linkage. For example, "75% less calories × 84% less filling 62% linkage" between this attribute and this consequence. This procedure is completely arbitrary. Better, but still imputed, is Gutman's suggestion of asking consumers to estimate the conditional probability that a linkage exists, such as "What is the probability that a beer would be less filling given that it contains less calories?"

This is closer to the imputation or inference that consumers as advertising audiences have to make when confronted with a hypothetical ladder proposed in an ad. Again, however, Gutman's example shows the implausibility of values being universally engaged. He gave an example of the probability of success given one's being refreshed by Pepsi's Slice beverage. This is an unrealistic c-v linkage, which Gutman realized was stretching the theory and would not work in practice.

Finally, the a-c-v and MECCAS models omit importance weights. The aggregate percentages calculated at each level of a ladder probably represent only an aggregate belief strength measure (sum of 0, 1 mentions), or perhaps a tangled aggregate estimate of belief × importance if one assumes that the proportion of individuals mentioning this level indicates importance. It is impossible to clearly evaluate the worth or persuasive potential of one ladder versus another without knowing the importance weights.

For instance, the abbreviated ladder "fruit juice" ("being refreshed") is probably more prevalent than "fruit juice" ("daily vitamin C intake, ") but is it more important? In contrast, our a-b-e model includes attributes, benefits or emotions in an ad only if they are known from prior research to be important, deliverable, and unique. This is our I-D-U model of benefit emphasis Rossiter and Percy, 1987). We cannot see how an advertising strategy can be formulated or evaluated without knowing benefit importance.

Overall Conceptualization Problems. The means-end a-c-v and MECCAS models have a number of overall conceptual problems. First and foremost, in comparison with the a-b-e model, is the assumed linear, causal sequence of attribute-consequence-value. In Reynolds and Craddock's words, the consumer must be "forced up the ladder of abstraction". We have already argued that values are not the inevitable end-points of consumer choice behaviour. Even if we substitute our terms, attribute-benefit-emotion, it is clear that this causal sequence is not universal. We do not have this restriction in our model. For one thing, levels may occur on their own.

For instance, consider the placebo-based effectiveness of many over-the-counter drugs for many consumers. On what attribute does this benefit depend? Similarly, consider the emotional feeling that Levi's are a psychologically comfortable brand of jeans to buy — on what attribute or benefit does this depend? For another, the links may be reversed.

Notably, *problem/solution advertising* basically works because a (negative) emotion occurs first (the problem) followed by a benefit (the solution): an e-b sequence rather than a b-e sequence in our model or the unidirectional c-v sequence in the a-c-v model. For instance, reminding the consumer of a value prior to the attribute may be necessary for the ad to work, such as ecological concern (look for "no hydroflourocarbons" on the label. The concept of a necessary a-c-v sequence and a one-way sequence, at that, is not justified.

Related to this is the notion (in the MECCAS model) that all levels — a, c, and v — must be represented and hierarchically linked in an ad. Even if the "all-levels" hypothesis were true, surely it is more important that the consumer makes the links (by inference or cognitive response again, or even subconsciously) rather than spell them out in the ad. Indeed, in the studies reported to date, the declining perceptions of the existence of a, c, and v in most ladders would require that the missing levels be subconsciously operating.

More basically, as we show in our a-b-e model, there are situations in which the ad would deliberately *not* mention higher levels (notably, attribute-only ads aimed at experts, who know or infer their own idiosyncratic benefits). Also, some ads might use a benefit for which there is no attribute foundation (as for many image brands). The all-levels assumption in the means-end model is in many cases forced and unnecessary. Even if this assumption is relaxed to allow implicit if not explicit representation of all levels in the ad, this makes the specification of what should be in the ad very vague indeed.

In the early work based on the a-c-v model, its proponents implied that the desirable position was always on the value end of the chain. This came from the insistence that ads must force consumers "up the chain". However, this has been modified in at least one recent study that recognized different foci may be appropriate. But their revised a-c-v model is inadequate in specifying conditions for alternative levels of focus. In the Perkins and Reynolds model, only one condition was given — light-user target audience versus heavy-user target audience.

They hypothesized that light users of the brand would be more likely to be persuaded by the attributes start of the chain, whereas heavy users would be most influenced by the values end of the chain. Some support for the hypothesis was obtained at the attribute end but not at the value end. More generally, they hypothesized that novices would respond to attributes, and experts respond to values. Our a-b-e model makes the opposite prediction and specifies other conditions for either an a, b, or e focus.

The a-c-v and MECCAS models also seem unable to hand le pure transformational advertising. Rather, the means-end approach assumes an informational persuasion model. As Reynolds and Craddock stated: "the attribute-based 'reason why' is required by the consumer to rationalize his or her choice behaviour".

Whereas we would agree that information is often used for this purpose in high-involvement and transformational ads, such as for luxury cars, it certainly is not required. In low-involvement and transformational ads, information rarely is even desirable. Coca-Cola ads, for instance, would not be feasible according to the MECCAS formula.

In summary, our opinion is that the means-end model is problematic theoretically and is overly restrictive for advertising applications. Certainly the claim that MECCAS is the complete theory of advertising strategy is ill advised. We would not make such a claim for our a-b-e model, which is only one small part of advertising strategy and indeed is only one part of advertising positioning strategy. The a-c-v model's limitations open the way for our a-b-e model to be proposed as a significant improvement. The discussion is now turned in detail to the new model, examining the conditions for a, b, or e focus.

ATTRIBUTE FOCUS

The standard dictum in marketing and advertising texts is to emphasize the benefit to the customer. This means the emphasis should be on the subjective reinforcement from the (actual or perceived) attribute rather than on the attribute itself. However, the a-b-e model posits that there are positioning situations in which the attribute itself should be the focus. The main situations are expert target audience, *intangible service,* and as an alternative to emotion focus for homogeneous-benefit brands. Explained next is each of these situations for which attribute focus is recommended.

Expert Target Audience

Attribute focus is appropriate when positioning the brand to an expert target audience because experts know the benefits that derive from the attributes. Indeed, it can be argued that it is more effective to present only attributes to experts because their perceptions of the importance or emotional weights of these attributes, an e element in our model, probably will vary, and therefore experts are more likely to self-persuade based on the attributes presented alone.

Sujan provided a demonstration of the attribute effect with expert consumers. She presented descriptions of two cameras — one a simple instamatic camera and the other a more advanced 35mm single lens reflex (SLR) camera. Based on their prior knowledge of cameras, the consumers in this study were classified as either experts or novices. For half of the consumers Sujan switched the labels on each description, so that these consumers saw the simple camera description with the complex-camera label "35mm SLR" and the complex camera description with the simple-camera label "110 camera." The experts were not fooled; they preferred the more advanced camera regardless of whether it had a correct or misleading label. Novices, on the other hand, judged by the label, regardless of the actual attributes.

Maheswaran and Sternthal provided another good demonstration of the attributes-for-experts effect. In their study, they prepared three product descriptions for a fictitious new personal computer: attribute focus, attribute-plus-benefit focus, and benefit focus. Examples of the attribute claims and the benefit claims for the personal computer are shown in Table, along with the results.

Again, consumers in the experiment were divided into experts and novices, based on a pretest of their computer knowledge. Maheswaran and Sternthal manipulated involvement in the experiment, telling half the consumers that they were participants in an anonymous survey, thus making their brand choice low involvement. They told the other half of the consumers that their opinion would decide whether or not the new product would be introduced, and they could expect to be contacted later by the manufacturer for a demonstration of the product, thus making their brand choice high involvement.

We selected the high-involvement results for novices because they would probably only be looking at a personal computer ad if they were seriously planning to buy a personal computer. On the other hand, we selected the low-involvement results for experts because their product category knowledge means that they would probably look at computer ads anyway in forming their future consideration sets. The high-involvement results for experts were similar to the low-involvement results in that an attribute focus was still highly effective, although the combination of attributes plus benefits was equally good when experts are closer to the purchase decision, both being better than benefits alone. As the results show, the novices' brand -attitude ratings of the new product were highest when the benefits were pointed out to them, whereas the experts' brand attitude ratings were highest when only attributes were provided.

An example of an extreme attribute-focus was a 1992 Australian newspaper advertisement for the Audi 90 automobile. The ad showed a small illustration of the car surrounded by descriptions of no less than 80 attributes. This ad may have been too extreme in terms of information overload because, two months later, the company ran a simplified ad showing the same image of the car along with a greater benefit focus in the headline.

However, the revised ad still had a considerable attribute focus with a listing of some 20 attributes. Presumably, these attribute-focus ads for Audi were aimed at luxury car buyers who see themselves as experts in discriminating the available makes and models in terms of their various features. It also is possible that these ads would work with novices, by impressing them with the sheer number of attributes.

Intangible Services

A second situation in which an attribute focus is recommended is when positioning a product that is not a product in the concrete sense but rather is an intangible service. Financial services, insurance, and auto servicing and repairs are typical examples of *intangible services.* Of course, the end result of these services is quite tangible. For instance, at a bank, you actually experience polite or rude service, or accurate or inaccurate service.

If your house is robbed, you will abruptly experience precisely what home- and -contents insurance covers, and poor or good car servicing is evident in a fairly concretely way, as well. However, the point is that when you first make the decision to purchase one of these services, the benefits are not yet forthcoming and thus are intangible.

An innovative hypothesis proposed by Shostack is that the more intangible the product or service, the more it requires tangible attributes in its promotion. This is because the tangible attributes serve as surrogate indicators of the yet-to-be-experienced benefits. This hypothesis has not, to our knowledge, been put to a formal experimental test, but real-world observations suggest that it is valid. For instance, consumers are more likely to initiate and maintain a relationship with a bank whose facilities are modern and whose employees are neatly dressed and polite, although these attributes may have little to do objectively with the ultimate service that is provided.

Insurance companies that are perceived as large are probably more successful than those that are not. Car service garages that are tidy and where the employees are not disheveled and grubby are more likely to get your business than places that look like backyard operations, and so forth. In sum, it seems a reasonable conclusion that companies offering intangible services have a greater need to demonstrate that their services are worth patronizing, by focusing on attributes as evidence of good service.

Alternative to Emotion Focus for Homogenous-Benefit Brands

When brands in a product category are virtually identical in terms of benefits, one well-known strategy is to attempt to differentiate the brand on emotional associations. An alternative strategy is not widely recognized — if most brands in the category are advertising the same benefits, it may be effective for our brand to go back to attributes as a means of differentiation.

The theory is that a distinctive attribute can serve as a parity-breaker even if the attribute is fairly trivial in terms of delivering a benefit to the consumer. This strategy has been used for many years in advertising. Classic campaigns include Budweiser's "beechwood-aged, " Shell gasoline's "X-100, " Procter and Gamble's Folger's coffee, with "mountain grown" beans in its regular coffee and "flaked coffee crystals" in its instant coffee. Or, consider Ivory Soap's "99(44)100(% pure, " a famous Claude) Hopkins claim from the turn of the century that the brand still uses.

Another successful example is in the ketchup category, where most leading brands' benefits are much the same. Heinz seems to have gained an advantage by focusing on the thickness of its ketchup, an attribute that makes it "slow-pouring". Slowness in pouring is hardly a benefit for adults, although it may be for those who have sloppy kids! Of course, the implied benefit from the sauce's thickness is that it is "richer." Notice that the Heinz ketchup ads do not mention the benefit, contrary to the stipulation in the MECCAS model that each level is explicitly addressed in the ad. Whether mention of the benefit would make the ads more or less effective is an obvious question that Heinz probably answered in pre-testing and settled on attribute focus.

Until recently, the effectiveness of the trivial-attribute-as-parity-breaker strategy had not been proven under controlled experimental conditions. Carpenter, Glazer, and Nakamoto provided an experimental demonstration of this strategy. They found consumers were much more likely to prefer a brand that, among otherwise identical brands, added a trivial attribute. The effect was shown for all three product categories studied—a brand of ski-jacket that advertised "alpine-class down fill, " a pasta brand described as "authentic Milanese style, " and a compact disc player that advertised a "studio-designed signal processing system." We note that deception or consumer misunderstanding is not the explanation. Half the consumers in the experiment were told that the added attribute was irrelevant or meaningless, yet most of these consumers still strongly preferred the brand that offered it. Thus, attribute focus, like emotion focus as described later, is worth considering when competitive brands are emphasizing much the same benefit or benefits.

Altogether, then, we have seen that there are at least three advertising situations in which the attribute point in the a-b-e model is the recommended focus:

- When advertising to an expert target audience,
- When advertising an intangible service,
- As an alternative to emotion focus for homogeneous brands. We now consider the next level, benefit focus.

BENEFIT FOCUS (ATTRIBUTE BENEFIT OR EMOTION BENEFIT)

Benefits, in the specific sense that we are using the term

here, are subjective reinforcements that are perceived to be provided by the brand. These subjective benefits may or may not derive from the objective attributes that the brand has. Yi noted that benefits can be either physically caused by attributes (e.g., the size of an automobile, an attribute, causing the comfort benefit and also the safety benefit) or be merely correlated with them (e.g., for automobiles, European, an attribute, and prestigious, a benefit, are correlated in the minds of many U.S. car buyers). Also, an attribute that the product's designers see as important can turn out not to be a benefit to the prospective buyer.

An apparent example of a benefit that is only vaguely related to attributes is the ubiquitous claim, "natural, " apparently a meaningless word. A.C. Nielsen Company conducted a content analysis of "natural" claims in food packaging. They found an incredible variety of meanings (attributes) for the claim "natural, " including "no preservatives, " "no added salt or sugar, " "no cholesterol, " "low in calories and low in sodium, " "made with honey instead of sugar, " "unprocessed cheese, " and even "decaffeinated" (for a brand called All Natural Tea Bags).

However, the vague attribute basis of "natural" does not mean it is any less effective as a benefit. An amazing campaign in Australia substantially reversed a 40% per capita decline in sugar consumption by emphasizing that sugar is natural. Sugar does, after all, grow naturally; it occurs naturally in fruit, it is naturally present in the body via blood sugar, and so forth. (However, the chemical difference between natural and artificial foods is, of course, nonsense.) The campaign theme, "Sugar, a natural part of life, " was largely responsible for restoring Australia's sugar consumption levels by disinhibiting people from adding sugar to food and beverages. A continuation of the "Sugar is natural" campaign then successfully held off the threat from artificial sweeteners that had entered the market as a diet aid. This is all the more remarkable considering that many other products claim they are natural precisely because they do not contain (or add) sugar.

Accordingly, benefit focus can be regarded as being either a sole focus on a benefit (point 3 in the a-b-e model) or as linking benefits to underlying attributes (attribute benefit, path 2 in the model). Also, as seen later, a benefit may be linked to a prior emotion.

Usually this is a negative emotion with the benefit providing relief (emotion-benefit, path 4). The common element is that the ad ends by stating or portraying a benefit. There are three situations in which we recommend benefit focus: brand with hard-to-imitate benefit, negatively-motivated (informational) brand, and logical attack on entrenched emotion-based attitude. The first situation, perhaps, is fairly obvious, but the second and third are not so clear. All three are discussed in the following.

BRAND WITH HARD-TO-IMITATE BENEFIT

Clearly, if a brand has one or more differential advantages that are hard for competitors to imitate, those benefits should be the focus (point 3 in the model). This is the normal recommendation in marketing, but the hard-to-imitate aspect is crucial. Benefits in the form of price and also price promotions, usually do not qualify, as they are easy to imitate, unless the company has a low-cost advantage and is prepared to sustain a predatory price position (as has been the case in some markets presently dominated by Japanese manufacturers). We should emphasize that for a brand with a *superior* benefit or benefits, the advertising focus should be on the benefit (the subjective relief or reward for the buyer) and not on the attribute or the emotion. This is because differential attributes are not necessarily differential benefits from the customer's stand point. Also, at the other extreme, differential emotions are, by and large, a less sustainable means of differentiation than if the brand has a differential benefit or benefits.

BRAND CHOICE BASED ON NEGATIVE (INFORMATIONAL) MOTIVES

Informational advertising, which is recommended when

brand choice is based on a negative purchase motivation (relief), should hype the negative emotion first (the problem) and then demonstrate the benefit (the solution). In terms of the a-b-e model, the sequence is e -b. That is, the negative emotional state caused by the problem is relieved, sequentially, by the benefit. It is optional, not necessary, that the benefit be further accompanied by a positive emotional state after its delivery. To illustrate the effective e -b sequence, consider two ads for liquid laundry detergents from the early 1990s.

One ad, an ad for Wisk, hyped the negative emotion of washing clothes by listing various ways to avoid "tsks" (life's little problems that occur when dirt or stains get on clothes) — "don't work, " "don't eat, " "don't drink, " "don't kiss, " "don't play, " and so forth. The ad went on to say that one could "use Wisk liquid laundry detergent to dissolve the dirt bonds that lock 'tsks' to your clothes and get your whole wash clean." This ad showed the negative emotion (of having to avoid fun or necessary situations to remain clean) but did not visually show how the benefit provided by the brand is the solution to the problem.

We think another ad, an ad for Tide liquid detergent, would be more effective, because it was better balanced. The Tide ad, using a before- and -after format, portrayed the negative emotion by showing a shirt stained with "dad's secret recipe, " a bar-b-que sauce, and then portrayed the benefit by showing the same shirt now clean after laundry with "mom's secret weapon, " Tide. Moreover, the tag-line for Tide was also benefit-focused: "If it's got to be clean, it's got to be Tide."

LOGICAL ATTACK ON ENTRENCHED EMOTION-BASED ATTITUDE

Consumers who have an entrenched brand attitude are particularly resistant to approaches by competing brands. This is because they perceive high risk in switching from their current brand and also consider alternative brands as inferior. If their entrenchment is based on strong emotional consequences of using the brand, it could be argued that the only way to shift the entrenched attitude is to mount a logical or rational attack rather than an "emotional" one. An emotional attack would stimulate the ready supply of emotion that the buyer has for using the brand and thus could be easily rejected.

A logical attack, on the other hand, might catch the buyer less prepared to defend his or her attitude. This would be an attribute (benefit approach (path 2 in the model). Here, our position is counter to the functional theory of attitude, which would recommend a same-function attack. For instance, if the motivational base of attitude is ego defence, then Katz' theory would recommend an ego-defence attack. The opposite function attack theory for negative target audiences has been proposed most recently by Millar and Millar, although their experiment provided only marginal support for the hypothesis. However, they used a mainly low-involvement product, soft drinks, and we believe that the idea is valid only for high-involvement choices.

Our view is supported by Pratkanis and Aronson's review of the "latitude of rejection" research wherein a high-credibility presenter may be able to override the narrow latitude of acceptance that is held by an entrenched target audience. The effectiveness of the attack is due to blocking of counterarguments; therefore, by the same process, we would expect that the opposing function attack should be similarly successful. Social problems such as teenage smoking, heroin use, and AIDS are examples of buyer behaviour that is reinforced by strong, emotion-based attitudes. To change these behaviors, a logical (benefit-based) approach by social agencies may offer the only hope.

Consider the case of AIDS, for example. The revelations by public figures, such as Rock Hudson, Anthony Perkins, Arthur Ashe, and Magic Johnson, that they had contracted the disease should be regarded as rational benefits in that they dramatically changed many people's personal estimate (subjective probability) of their chances of contracting AIDS. Most people already know the negative emotional consequences of the disease, and preventive campaigns based simply on negative emotion seem less likely to be effective.

Overall, the benefit level in the a-b-e model is the most frequent focus for advertising. A major reason for its frequent use is that it fits informationally motivated products, which are the most prevalent category in buyer behaviour. However, we identified two other advertising situations where benefit focus is recommended. One is where the brand has one or more hard-to-imitate benefits (whether informational or transformational). Another is when mounting a logical attack on an entrenched emotion-based attitude. We look now at emotion.

EMOTION FOCUS (BENEFIT EMOTION OR HEAVY NEGATIVE EMOTION BENEFIT)

The final option to be considered in the a-b-e model is emotion focus. This can take two forms: a benefit-positive emotion path (path 5) or a pure emotion focus (point 6), which would normally be e^+ but could be e'' if the ad is intended to discourage a certain behaviour, as with the previously mentioned social problems. However, we also distinguish a third form, which is the same path as e'' -b in benefit focus (path 4) but where the initial emotional emphasis is very heavily negative and pronounced. The situations in which emotion focus seems most appropriate are:

- Brand with easy-to-imitate benefits
- Positively-motivated (transformational) brand
- "Emotional" attack on entrenched attribute-based attitude

BRAND WITH EASY-TO-IMITATE BENEFITS

A large number of brands compete in basically homogeneous product categories where the benefits delivered by competing brands are essentially identical. One positioning option in this situation is to go back to attributes, as we saw in the example of Heinz ketchup. The other is to go forward to emotions or emotional consequences of benefits. The latter is sometimes skeptically referred to as the "If you've got nothing to say, sing it" school of advertising, but it works! For a brand whose attributes or benefits are easy to imitate and are likely to be imitated quickly by a competitor, emotional positioning provides an additional differentiation that may help preserve its uniqueness. For this purpose, the benefit-positive emotion sequence would be used, but with focus on the emotional consequence of the benefit, which the brand should try to make unique.

A well-known example of benefit-positive emotion (with emotion focus) that has apparently been successful for many years is the campaign for United Airlines, "Fly the friendly skies of United." Another example that is quite touchy with Australians is the practice of auto manufacturers selling identical cars under different manufacturers' badges.

Amply demonstrating that there is differential equity in a brand name alone, the same car can comm and a $1, 000 or so price difference depending on which manufacturer's name it carries. Another excellent example of benefit-positive emotion with emotion focus is Toyota's creative device, "Oh what a feeling" (accompanied by euphoric jumping), used as a clearly emotional ending for its otherwise benefit-oriented car ads.

Although we may question the ethics of the emotional differentiation approach, it could be answered that, if buyers are subjectively happy with their emotional choices, the approach is justifiable. Several schools of moral philosophy, such as Bentham's utilitarianism, would make this argument.

PURE EMOTION FOCUS

The interesting option of "pure emotion" focus (the single point 6 in the model) is one approach that has been perfected by the late German researcher Werner Kroeber-Riel. The pure emotion-focus approach, almost always e^+, might be expected to apply only to low-priced products such as soft drinks, beer, and cosmetics. However, Kroeber-Riel applied the approach successfully to higher-priced products such as kitchenware and to services such as banks and insurance companies (personal communication). For example, an ad for a German insurance company, developed with the help of Kroeber-Riel's advertising expert system, contained the headline, "We're opening the horizon."

There was no explicit benefit. Essentially the ad contained only an attention-getting and emotionally-arousing illustration of a young woman in a gauzy dress stand ing in front of an open door with light streaming through the opening and the wind blowing her dress and shawl. Benetton, too, has used a similar "pure emotion" focus approach, although this time daring to use e″ explicitly (the social controversy theme of Benetton's ads is well known) although the inferred end result is almost certainly e^+. The ads have met with great success everywhere except in the United States where most of the ads were banned. In 1991, the first year of its controversial campaign, Benetton's profits grew by 24% worldwide, but fell to near break-even in the United States.

It could be argued that many cases of apparently pure-emotion focus, such as the German insurance company ad and the typical Benetton ad, are in effect benefit emotion ads in that consumers are likely to interpret a benefit belief although none is explicitly stated.

For instance, consumers exposed to the German insurance ad might have inferred that "We're opening the horizon" means that the company is promising to make your future less worrisome. Similarly, consumers may infer benefit beliefs from the Benetton ads such as the company is socially responsible, or simply the brand has avant-garde advertising. If so, then these examples could be seen, not as a pure emotion focus (point 6), but as the e″ -b path (path 4) in both instances. However, this argument is not strictly valid, because the a-b-e model only indicates what messages to put (explicitly) in ads; it is not a model of how consumers, or anyone else, will interpret the ad.

Worth discussing is the use of subliminal sexual imagery in ads. This is certainly a demonstration of pure emotion in advertising, because the persuasion process is evidently not based on conscious cognitive consideration of attributes or benefits or conscious consideration even of the emotion. The more sensational, unproven claims by Key of subliminal sexual imagery or death imagery in ads (corresponding to the Freudian theory of Eros or sexual drive and Thanatos or death-wish drive) have rightfully been dismissed. However, subsequent experiments by Freudian psychologist William Ruth and his colleagues suggest that the sexual arousal effect is real, that it can occur unconsciously, and that it favorably affects brand attitude.

Ruth and his colleagues conducted their experiments with ads for liquor, a product category where the benefits are similar across brands. Moreover, it could be maintained that, for liquor products, sexual arousal (usually a sensory gratification motive, but sometimes social approval) is a relevant benefit (emotion focus).

In the first experiment, consumers were shown six one-page liquor ads taken from weekly news and sports magazines. Three of these ads were judged by the experimenters to contain phallic and vaginal symbols — indeed, two phallic symbols and two vaginal symbols per ad (experimental group). The other three ads contained no such symbols (control group). All of the ads depicted objects only, not people, so there was no explicit portrayal of sex in any of the ads.

Consumers were told there would be a recall test after looking at the ads. However, they actually were administered a psychoanalytic Thematic Apperception Test (TAT). The TAT is an ambiguous picture projective test (like the famous Rorschach Inkblots but with people in the pictures) in which the individual is asked to write a story about what was going on in the TAT picture. The stories were then scored, blind as to experimental condition, for presence of sexual imagery, using the standard TAT coding scheme. In a postexperimental interview, none of the consumers showed awareness of the true purpose of the experiment.

As predicted, consumers who saw the liquor ads containing phallic and vaginal symbols exhibited approximately twice as much sexual content in their subsequent descriptions (of the ambiguous TAT cards, not the ads) as those who saw the nonsymbolic ads. Men and women both showed the effect. This first experiment demonstrates that sexual drive can be unconsciously aroused by normal but symbolically-particular stimuli in ads.

In the second experiment with a new sample of consumers, the effect of sexual symbolic content was taken one step further by examining purchase intentions for advertised liquor brands. Seven paired ads were selected — again actual ads from consumer magazines. Although no people were shown in either ad, one ad in each pair contained copulatory symbolism (implying male-female intercourse), whereas the other ad had no sexual content.

The ads used in the experiment were quite normal. For example, the copulatory symbolism ads used illustrations such as a bottle protruding diagonally from a Christmas stocking and the nonsexual ads used illustrations such as a winter snow scene glimpsed through a frosty window.

The ingenious prior step was that the brands and liquor types in the pairs were matched beforeh and for purchase intentions based on the name alone, rated by a separate but similar group of consumers.

In this pretest, the brands in the pairs differed by less than 0.2 of a rating point on the 7-point purchase intention measure. The experiment, with a new sample of consumers, followed the pretest. Purchase intentions for brands advertised in the Freudian copulatory symbolism ads were rated approximately 1 rating point higher on the 7-point purchase intention measure than the brands in the nonsymbolic ads.

Moreover, demonstrating generalizability, this highly significant effect was observed for men in the experiment on five of the seven ads and for women on six of the seven ads. It is unlikely that other factors such as the esthetics or likability of the ads produced these differences because the control ads were probably more attractive than the experimental (symbolic) ads.

Unconscious sexual arousal (an effect of e^+ focus in the Freudian ads) is the most likely explanation. We note that the effect was obtained with only one exposure to the ads, although the laboratory-like forced exposure conditions of the experiment probably translate to about three real-world exposures. Pending replication, we accept these experiments as valid demonstrations of subliminal sexual imagery working in ads — and as an intriguingly successful demonstration of pure emotion focus.

BRAND CHOICE BASED ON POSITIVE (TRANSFORMATIONAL) MOTIVES

The positive reward motivations in Rossiter and Percy's theory were sensory gratification, intellectual stimulation or mastery, and social approval. For brand choice based on these motives, transformational advertising is recommended. An important line of research by John Deighton suggested that advertising that focuses on the emotional consequence of a benefit can actually affect the buyer's experience of that benefit when the brand is subsequently purchased and used.

Thus, if the advertising has portrayed the positive benefit in an emotionally authentic way, then those exposed to the advertising are more likely to rate the brand's benefit delivery as better when they experience it later, compared to those not previously exposed to its advertising. Perhaps this is why Coca-Cola works so hard to achieve emotional authenticity in its TV commercials (the company tests only finished TV commercials, not rough versions, because roughs do not have sufficient emotional authenticity.

More generally, the transformational style of advertising in which almost all advertisements that make a promise are regarded as transformational) depends vitally on a positive emotional end state. The sequence is usually b-e^+ (path 5), or simply. For the negative motivations, the end state can be emotionally neutral (relief or relaxation). For the positive motivations, on the other hand, the end state *must* be a positive emotion.

EMOTIONAL ATTACK ON ENTRENCHED ATTRIBUTE-BASED ATTITUDE

Again, let us consider the entrenched buyer of a particular brand, in which the brand could be some form of personal or social behaviour instead of a brand in the commercial product or service sense. If the buyer's brand attitude is rationally based on an attribute, and we want to change it, then an emotional attack is worth considering. In terms of the a-b-e model, this is a-b attacked by e″ -b (path 4). Although technically this should be labeled as a benefit path because it ends in a benefit, the key is the heavy, negative (emotional beginning; hence we classify it as emotion focus.

Threat or fear appeals in advertising (or in personal selling) are the best-known application of this approach. The effect of fear, a negative emotion, is to distract the person from mounting rational counterarguments. Well-known examples of fear appeals in advertising include the TV commercials for American Express Travelers Checks in which overseas travelers are robbed ("What kind were they?") and the Prudential Insurance TV ads of the early 80's in which a father dies on the operating table or a mother drowns, thus emphasizing the need for life insurance.

The overall conclusion from many years of research on fear appeals is that the higher the fear level, the more effective the attack on brand attitude will be, provided that the recommended behaviour change is perceived as do-able by the individual. If the behaviour change is not do-able, any level of fear will exacerbate the original behaviour. The "do-ability" proviso is important. Perhaps the best examples are not in the areas of addictive habits such as smoking and drinking, whose consequences are largely emotionally reinforcing, but rather in the example of voting behaviour.

Voting is easily do-able. Whereas one would think that the public's political choices in state and national elections should be based on rational appraisal of the issues (attributes), many recent elections seem to have been strongly influenced by opposing parties' emotional attacks on the personal background of the candidates. Pratkanis and Aronson provided an interesting discussion of how emotional positioning can be effective in otherwise attribute-based arenas.

Summarizing the advertising situations in which emotion is the recommended focus, we see that there are at least three: (1) when the brand has only easy-to-imitate benefits, remembering that attribute focus is also an alternative; (2)

when the brand choice is positively motivated (the b-e^+ sequence); or (3) for an emotional attack (e″-b, but with heavy e″ focus) on an entrenched attribute-based attitude. These quite diverse but conditionally specific situations go beyond the simplistic exhortation to use "emotional" advertising.

Chapter 5

Communications Strategy and Advertising Practice

The majority of marketplace competition centers around the "attribute versus attribute" level. In contrast, with a means-end communications strategy, the axial challenge is to determine the personal value or goal that best fits with the distinctive attributes of the product, forge a strong connection between personal value and product attribute, and fight off competitive products that want to do the same.

A stream of academic research starting as early as Cartwright has consistently reported results indicating that a product's success at tapping into personal needs, goals, or values tends to be the best predictor of consumer preference. The basic finding is consistent across many different types of products and situations. For example, Reynolds, Gutman, and Fiedler found the result among restaurant patrons: Reynolds and Jamieson among department store patrons; Perkins and Reynolds for snack chip consumers; Jolly, Reynolds, and Slocum with respect to the performance appraisal of subordinates.

Means-end theory asserts that effective advertising will link together several levels of product information, that is attributes, consequences, and values. Moreover, means-end theory asserts that advertising will be the most persuasive when the psychological and sociological benefits of consumption, that is, psychosocial consequences, are shown to develop rationally and consistently from a set of distinctive product attributes. Reynolds and Gengler reported that it is unusual for an ad to generate significant product affect unless the ad can make at least one strong connection between an adjacent pair of communications levels.

MEANS-END FUNDAMENTALS

The means-end model classifies and links together four levels of information that underpin consumer decision-making. At the most concrete level, attributes are the physical, tangible features or characteristics of a product. In the mind of the consumer, these tangible features translate into functional consequences. Functional consequences can be described as the physical, tangible experiences associated with product consumption. At higher levels of abstraction, product attributes and functional consequences tap into personal values or goals through satisfying key psychosocial consequences. Psychosocial consequences, themselves, spring from the emotional experiences of consumption driven by psychological and/or sociological rewards or punishments.

The means-end chain traveled by a consumer when connecting product attributes with personal needs or goals represents their perceptual orientation with respect to the product and the buying situation. It shows why the product is self-relevant or involving. Consequently, one might argue that the perceptual orientations depicted by personalized networks of means-end chains provide the key str and s of information needed to explain product-related attitudes and behaviour.

The strength of connection between person and product is reflected by the level of involvement a consumer has with the product category. Consumer involvement grows when marketers bring out personally relevant psychological and sociological reasons for consuming their products, and consequently, involvement can be manipulated by marketing programs. For example, small-package delivery was a low-involvement, low-loyalty commodity business until Federal Express introduced the overnight delivery of small packages and made it self-relevant by showing the important psychosocial consequences associated with using their delivery service for business-related packages. Indeed, the primary goal of a means-end communications strategy is to build consumer involvement.

MEANS-END RESEARCH

Distinctions From Consumer-Attitude Survey Research

The key distinction between means-end research and traditional consumer-attitude research is the relative emphasis the two approaches put on determining the specific reasons why product attributes are important to consumers. Traditional attitude research focuses on determining the relative importance of attributes and measuring perceptions about how well products perform with respect to important attributes. Means-end research focuses on determining the key choice criteria underlying a purchase decision, identifying how the choice criteria relate to product attributes and understanding the reasons why the product attributes and related choice criteria are important or personally relevant to consumers.

Marketing research that addresses attribute importance and performance becomes much more actionable when marketers also learn how the consequences of product attributes can be communicated effectively and how to link product attributes with reasons why superior performance of an attribute matters to the decision maker. Furthermore, with a consumer-relevant context that relates a product to the real needs underpinning product purchase and consumption, the marketer gains more insight into how to use marketing research to create a sustainable competitive advantage.

Means-end research can provide new ideas for product development, consumer promotions, communications strategy and advertising execution, pricing, distribution, and many other important marketing issues. Intuitively, successful marketers know that product attributes and the functional consequences of those attributes are not the motivating "end-states" leading to trial, repurchase, and positive word-of-mouth. They sense that product traits are a means to some end but are unsure about how consumer end-states change depending on the event triggering the buying situation, the target audience, and other aspects of the purchasing context relevant to the consumer.

GUIDELINES FOR LADDERING INTERVIEWS

In-depth laddering interviews provide the primary machinery for conducting means-end research. Although often misused by marketing research companies, this style of interviewing amounts to much more than just unstructured note taking directed at recovering a respondent's general knowledge about a product or product category. It also markedly differs from narrowly-drawn, open-ended questions about important reasons for selecting a product. To be effective, laddeiing interviews must be in-depth, yet crisp and pointed. Unlike survey research that is often shallow and broad (dozens of short-answer, closed-end questions asked across a large sample of respondents), means-end research and laddering should be focused and deep (five or six interdependent, closed-ended and open-ended questions asked across a small, targeted sample).

Laddering research works best and produces the most actionable results for marketers when it is directed at achieving a specific marketing goal such as increasing sales revenue through increasing the number of people buying in the product category, attacking a leading brand, or encouraging current customers to use the brand more often. To accomplish such a goal, marketers must utilize a well thought out research design consisting of a purposive sample, context-specific interview drivers, appropriate elicitation techniques for detecting choice criteria, suitable methods for uncovering personal relevance, and unbiased ways to measure competitive strengths and weaknesses.

A purposive sample is selected to create contrast between different consumer points of view and to isolate factors that will "tip the balance" in favour of buying from a product category, selecting a particular brand, or increasing one's frequency of brand use. Furthermore, the interview itself and the method for eliciting reasons for choosing one product over another must be dimensionalized to include relevant people, places, social occasions, and purchase or consumption timing. Distinctions between alternatives, that is, choice criteria, can be elicited in several different ways, including triadic sorting, but are usually determined by asking about reasons for choosing one alternative over another. Reynolds and Gutman provided detailed explanations of alternative elicitation methods. Finally, the full set of choice alternatives, whether they are direct competitors like Coke and Pepsi or indirect competitors like Coke and tap water, should be included in the choice exercise. Furthermore, marketers should resist the urge to myopically focus their total effort on brand competition where gains are the hardest and competitive reactions are the strongest.

Choice criteria elicited in the laddering process must be linked with tangible product attributes as well as to the intangible reasons why the criteria matter to the consumer and their value system. This often requires interviewers to ladder down before they can ladder up. In our experience, respondents only occasionally mention concrete product attributes as the reason for selecting one product over another. Respondents are more likely to mention a functional or, in some cases, a psychosocial consequence as the choice criterion. Untrained or poorly trained interviewers often take consequences as the starting point for a ladder. Consequently, they frequently do not differentiate between attributes and the functional consequences of attributes. As a result, they have difficulty uncovering the connection between product and person and seldom identify the respon-dent-specific cues that can clearly communicate a functional consequence.

In conjunction with the laddering interview, competitive strengths and weaknesses must be measured with respect to key choice criteria and the means-end chain of attributes, functional consequences, psychosocial consequences, and personal values to which they relate. Effective communications strategy fundamentally grows out of playing to strength. Consequently, without a pattern of competitive strengths and weaknesses to overlay on the network of means-end chains resulting from laddering interviews, there is no basis to judge whether a particular communications strategy can help build or sustain a competitive advantage. In short, marketers need more than an aggregate map of means-end chains to formulate, specify, and execute an effective communications strategy. Understanding competitive strengths and weaknesses and the barriers and opportunities they create also is critically important.

ANALYSIS OF MEANS-END RESEARCH

Laddering interviews uncover means-end chains associated with consumer-specific product meanings. These product meanings represent the different perceptual or buying orientations of various benefit segments within the target market. Understanding the key product elements and connections between elements together with the associated overlay of competitive strengths and weaknesses forms the basis for devising a customer-focused communications strategy.

There are four general approaches to creating competitive advantage through an analysis of means-end chains:

- Uncovering an Untapped or emerging buying orientation that represents a significant market opportunity. As examples, consider the emerging buying orientations of the elderly living as retired people many more years than anticipated, the baby-boom generation going through mid-life crisis, or the large numbers of young people now gaining unprecedented buying power.
- Strengthening Ownership of a buying orientation that is already, or at least somewhat, associated with your product. It is not unusual for new products to sell successfully in the marketplace without the marketing manager knowing exactly why. Similarly, many marketers cannot easily specify the higher level reasons underpinning the purchase and consumption of their brand. In these situations, understanding the importance in a consumer's decision-making process,

means-end orientation that attracts consumers provides the stepping off point for reinforcing and defending one's market position.

- *Creating a new Buying Orientation that better fits the Distinctive Traits of your Product.* New buying orientations may be created by either connecting yet unrelated concepts or interjecting new attributes or context-specific consequences into the network of choice criteria. This general approach to strategy can create marketing miracles along the lines of Honda who revitalized and dramatically expanded motorcycle sales in the United States by making a new connection between small motorcycles, convenient transportation, and young-at-heart, friendly riders.
- *Reframing a buying Orientation Initially owned by a key competitor.* Turning a strength into a weakness is one of the most powerful strategic ideas a marketer can employ. In a means-end world, this can be done most effectively by playing to the relevant set of psychosocial consequences. Consider the resounding success of Cannon personal copiers against Xerox relative to the very limited success of the larger, stronger competitors Kodak and IBM. Kodak and IBM tried to compete on the basis of superior product attributes and consequences in the context of centralized copying which Xerox owned. On the other hand, Cannon turned the distinctive competence of Xerox in centralized copying into a liability for many potential customers by stressing distributed copying that gave more personal control, a psychosocial consequence, to employees and business managers.

COMMUNICATIONS STRATEGY AND ADVERTISING PRACTICE

Aside from the general approaches to creating competitive advantage previously outlined that can be uncovered by means-end research, which have been to some extent discussed in several papers, few specifics or examples have been published explaining how one can translate means-end research into effective communications strategies and executional ideas.

We offer the following strategic principles and contemporary examples as a help to marketers, communications consultants, advertising executives, and public-relations practitioners interested in applying the lessons of means-end marketing. The practical lessons outlined in this chapter are an outgrowth and extension of principles and research findings previously published by several authors. We also draw heavily from our personal correspondence with these and other leading professionals in the field of advertising and communications.

Guidelines for the Strategic Assessment of Advertising

To assess the fit between communications strategy and advertising execution, the content of the desired communications elements, relative weight among elements, and desired executional effect must be prespecified. There are several published examples of how to apply the MECCAS model to the assessment of communications strategy. Beyond the mechanics outlined in the previous chapters there are several simple and practical rules-of-thumb to keep in mind when devising a system to strategically assess advertising.

First, the biggest hazard of formally specifying and assessing a communications strategy is allowing the ads to rely too heavily on using words to make their points. When it comes to communications and the spoken word, more is often less. It is estimated that less than 20% of what gets communicated in our society is verbal. Perhaps people simply do not have the patience to listen to a lot of advertising copy because, in general, advertising is not considered by consumers to be a very credible information source because of the marketer's vested interest in selling the product.

Advertiser's can not depend on copy alone to persuade consumers. In fact, too much copy can get in the way of an effective ad. In today's society, it appears as though the more an ad relies on images and music to convey its message, the more persuasive the ad will be. This may put ad agencies in a difficult position when working with the MECCAS model. On the one hand, the creative group wants to put together what they think will be a persuasive ad, on the other, they may want to include copy speaking directly to the MECCAS framework to show their work is "on-strategy."

However, such problems can be avoided if one remembers the goal of the advertising is to effectively communicate and link the key strategic concepts and not necessarily to use the exact words specifying the communications strategy or, for that matter, use any words at all.

Another serious and frustrating problem is the tendency of respondents to become advertising experts. One way to address this issue is to show several ads together, one after another, then ask about the impact, content, and communications characteristics of the ads. Having respondents compare several ads, two at a time, also may be effective. Moreover, a laboratory setting for conducting ad assessments may help because one viewing of an ad often is not enough to gather all the pertinent information.

An ad assessment should also provide a foundation for learning how to make better advertising executions in the future. Consequently, the success of the executional framework in showing key points and creating the right mood must be measured. In addition, one may want to measure shifts in viewer attitudes toward the product, behavioral intentions, and how well viewers like the ad so that these factors can be related back to specific communications and executional elements.

Strategic Assessment of Competitive Advertising

Working on your own advertising is often so personally involving that it is easy to overlook the opportunity to learn more about competitors and how to position your product in the competitive environment by conducting a strategic assessment of competitive advertising. Assessments of competitive advertising bring out the strengths and weaknesses of competitors in the marketplace. Moreover, these assessments can clarify the nature of the target audiences being addressed by competitors and the buying orientations into which they are trying to tap.

In our experience, taking the time to look critically at and understand competitive advertising and positioning strategies has been among the most effective ways to leverage means-end research into an effective communications strategy that builds on strength, stresses defensible points of distinction, and reframes the consumer decision-making process in a way that creates competitive advantage.

The first step in assessing competitive advertising is expressing the content and executional elements of competitive ads in the MECCAS framework. An assessment can then be conducted with respondents evaluating a set of competitive ads along with the your own ads. In addition, similar to drawing a sample for a means-end laddering study, the sample for a competitive ad assessment should be targeted to include people with differing buying orientations, product preferences, and usage patterns.

Chapter 6

A Strategic Framework of Advertising

Advertising expenditures for individual firms, particularly consumer goods firms, continue to increase, representing a significant portion of revenues.

For example, in 1988 Philip Morris became the first single company to crack the 2 billion dollar mark for annual advertising expenditures. The immensity of these annual commitments to advertising expenditures reflect the importance that industry places on the role of advertising in the marketing process. The management of this critical marketing function demands that the maximal efficiency, or strategic quality, be sought.

Current trends indicate that one area in which firms are aggressively seeking to better manage their television advertising expenditures is by evaluation of ads at earlier stages of the production process through the use of rough prototypes of the finished advertisements, termed animatics, photomatics, or steal-a-matics.

Because the average production cost of a television commercial usually ranges from $250, 000 to $500, 000, the reduction of expenditures on ineffective advertisements represents a goal, early on in the creative process, by which the goal of maximal efficiency can be formally investigated. Of primary interest, then, is how the complex concept of advertising efficiency, or strategic quality, can be assessed early in the creative process, at the animatic stage of copy development.

BACKGROUND

Many methods of assessing the effectiveness of advertising have been advocated and implemented. Yuspeh presented the views of a group of the leading advertising agencies on the topic of advertising copy testing. Of the nine principles that were the consensus of these views, the preeminent, first principle cited is that "A good copy testing system provides measurements which are relevant to the objectives of the advertising".

Along this vein, Seggev suggested that "... the primary goal of advertising is to effect positioning." Thus, if positioning is the primary goal of advertising, then a major component of the evaluation of copy should therefore be the assessment of the strategic positioning message communicated, reflecting its strategic quality.

At present, a majority of copy is assessed after the final stage of production. Obviously, several aspects of the communication process are all at question simultaneously at this point. The advertisement must gain an audience's attention and must communicate the desired message to the consumers that they will remember. Measures of whether or not a particular aspect of the message was delivered or whether the ad was remembered typify traditional copy-testing research methodologies. However, these types of research methods often ignore the specific, strategically based positioning content of the message.

The fact that no a priori framework of strategic positioning is utilized for the assessment forestalls any direct assessment of the relative effectiveness of the execution or any systematic contrasting of the quality of alternative executions. Clearly, advertisements should be assessed to monitor the degree to which they communicate the desired positioning, or in other words, to assess how well these messages deliver the intended strategy. Following this argument, Reynolds and Rochon stated:

Standard copy testing methods adequately measure intrusiveness, be it known as recall, recognition or simple memorability of key copy points. Standard copy testing fails to measure, however, the degree to which the desired strategy was communicated.

It is proposed that the most consistent, and most important, aspect of an advertisement across all stages of production is the particular strategy-related positioning message it contains. Obviously, standard intrusiveness measures, although important in their own right, are inapplicable for animatics, as is any related form of recall or recognition research. The strategic evaluation of animatics is primarily a judgment of quality of the *content* of the communication, reflecting the extent to which a desired positioning was obtained. Dual research issues emerge:

- Specify a theoretically sound framework for the assessment of advertising strategy;
- Assess the correspondence of the analysis of the strategic message represented in animatics with respect to analysis of the message communicated in the final production.

DEFINING ADVERTISING STRATEGY

Reynolds and Gutman described advertising communication as "the set of meanings and associations that serve to differentiate a product or service from its competition." With this in mind, advertising strategy is simply defined as "the specification of the manner by which the brand will be meaningfully differentiated by the target consumer". A specific strategy, then, is the particular set of meanings and associations linked to the brand, or cognitive structure, which is being communicated.

Several structural viewpoints of communications, with respect to how meaning or cognitive structure is derived, have been proposed. Cart-wright proposed a goal orientation in understanding motivational structure communicated in advertising. Young and Feigin presented the Grey Benefit Chain, which links physical traits of products to more personal "emotional payoffs, " which represent, similarly, the motives of the consumer. Consistent with the motivational approach, Levy presented a structural perspective of product meaning based on social structure in which products are linked to individuals' perceptions of the type of people they feel use those products. Another related model of meaning was presented by Cohen, who linked product attributes to valued outcomes.

Similarly, Chattopadhyay and Alba studied levels of abstraction in cognitions generated from advertising, ranging from "Factual Details" through "Single-Fact Interpretations, " "Abstractions, " to "Global Evaluations." Seeking a more comprehensive research paradigm, means-end theory proposed a structural viewpoint of meaning based on consumer cognitive categorization processes, which are the essence of product differentiation.

Means-end theory is based upon a personal values orientation, where personal values are the motivating "end-states of existence" that individuals strive for in their lives. The core of an individual's self-concept can be viewed as a bundle of values, which govern perception, memory, and ultimately behaviour. Products are viewed as a schema of physical attributes. Means-end theory simply suggests that the way in which these physical attributes of products are linked to personal values of individuals is the manner by which products gain personal relevance, essentially, the manner in which meaning is established.

Thus, a physical attribute of a product is important only to the extent to which this attribute delivers a benefit or consequence to the consumer through the perception of product usage. The perceived consequence of product usage, then, is important only to the extent that this consequence is linked to another higher level, psychosocial consequence and, ultimately, to an individual's personal value orientation. A technique known as laddering has been demonstrated as a methodology for eliciting from individuals what their individual meaning structures are for a product category defined by attributes, consequences, and personal values.

Essentially, laddering provides the basis from which an individual's cognitive structure can be obtained, including both content and structural components. The aggregation of ladders across a sample of consumers, then, yields a representative cognitive structure for an entire product category.

Following this theoretical perspective, a model to define the cognitive components of meaning for advertising strategy has been presented, termed the MECCAS model. This model, predicated on means-end theory, presents four conceptual elements of an advertising message that should be considered in strategy development and specification. In the model, Message Elements refer to the differentiating physical attributes of the product that are communicated. Consumer Benefits are the direct consequences consumers could gain through product usage.

Leverage Points are the ways in which the message taps into, or activates, the individual's personal value system. This level is oftentimes considered to reflect brand personality traits of the product that serves to provide the link from the physical descriptors of the product to the higher level definers of "self." Driving Forces, then, are the high-level value orientations, that define self, communicated or activated by the ad.

The final component of MECCAS, the Executional Framework (EF), is the specification of the delivery vehicle for the four fundamental strategic components and, as such, is not considered part of strategy specification. It is important to note that *not* all ads are required to communicate at each of the strategic levels; rather, MECCAS represents a framework which is broad enough to deal with all types of advertising strategic specification and assessment.

To illustrate how strategy can be specified with MECCAS, a summary derived from an assessment of telecommunications ads is presented. Note that the key strategic elements corresponding to the MECCAS definitions are specified in the appropriate boxes. The blank box for EF represents the unique contribution of the advertising agency, namely, the optimal executional story or device to communicate and link together in an impactful way the four strategic elements.

A strategic specification in this form, then, indicates what the key meanings that are to be communicated by the ads, which essentially defines how the telecommunications product or company is going to be made personally relevant to the viewer. In a real-world environment, the specification would also include the relative strength desired at each respective level, thereby providing the marketing strategist the ability to communicate to the agency the particular area of focus desired for the desired positioning. Interestingly, the responsibility of the advertiser can be defined as one of developing and specifying a positioning strategy, whereas the dual responsibility of the advertising agency is to simultaneously provide the meanings desired as well as maximizing the connections or associations between these meanings.

The MECCAS model has been used to assess strategic components of specific advertisements. Reynolds and Trivedi studied the relation between components of the MECCAS model communicated and the overall affect generated by the ad in the snack-food product category. In their research, significant correlations were found between components of the model and overall affect.

Two key omissions were made, however, in design of the initial Reynolds and Trivedi study. First, an aggregate affect measure was used that combined both ad affect and brand affect, although these have been demonstrated to be separate constructs. Second, and of equal importance, the Reynolds and Trivedi study concentrated entirely on communication of meanings at the levels of MECCAS and ignored measures of association between conceptual meanings communicated in the ad. It is this latter point that offers unique potential in the assessment of advertising quality from a strategic perspective, both for finished as well as animatic ads.

Recently, Gengler and Reynolds addressed both of these issues in a new approach to assessing the meaning on which product positioning and advertising strategy is predicated. A separate construct was designed for brand affect generated by the ad and for affect for the ad, and subject perceptions of the associations communicated between the strategic components of the advertisement were gathered. Their findings indicate that both the MECCAS components and the associations between components were found to offer independent contributions to the prediction of brand affect for ads in the telecommunications category. The critical finding showed that the associations communicated between strategic elements, thought to be the basis of meaning, were indeed related to affect for the brand. Furthermore, a pattern was observed in the results that indicates that for the ads in which stronger contribution from associations was found, the affect generated for the brand by these ads was systematically higher.

This basic finding with respect to the importance of the levels of abstraction in communication, as represented by the MECCAS model, and the connections or linkages between the strategic elements at the respective levels presents a unique opportunity to develop a new data presentation format that summarizes both the relative strength of a given set of strategic elements as well as the myriad of potential connections between adjacent levels.

The opportunity presented here is to develop a data presentation framework that, in essence, provides a complete summary of the cognitive elements and associations activated by a given execution. From the Gengler and Reynolds data, a diagrammatic model representation of the strength of the communication of both the strategic elements corresponding to levels of the MECCAS and the strength of the associations between each pair of elements is developed.

METHODOLOGY

To address the basic research issues, animatics were obtained for two of the finished telecommunications ads analyzed by Gengler and Reynolds (in press), hereafter referred to as Ad A and Ad B. The finished ads were very consistent with the animatics in terms of the similarity of scenes presented and accompanying voiceover.

A sample of 49 subjects recruited under the same sample specifications as the sample from the finished ads – from a geographic region where the finished ads had not been aired – was utilized, thereby ensuring no previous exposure to the finished ads. Subjects were administered a questionnaire in exactly the same fashion as was performed in the original assessment of the finished ads, a personal computer-based procedure, termed strata. This system integrates a personal computer and a video cassette recorder such that the ads being assessed and the questions directed to the subjects can be shown alternately on the same colour monitor. Responses are given verbally by subjects to a trained interviewer, who then enters them into the computer. The average amount of time required to complete the task, assessing both ads, was 53 minutes.

Strata is designed to assess the strategic communication effects of advertising through implementation of the MECCAS model discussed earlier. Prior to the initiation of a research study, the key elements for the entire product/service category, usually jointly obtained from the laddering process and a strategic review of competitive advertising, are translated into statements corresponding to the levels of abstraction prescribed in the MECCAS format. An outline of the presentation format of the different types of questions is detailed in Appendix A. R and omization of questions within the question categories is performed.

The scale utilized in strata for assessing the strength of a specific strategic element has three response options: (0) "does not apply, " (60) "clearly applies, " and (100) "perfectly applies." Pretesting was performed and the resulting scale point weights were assigned. Of note is prior research conducted by Reynolds and Trivedi that showed little difference between a two-point and a five-point scale in a similar study. The scale utilized for the strength of association between key elements, defined as those that are endorsed as either "clearly" or "perfectly" applicable to describing the specific ad, also has three points:

- "Little, "
- "Somewhat, " and
- "Totally" connected. These questions are presented in the form of a graphical scale using colour-coded Venn diagrams with differing degree of overlap

between each relevant pair of strategic elements (approximately 5%, 35%, and 75%, respectively). The resulting associations score is derived from a multiplicative form of the three scores (element i, element j, and their direct association measure ij), which is rescaled using a probabilistic function to a 0 to 9 scale. More specifically, the scores for a given pair of statements representing adjacent levels of MECCAS are multiplied by the score reflecting the strength of connection (1, 2, or 3). This multiplic and is then scaled on a 0 to 9 scale with each increment corresponding to probabilistically equal steps.

The primary quantitative output of the strata methodology, the strength of communication of the key strategic elements, and their pairwise strength of associations between adjacent levels can then be summarized in the new stepwise data format developed above.

RESULTS

Following the previous Gengler and Reynolds research, this study was concerned only with potential differences in the measures of brand affect. The same two statements, namely, "This ad makes me feel even better about using the product/service" and "This ad makes me really want to get the product/service, " were used.

The scores of these two statements across both ads yielded a Cronbach alpha reliability in the previous study with finished ads of.70 as compared to.73 in this study with animatics, indicating no significant difference. (Of note is that what are termed as brand-affect questions in this research paradigm closely resemble what many refer to as persuasion scores, possibly broadening the interpretation of these findings to persuasion-like scores.

Level of Meaning

For both ads assessed, the overall pattern of scores between animatics and finished were quite similar, except for consistently stronger scores at the Message Element level. This difference, noted for five of the six lower level elements across both ads, was likely due to the difference in executional format. That is, the reason animatics are scoring higher at the Message Element level is apparently due to increased attention being paid to the more concrete product-related aspects, stemming from the lack of distraction from becoming involved in the story line of the finished execution.

Said another way, the viewer involvement with the story flow in the finished execution causes the viewer to attend to more of the dynamic flow of information and images as opposed to the more static "picture" approach executed in animatics. As such, the assessment of animatics will probably result in more perceptual emphasis on the concrete aspects of product information of the communication.

At the higher levels, two significant differences of the 16 possible for both ads can be observed. For Ad A, "Commitment to Positive Change" at the LP level scores significantly higher for the animatic (58) than for the finished (35). The stronger ME communication may well account for this net result. Similarly, the LP element of "Care" for Ad B is again more strongly communicated by the animatic, 64 and 45, respectively. In total, the scores for the strategic elements on the higher levels do appear to correspond closely between the animatic and finished executions.

Analysis of the differences in the strength of associations is generally consistent with the above findings: Differences emerge at the lower levels. The explanation is obvious. Given that the absolute magnitude of the ME is significantly more strongly communicated, the likelihood of making a connection to higher level elements is also significantly increased.

For Ad A, two significant differences appear, which, interesting for one of them ("Save Time" to "Care"), is not a result of a significant difference for either of the strategic elements. This difference cannot be readily explained. However, the other difference for Ad A, "Can Count on to Work" to "Commitment to Positive Change, " appears consistent with the prior explanation, namely, the strength of the lower level communication produces potentially higher connection scores to the higher levels. With this specific example, however, the observed strength of communication for the statement "Can Count on to Work" is not significantly different between animatic and finished, suggesting that the network of cognitive meanings may not be perfectly linear and stepwise in nature as proposed by the specification format of MECCAS. Different networks of connections may well produce different types, connections, or routes of meaning in producing persuasive communications. For Ad B, no significant differences in associations at the higher levels between animatic and finished were found.

Brand Affect

No statistically significant differences were found between the animatics and the finished ads. The scale used to assess brand affect was the same three-point ordinal scale as was utilized in the measurement of the strength of strategic elements. The brand -affect summary scores for Ad A were virtually identical, 47 and 51, respectively. For Ad B, the animatic scored 36 as opposed to a slightly lower score of 28 for the finished execution, again indicating little difference in the overall affect measures.

Decision-Making Value

To address the second research issue, namely, contrasting of alternative execution vehicles for the same strategy at the animatic stage with the purpose of deciding which offers the most potential to deliver the desired strategy. Contrasting of the summary affect score, although not statistically significant, does give the animatic for Ad A a slight advantage.

More importantly, the scores for Ad A do significantly outscore Ad B on one element at each of the four strategic levels: "Wide Selection of Product/Services" (ME), "Make My Life Easier" (CB), "Trust" (LP), and "Personal Security" (DF). Depending, of course, on the desired positioning strategy, the stronger communication of these key strategic elements in combination with the stronger set of associations between levels, does appear to suggest that the animatic for Ad A offers significantly more strategic quality potential. The research question of assessing strategy or positioning in this way strongly suggests that an a priori specification of strategy be made. The primary application of strategy assessment is to determine to what degree a given animatic delivers against the desired strategy.

Desired strategy, in this case, means predetermining the key strategy elements and their relative strengths. Secondarily, however, the ability to assess the strength of the connections "of meanings" between and across key strategic elements presents a diagnostic that can serve the creative process, either in terms of indicating a potential weakness prior to final production, or, to serve as reassurance that a particular executional device does in fact deliver the desired linkage or connection.

Experience with the strata methodology with animatics across a broad range of executional types yields two basic findings. One, rarely do ads that do not have at least one strong connection between at least two MECCAS levels generate significant affect for the brand (for both animatic and finished execution). and two, the only real differences that exist between animatic and finished occur only where the execution cannot or has not been captured in the animatic. For example, an execution that relies totally on borrowed interest from a unique aspect of a celebrity endorser is difficult to represent in animatic form and, as such, typically scores more strongly in the finished form.

The results of this study have demonstrated that strategy assessment is feasible at the animatic stage of copy development. Both the strength of communication of the strategic elements and the associations between those meanings that subjects interpret from animatics correspond, in general, closely to those for the finished executions. This implies that a positioning strategy can be assessed early on in the advertising process, thereby providing management with a tool to assist in the development of effective, strategically sound executions.

The very nature of animatics, however, does create a

positive bias in terms of the assessment of concrete, product-attribute-related strategic elements. The static nature of an animatic, as compared to its more dynamic finished counterpart, permits the viewer to attend more fully to the basic product characteristics, thereby inflating the communication scores on those elements, and on their respective strength of associations to the higher level meanings.

Chapter 7

Motivating the Sales Force

Marketing solutions that work have one thing in common: a customer orientation. Success, however, depends not only on orientation, it depends also on understanding and action. Despite the rapid evolution of marketing methods toward a more accurate and detailed understanding of the marketplace, managers have difficulty translating the results of the research process into effective marketing solutions. Success and failure often hinge on the manager's skill at implementation. Marketers have not provided clear answers to the manager's fundamental question: How do I really know what to do? Managers need a problem-solving framework that allows them to break away from old habits and tap into the power of customer-oriented marketing practices.

Mary Kay Cosmetics, made use of means-end marketing to solve a major strategic problem that threatened the continued viability and growth of the company. In presenting this case, we detail a problem-solving process that can help almost any company identify and adopt an effective customer orientation. To be successful, a customer orientation must embrace all of the relevant details surrounding the customer during the critical moments when that customer makes a choice, and then focus on the customer's decision-making process to find out why the choice was made.

The managerial problem-solving process involves answering six critical questions. The first four help managers frame the marketing problem from the customer's perspective. The last two then motivate in-depth customer research. The information is used to construct a template or map of the perceptual marketplace, including the reasons that customers both choose and reject alternatives. Based on the template, management can specify positioning strategy in customer language, which allows direct translation into communications and other marketing activities. An important characteristic of the process is that these communications address the personal motivations and beliefs that drive customers' behaviour.

IN EARLY 1986, MARY KAY COSMETICS, INCORPORATED

was in trouble. A recent management buy-out left them heavily in debt, with interest and principle repayments scheduled to begin at the end of the year. A 22% decline in sales over the previous 2 years, from $325 million to $249 million, required that management take immediate and substantial action to meet debt payments and remain solvent.

At the time MKCI was the eighth largest cosmetics and toiletries company in the United States. The highly fragmented and mature cosmetics industry had grown at an inflation-adjusted annual rate of less than 2% since the mid-1970s. MKCI products were sold through a network of independent sales consultants, not in retail stores. Thus, MKCI competed not only other direct-sales cosmetics companies such as Avon and Amway for salespeople but with cosmetics companies such as Estee Lauder who distributed through retailers.

Mary Kay's sales consultants were organized into a hierarchy consisting of four levels: beauty consultants, sales directors, senior sales directors, and national sales directors. All sales people started as beauty consultants and could be promoted contingent on meeting sales and recruiting goals. Sales consultants purchased products from MKCI at a wholesale price and then resold them to customers at the suggested retail price. Periodic promotional events gave consultants additional opportunities to earn bonuses and prizes.

MKCI also provided substantial incentives to the sales force to recruit and train new beauty consultants. Although the beauty consultants purchased products directly from

MKCI, the recruiter was paid a percentage bonus based on products purchased by people she recruited. Sales directors also received bonuses based on the number of beauty consultants recruited into her unit as well as products purchased by all consultants in the unit.

Recruiting is critical to any direct sales organization, including MKCI. In the past, both revenues and operating profits were determined primarily by the number of consultants and directors in its sales force. During the recent revenue decline, sales revenue earned per consultant at MKCI had actually increased slightly, but the size of the sales force had gone down. Also, recruiting tended to be countercyclical. When the economy was doing well, fewer people wanted to work as sales consultants. When the economy faltered, recruiting for direct-sales organizations tended to increase.

But the problem was more complex than just recruiting. Indeed, a primary motivation behind the MKCI buyout was to reduce the effects of reported performance and stock price on recruitment, retention, and productivity. To become a beauty consultant, the new recruit had to invest $600 in product inventory at the outset. When Mary Kay's stock price was down, potential recruits became skeptical about investing in the company. Existing sales consultants also lost motivation, which contributed to further declines in performance and profitability. Although the buyout reduced future negative effects of stock price on performance it did not halt the decline in sales. At a meeting of top managers, both immediate and long-term solutions to increase cash flow were proposed. Operating, efficiency, a more diversified product line, and new product development were discussed, but all practicable near-term solutions focused on marketing related issues. The principle options considered included the following:

- Raising both retail and wholesale prices;
- Increasing sales force recruitment, sales productivity, or the length of time that a consultant stayed with the firm;
- Increasing product availability through retail channels;

- Developing advertising and other consumer communications to boost the image of the company and its product line. Options were discussed in detail and many issues were raised. For example, management knew that product imagery was old fashioned, dominated by pink Cadillac's, although technical product quality was as high as that of premium retail brands. It was further noted that MKCI was spending literally nothing on advertising.

Management had to take some form of action but realized they needed more information. To this end, they decided to commission a market research study to more fully explore the potential consequences of the options they were considering. Learning from the research, they decided, would help them come to a decision about how to solve the problem of declining sales. Before the research could begin however, MKCI management had to answer some tough questions about the market environment in which they were operating.

FRAMING THE MARKETING PROBLEM

Solving marketing problems by adopting a customer orientation must begin with framing the problem from the customer's perspective. First, MKCI management had to identify who was their key, customer. To identify their key customer, management had to consider a fundamental marketing concept — the two primary methods of selling a product. In the *pull* method, the manufacturer directs its marketing efforts at the end-user, who then actively seeks out the product and "pulls" it through the distribution system. In the *push* method, the manufacturer motivates the distribution system with incentives and promotions, relying on the distribution system to get the product into the end-user's hand s. Mary Kay management had to decide where they should focus their marketing efforts to have the most influence. If pull could become the primary driver of sales, then the end-user would represent the most important customer. On the other hand, if push could provide the highest returns, then the salesperson would be key. From the beginning for MKCI, revenues correlated almost perfectly with the number of sales consultants. Management also knew that productivity had increased slightly over the past few years, but recruitment and retention were what had really suffered. Management correctly reasoned that consumer acceptance was not the problem, rather motivating the sales force was. Hence, MKCI's key customer was the sales consultant, not the end-user. Management, then, had to develop a marketing strategy that focused on the needs of the sales force.

Next, management had to determine what were the relevant behaviors of the sales force that subsequent marketing activities would have to address. *Marketing* can be described simply as a process of either changing or reinforcing people's behaviors. Therefore, relevant behaviors can include what management wants key customers to do and what customers actually do. Behaviors are not always physical actions. They can be decisions that later on become actions.

For example, eating at a destination restaurant usually requires a decision about where to go before the actual behaviour of going there. Also, behaviors and the decision about behaviors can be singular or take multiple steps. Drinking a cold beer might simply involve opening the refrigerator and pulling one out. In contrast, buying a car might first include deciding what decision criteria are most important, and then what car magazines to read, what people to talk to, what dealer-ships to visit, and what models to test drive before dickering over the price. These behaviors must be understood so that subsequent marketing activities target the most critical behaviors.

The relevant behaviors for MKCI were not complicated. Management needed to know about three primary outcomes or events that corresponded to being a sales consultant. The first two were desired behaviors that had to be reinforced in order to duplicate the company's past success. These were becoming a sales consultant and continuing as a sales consultant. The third behaviour, quitting as a sales consultant, represented the other side of the coin, the undesired behaviour. Understanding this dark side was just as important as understanding the positives because much decision behaviour is motivated by avoiding undesirable outcomes. Each of these behaviors further defined that the key customer becoming a consultant was a relevant behaviour for new consultants, continuing as a consultant was a relevant behaviour for those who were experienced and successful, and quitting was a relevant behaviour for former consultants.

Identifying behaviors provided guidance for developing hypotheses for further investigation. MKCI management realized that they must understand why people joined Mary Kay and then what factors contributed to their success. Also, because many consultants quit after just a short time with the company, management realized that there were inconsistencies between what these people expected and what they actually experienced. In this case, management deliberately avoided getting involved in how the sales force actually sold their products. All consultants received training and sales support from the sales directors and the company, but to sustain the entrepreneurial spirit that MKCI represented to women, consultants were encouraged to use their own ingenuity and ambition to develop a client base.

Once MKCI management identified their key customers and relevant behaviors, the third question that management had to answer was: What were the relevant contexts of the key behaviors? Behaviour does not occur in the abstract. All behaviour is contingent on situational factors that, in part, determine the behaviour. Thus, the relevant context can refer to the situation or physical occasion in which the behaviour occurs. Context can involve consumption of products or services, purchase of products or services, or information gathering. In this case, it was the need for a job.

Defining variables of an occasion context can include the physical time of day, location, activity, and participants. For example, an occasion for restaurant choice could be described as, "during breakfast, weekday, near the office, with a client, setting up a new account." Such an occasion would likely result in a very different choice of restaurants compared to, "during breakfast, with the kids, weekend, near home, suffering from a hangover." Situational variables might be psychological, physiological, demographic, or cut across multiple occasions. An example of a psychological situation could be, "approaching midlife crisis and questioning your self-worth, " whereas a physiological situation might be, "over 40 and getting wrinkles."

Preliminary research identified the relevant contexts for women deciding about becoming a Mary Kay beauty consultant. One such context was an "earn money" orientation, described by "I've got kids and my husband earns enough to support us, but I want to contribute." Another was a career orientation, illustrated by "I've worked a lot of dead-end, low-paying jobs, but now I want a career." A third was a personal growth orientation — for example, "I want to be self-sufficient, but I don't have the necessary skills."

Each of these orientations represented a lifestyle or life situation context. Several personal factors including age, family status, and educational background helped determine these lifestyle situations. Understanding context was important because it influenced the beauty consultant's decision about joining staying with and quitting Mary Kay Cosmetics. Context was part of the cognitive process that resulted in these three key outcomes.

Because making decisions is predicated with having options, the fourth framing question that Mary Kay management had to answer was: "What were the options that required the decision?" Behaviour is almost always a choice between competitive alternatives. Alternatives can be similar, for example, "should I drink Coke or Pepsi." Or, they can be dissimilar, "should I drink Coke or coffee?" Alternatives can even be completely unrelated, "should I drink Coke or go to the gym?" Competitive alternatives relate to the behaviour of interest and they frequently differ by context and by key customer group. Because Mary Kay beauty consultants could either choose or reject Mary Kay as an employment opportunity, their competitive choice alternatives included other jobs that were available to them. For many of these women, the most realistic job alternatives included:

- Working for another direct-sales organization such as Amway or Avon,
- Working a secretarial 9-to-5 job,
- Working shifts in retail sales. Understanding what alternatives the potential beauty consultants were considering allowed management to focus on the critical reasons for choice, which for many consultants differed from the reasons that they liked different alternatives. For example, a consultant liked both Mary Kay and Avon because direct sales provided flexible working hours, but this same person chose Mary Kay over Avon because Mary Kay offered more opportunity for personal growth.

To review, MKCI management had to answer four problem-framing questions: Who were the key customers? What were the relevant behaviors? What were the relevant contexts? and what were the competitive choice alternatives? Although the process has been demonstrated by answering the questions in sequence, an iterative approach was followed in practice, with management confirming answers to previous questions when answering the later ones. At this point, management could have written a formal problem statement in terms of their answers to the framing questions. For example, a useful statement might have read: Develop a marketing strategy that;

- Provides both immediate and long-term sales growth
- By focusing on the relevant life experiences that Mary Kay can provide
- Versus alternative job or career options
- That will motivate new salespeople to join Mary Kay and that will give them the orientation that will influence their chances of finding long-term success in the company.

UNDERSTANDING CONSUMER DECISION MAKING

Having framed the problem, the next step for management was to understand the decision-making process of their key customer, the beauty consultant. Understanding decision making included two parts: The first was to determine what choice criteria consultants used to distinguish among their job alternatives, and the second was to understand why the choice criteria were personally relevant to the consultants.A research study was designed to get at these critical issues. During interviews, consultants were asked three questions to elicit underlying factors driving key choices made with respect to MKCI. The three questions were:

- Why did you join Mary Kay?—asked of all consultants in the sample;
- Why do you stay with Mary Kay?—asked only of successful consultants who stayed with the company; and
- Why did you quit Mary Kay?—asked only of those who had quit.

During actual interviews, these questions were customized for each respondent, depending on the respondent's predetermined behaviour classification, context, and competitive alternatives. For example, an interviewer might have said, "Why did you join Mary Kay instead of staying with your secretarial job with IBM?" Reasons for joining and staying with Mary Kay represented the positive aspects of being a Mary Kay beauty consultant, whereas reasons for quitting Mary Kay represented negative aspects of the job and the company.

Most of the responses given by consultants were grouped into three broad categories: financial, social, and job characteristics. Financial reasons included having one's own money and having additional money for the family. Social aspects were being able to teach others about skin and beauty care, and the people orientation of the job, embodied in characteristics such as meeting new people and working closely with other people. Finally, the job characteristics focused on being one's own boss, which provided considerable job flexibility.

Once these initial choice distinctions were identified in the interview, the interviewer had to understand *why* the distinctions were important to the respondent. Identifying choice criteria is only an academic exercise, unless we also determine why the criteria are important. Knowing the reasons why makes the research more actionable and provide the means for making stronger ties between the characteristics of the job and the psyche of the sales consultant.

For example, a successful consultant indicated that she stayed with Mary Kay because "I am able to help my customers." Being able to help customers was important to this person because it makes me feel like I've got a special role with them.

Having this special role was important because it meant, "I'm learning more myself, " which in turn was important because it provided a "feeling of açcomplishment." Accomplishment was the motivating internal drive or personal value behind the choice criteria.

Another consultant who had quit Mary Kay did so because "I didn't earn much money." Not earning money was important because it meant that "I wasn't contributing anything to our household income, " which then led to dissatisfaction because "I wanted to prove that I could do it... that we could afford to buy a few luxuries." Not being able to afford luxuries caused her to "still feel dependent on others, " which is exactly the opposite of the independence value that she wanted to achieve.

These chains of connected ideas, from choice criteria to personal values, are called ladders because the interview process involves moving up the ladder of abstraction from concrete choice criteria to abstract personal values. The closer one gets to personal values, the more internal and feeling-oriented the remarks become. Eliciting these ladders is usually done by asking some form of the question is that important to you beginning with the initial choice criteria.

Beauty consultants from the three key groups — new joiners, successful consultants, and quitters — were interviewed in this manner to uncover the personally relevant reasons associated with their choice criteria. Once the full range of these connected associations and ideas were uncovered, they were summarized in a Customer Decision Map, a graphical presentation of the ladders. Each phrase or idea on the map was found in a substantial number of the ladders. The words on the map were simply coded responses that represented the actual verbatim remarks made by the respondents in the interview.

Each line on the map indicated that a substantial number of ladders contained both of the connected elements. Each pathway that could be traced, from the choice criteria at the bottom to the personal values at the top, represented a perceptual orientation of the market, in this case the beauty consultants' reasons for accepting or rejecting Mary Kay.

This map had five primary orientations — more than management had previously believed existed. One was financial: On the far left side of the CDM, Earn Money appears at the bottom, connected through Contribute to Household Income and Quality of Life to Independence at the value level.

A second orientation, in the centre of the map, was grounded in My Own Boss, which then led to Job Flexibility, Own Schedule, Time With Family, and finally Good Mom. A third branched from Time With Family to Special Role, Have Influence, Sharing With Others, Feel Good Emotionally, Self-Satisfaction, and finally, Self-Esteem.

A fourth orientation began at People Orientation and led through Special Role, Have Influence, Sharing With Others, Leaning, Accomplishment, Broadens Horizons and Independence. The fifth orientation followed the same path as the fourth through Broadens Horizons but then went to Feel Good Emotionally, Self-Satisfaction, and finally Self-Esteem.

Although informative, the map was incomplete without additional information about which orientations were associated with the three primary consultant groups in the sample and the positive and negative associations between MKCI and the choice criteria and other elements. Stepping back from the map, management had to understand the two sides of choice — selection and rejection.

Understanding the relevant ladders of consultants who had chosen and stayed with Mary Kay as well as the ladders of those who had rejected Mary Kay allowed management to identify the elements on the map that were perceptual strengths and weaknesses of the company compared with other job alternatives.

Once this was accomplished, it became evident to management why they had to first segment their respondents based on the consultants' relevant behaviors. To alter behaviour, management had to understand the differences in beliefs between those consultants with the desired behaviour and those without — that is, those that were successful sales people and those that were not and quit.

The perceptual strengths that represented the primary reasons that all consultants joined Mary Kay were labeled as common equities of Mary Kay. On the map, three key pathways existed here: The Earn Money to Independence orientation, the Be My Own Boss to Good Mom orientation, and the Be My Own Boss to Self-Esteem orientation.

The primary reasons that consultants left Mary Kay were called *disequities*. On the map, the elements that were reasons for consultants to quit were also among some of the same reasons that they joined. Specifically, MKCI's disequities were associated with the Earn Money orientation. This suggested that those consultants who quit did so because of unfulfilled financial expectations.

Recruiting had, indeed, focused primarily on the ability to earn money as a Mary Kay beauty consultant by pointing out those relatively few consultants who had done very well. The majority of sales consultants, however, never earn as much as these top performers. Many consultants quickly realized this and quit.

Leverageable equities were those elements that were the primary reasons successful consultants stayed with Mary Kay. These elements were unique to the successful consultants. Those who quit and those who had recently joined did not mention them. Somehow, successful consultants learned about this orientation, from People Orientation to Independence, during the time that they had been consultants.

For this group, achieving Independence through Learning

and Broadens Horizons supplanted the financial pathway to Independence. Armed with this understanding of the perceptual marketplace in which the company was operating, management next had to specify a positioning strategy that would become the basis for subsequent recruiting and sales force communications.

IDENTIFYING POSITIONING STRATEGY

Positioning strategy was defined as the specification of how Mary Kay would be meaningfully differentiated to their sales consultants. Specification required identifying the key components of the strategy in terms of the elements on the map. The CDM then became the game board to think about positioning strategy. Meaningfully differentiating Mary Kay required identifying how the company would appear special and superior to alternatives.

In general, effective strategies operate across all levels of the decision-making process. Differentiation, then, could occur at any or all levels. Also, effective strategies supplant disequities and leverage equities. Supplanting disequities could be accomplished by either convincing beauty consultants that the negatives they associated with Mary Kay were actually positives or by providing alternatives to the negative elements.

This second method in effect would reduce or eliminate the importance of the disequity. Leveraging equities could be accomplished by strengthening the current positive beliefs about Mary Kay and by introducing these ideas to consultants who might not have or associate these positive concepts with MKCI.

Following these guidelines, management specified a positioning strategy. The strategy had to focus on recruiting new sales consultants and then keeping them once they joined. Therefore, the elements that were selected for the core strategy included all of the leverageable elements identified on the map: People Orientation, Special Role, Have Influence, Sharing With Others, Learning, Accomplishment, Broadens Horizons, and finally, Independence. This core strategy was chosen because it supplanted the existing financial and job characteristic reasons for joining Mary Kay with the reasons that the successful consultants stayed.

This reduced unfulfilled financial expectations and at the same time provided management with the opportunity to differentiate Mary Kay from other direct sales organizations that also offered Earn Money and Be My Own Boss. Incidentally, both the Earn Money and the Be One's Own Boss orientations were still included in the strategy but the emphasis on these two pathways was greatly reduced.

Another advantage of the core strategy was that it tended to attract people who already had this orientation for success, for example, those people who placed higher value on the reasons that successful consultants stayed with the company and less on the financial ones. This helped reduce the high-turnover rate among beauty consultants.

COMMUNICATING POSITIONING STRATEGY

The final phase in the process was to translate the strategy into effective communications. MKCI management chose to produce a recruiting videotape called "Focus on Independence" that informed potential recruits about the key ideas and their connections from the positioning strategy. A video was selected because it could be quickly produced and distributed for nearly immediate results, and it demonstrated MKCI's commitment to current consultants by providing them with a tool that could help them succeed.

The video included a montage of interviews with successful consultants and exposition about MKCI's commitment to helping them achieve their independence. The video was made available to current consultants, and about 15% of them bought it during the year.

To assess the video's effectiveness, MCKI managers compared the results achieved by 1, 200 matched pairs of sales consultants. One consultant from each pair had used the new video while the other had continued using an old video that talked only about the financial potential of the job and the benefits of being one's own boss.

Recruitment increased by 42% in one year for the

consultants using the new tape over the old. Based on these impressive results, the company implemented company-wide distribution of the new tape.

Additional internal communications including a monthly newsletter and sales promotional material were produced and distributed that also focused on the key elements in the strategy. Both recruitment and sales almost immediately returned to their prior 16% to 20% annual growth rate. They have continued at this pace ever since and continued to do so at the time of this publication.

Chapter 8

Fund-Raising Strategy

Using a sample of 200 millionaires, a recently published book identifies personal motives underlying philanthropy among wealthy donors. Although there seem to be many different reasons for giving, what these millionaires want from charities apparently can be boiled down to different shades and mixtures of only two factors — degree of personal control and the need for public recognition.

By combining these two factors together with the types of charities supported, we can identify seven giving-types that range from *altruists* (people who provide unrestricted funds to support social causes and wish to remain anonymous) to so-called *communitarians* (people who want a big say in how their contributions are used to support local cultural, religious, or educational concerns and expect generous amounts of public acknowledgment and personal attention).

The basic insight of the research on wealthy donors is that both the characteristics of a charity and the personal motives of donors are important in understanding philanthropy. Our own experience in fund-raising tells us that personal involvement greatly increases when donors can see and feel a tight connection between the characteristics of a cause or a nonprofit organization and their own personal goals or values. Experience also teaches us that gaining the personal involvement of prospective donors is the key to successful fund-raising.

The purpose of this chapter is to show how to build personal involvement among current and prospective donors so as to solidify and expand a nonprofit organization's base of support. We suggest new ideas for how to make a tight connection between the characteristics of a nonprofit organization and the personal values of prospective donors. To formalize these ideas, we propose a definition of philanthropic strategy based on understanding the prospective donor's decision-making process, and then we explain and demonstrate the methods used to develop an effective strategy.

PRESENT AND FUTURE CHALLENGES FOR NONPROFITS

It is the rare nonprofit organization that has not suffered significant setbacks during the worldwide economic slowdown of the early 1990s. As the economy began to make a modest recovery, the roll out of delayed fund-raising campaigns threatened to overwhelm prospective donors especially in combination with the increase in the number of organizations looking for funding in the wake of governmental budget cuts.

Based on the experience of corporate America since the 1980s, more customer choice often means more customer power. Donors of all types now have more choices of where to put their time and money than ever before. In the short term, many nonprofits that laid low during the recession without investing in a more complete understanding of their donor constituency may face further reductions in financial support and losses of key personnel. In the long term, it will become critically important for all nonprofits to adjust what they do within their organizations and what they communicate both inside and outside their organizations in order to better satisfy the growing demands of current and prospective donors.

SEEING THE OPPORTUNITY

In a marketplace crowded with many alternatives, organizations must establish meaningful distinctions over their competitors. Meaningful distinctions are associated with delivering real value to their customers. Today's winning companies have been among the first to accentuate their distinctiveness by adopting customer-based marketing and positioning strategies. Such strategies help managers deal with their growing uncertainty regarding how to position a product and develop an action plan that will retain and cultivate established customers, and in some cases, attract whole new market segments. This approach to strategy is successful because it outlines the means whereby a close connection can be made between product qualities and the personal motives of customers. Tightly connecting product qualities with personal motives provides customers both the rational reason and the emotion-based motivation to purchase and repurchase the product. Such a basis for product positioning raises competitive barriers, reduces price sensitivity, and often increases frequency of use. As a first step in translating the concepts of "customer orientation" to nonprofit organizations, it is useful to start by defining and outlining the principles of a customer-based philanthropic strategy.

Philanthropic strategy is the specification of a customer-based template for guiding the operations, communications, and public relations activities of a nonprofit organization so as to differentiate the organization's case for support from other social or personal investments in positive and personally relevant terms among key donors and donor prospects, members of the community, and other important stakeholder groups. Adhering to the basic principles of strategy that arise from the preceding definition allows organizations to leverage a customer orientation into marketplace success.

PRINCIPLES OF A CUSTOMER-BASED PHILANTHROPIC STRATEGY

Principle 1: Philanthropic strategy guides a coordinated set of actions through the use of a strategic template. Strategy brings together and coordinates resources to accomplish highly focused objectives. A core strategic concept is to pick targets of opportunity that enable one to match many resources against a competitor's few. Also, successful organizations follow a strategic pattern or template, even if it is not written down, that enables them to gain efficiency by focusing all of their resources on the same target or goal. A *strategic template* is different than a formal strategic plan. A template succinctly captures the strategic intent of the organization in an outline form that facilitates the assessment of an organization's behaviour, communications, or appeals against a strategic standard of measurement.

Principle 2: Philanthropic strategy differentiates the organization's case for support from other social or personal investments. People contribute charitable donations and service for a wide variety of reasons, attenuated by their preferred area of support, preferred type of support, desired level of recognition, and the amount of personal control. Identifying the right mix of powerful, motivating reasons is critical. To attract substantial investment, an institution's case for support must be sharply drawn, distinct from other social and personal investments, and be centered in activities and practices that donors value.

Institutions differentiate themselves by communicating to constituents or donors that through contributing to or becoming an important part of the organization, the donor will receive psychological or social rewards that satisfy their important driving goals or values.

Principle 3: Philanthropic strategy uses positive terms. Many organizations dwell on how they have corrected past mistakes rather than moving on to stress their unique benefits. Problems must be fixed, but publicizing their repair will not guarantee success. Sharing a positive vision based on the delivery of unique benefits strengthens continuing support and attracts new investment. Unique benefits are defined in the context of competitive weaknesses. A good strategist will turn a competitors strength into a weakness and consequently find a competitive edge.

Principle 4: Philanthropic strategy uses personally relevant terms. Strategists make it a point to gain a better understanding of the "landscape" than their competitors, and clever use of the landscape creates competitive advantage. With a philanthropic strategy, one is competing on a mindscape. We can gain competitive advantage by using personally relevant words and experiences that tap into the ideas and associations forming the donor's mindscape. In this terrain, an experienced guide can uncover a case for support that prospective donors will find convincing and motivating. Of course, for a philanthropic strategy, one of the most important facets of personal relevance revolves around the peer group. Donors want to be sought out, but not by just anyone. A case for support will not be personally relevant unless donors believe they are being sought out by a befitting peer group or organization.

Principle 5: Philanthropic strategy focuses on key donors and donor prospects, members of the community, and other important stakeholder groups. Good strategists define the battlefield on their own terms, not someone else's. In philanthropy, the field of competition is the marketplace of donors and public opinion. A key to effective strategy is not simply identifying who these people are, but defining who we want them to be in terms of *external* factors (demographics and socioeconomic status) and *internal* characteristics (attitudes, beliefs, and values).

The need for fund-raising is often the impetus for taking a closer look at how a nonprofit is operating and communicating. To be truly customer-based, nonprofits need to have a master plan to bring all of their activities in tune with the physical and emotional needs of their constituencies. A philanthropic strategy is a master plan. Its development and use will bring a sense of uniqueness, consistency, and relevancy to the organization and its fund-raising activities.

Developing strategy requires three broad steps:

- Framing the fund-raising issues;
- Identifying the compelling reasons and associated physical and emotional benefits that underlie donor contributions, given the specific frame;
- Developing appropriate communications that link these compelling reasons with the organization, activity or fund-raising campaign.

FRAMING THE FUND-RAISING ISSUES

To uncover which physical and emotional needs matter

most to donors and therefore serve as reasons for choice and to determine how they can be used to link the characteristics of the organization or activity to the individual's personally relevant goals or values, we must answer four questions.

- What constituencies should be considered?
- What are the relevant behaviors of the constituents?
- What situational contexts are relevant?
- What are the constituents' choice alternatives?

Answers to these four questions help frame subsequent donor research that will yield actionable and successful marketing and positioning strategies. Consider the example of Mardan School, a case in which school officials ran a real risk of not keeping pace with the growing needs of the learning-disabled children within their community. The Mardan School is a day school for learning disabled children, offering many types of education ranging from special needs' tutoring to full-time instruction. In 1984, it had an enrollment of approximately 50 children and was marking its tenth anniversary in the former City Hall in the downtown area of Costa Mesa, California.

Enrollment growth led the school to purchase two mobile classrooms that were placed in the parking lot. The board of trustees commissioned an architect to prepare a plan for the building's renovation and expansion. However, although the community held very positive beliefs about the quality of the school and clearly felt that the service provided was very important, the level of fund-raising support for the expansion was judged as being poor to fair. What had the board of trustees overlooked in arriving at their decision to renovate the building?

Before the board could move forward, they realized they had to take a few steps back to assess the issue more thoroughly. Clearly, the problem was to understand the reasons for this apparent lack of interest and formulate a solution that enabled the school to fulfill its purpose. Following a customer-based approach, the first step was to answer the four framing questions.

First, the key constituencies needed to be identified. The

constituencies included all potential donors, of whom 10% would be expected to provide 90% of the dollars for the fund-raising campaign. Thus, the key constituency was the smaller group of anticipated large donors. Most of these donors were known to the board, so further identification research was not necessary.

Once the key constituencies were identified, Mardan's trustees needed to know what relevant behaviour had to be addressed. The obvious answer was to give generously, but in order to support this key behaviour, Mardan's board had to establish positive attitudes toward substantial giving to the Mardan school among key donors. Also, some of these donors in turn would be asked to solicit donations from their peers or associates. Thus, Mardan had to provide them with persuasive arguments to support the School.

The relevant context was the next issue to be addressed. Donors generally want to be recognized as worthwhile members of a worthwhile group. Consequently, the organizational mission, reputation for excellence, and quality of staff, physical facility, and business decisions made by Mardan School were matters of personal pride for key donors. In addition, a study of county records indicated that in the years ahead, school-aged children would be predominantly located in growing residential areas several miles south of Costa Mesa. To continue to serve its traditional constituency effectively, Mardan would have to move south with young families. Thus, the social context within which Mardan School's donors would be expected to contribute involved receiving civic recognition and seeing that the gift was used efficiently.

The fourth framing question involved identifying the choice alternatives available to the key donors. External to the school were numerous worthy causes, some offering similar services to Mardan. Within the school, there were several opportunities other than the original expansion plan. For example, potential donors knew that many schools in the community surrounding Mardan were vacant. To them, this meant that there were opportunities for Mardan to relocate to a nearby vacant school under a favorable long-term lease.

Once the framing issues were laid out, it became apparent that the next step was to better understand the personal values of key donors that made the renovation project unacceptable. Interviews with the potential donors revealed that many donors believed the renovation of an existing building was not at all warranted. Moreover, they were disturbed that board members had asked for renovation plans before they had obtained a better grasp of the situation.

From the potential donor's perspective, the renovation planned for Mardan School would result in a high-priced, clumsy-looking, ill-suited building in a location far removed from the growth area of the county. To them it felt like bad business, and they believed that once completed, it would become a source of public embarrassment, not public pride. What was needed was a one-time, long-term solution for the school that would reflect favorably on the judgment and leadership of the donors.

Once the perspective of potential donors was identified together with key situational factors and the choice alternatives, the campaign progressed rapidly. With the help of a local developer, school officials located an affordable three-acre site across from a park in a growing residential area. Because the existing location was ideal for low-income housing for elderly, the city of Costa Mesa repurchased the City Hall building from Mardan at a price that paid for most of the new site. A beautiful, modern new school was built that far exceeded any facilities envisioned or possible at the previous location.

What made the Mardan campaign a success? We believe the research effort to uncover the personal reasons for donor participation in the project made a big contribution. Clearly framing the problem situation, then uncovering the key donor-decision criteria, and then understanding why they were important helped Mardan's directors create a vision of what the project could mean to the major donors and the community. When Mardan's directors were able to communicate the vision to donors, they created a heightened personal involvement and enthusiasm for the project, which ensured a successful fund-raising campaign. Although the donor-based plan required more money than the original renovation plan, the donor plan received substantial support because it tapped into the personal goals of the donors.

LOOKING BEYOND THE DONOR CONSTITUENCY

Large corporations conduct business in an ocean of public opinion. Among other advantages, a favorable public image can help companies maintain sales during tough situations. For example, although stores to either side were burnt to the ground, McDonald's restaurants were left relatively untouched during rioting in Los Angeles, so McDonald's was open for business whereas competitors were still cleaning up debris.

The benefit of favorable public opinion and public trust is also evident in the ability of Johnson and Johnson to get past the Tylenol poisonings, as well as the speed with which major airlines rebound after devastating airplane disasters.

On the other hand, certain industries and companies have not invested in accumulating a deep well of favorable public opinion. For example, Exxon has lost competitive ground since the Exxon Valdez Alaskan oil spill because at least some consumers find it socially unacceptable to buy gasoline from a company that reinforces their perceptions that oil companies do not act responsibly toward the environment.

Public opinion is also one of the most vital elements for a nonprofit organization to consider when planning and implementing a fund-raising campaign. Few development officers would admit that public opinion has a serious impact on fund-raising activities because the majority of charitable support comes from so few people. Yet, public opinion should not be overlooked.

As already mentioned, what a key donor's peers think about the organization he or she supports or the group with which he or she affiliates is an important factor in explaining his or her philanthropic behaviour. What one's peers think about an organization or its governing board can be strongly influenced by public opinion. Consequently, when public opinion of a nonprofit turns sour, as was the recent case with the United Way, the organization can often face serious challenges for many years.

In some instances, the management of public perceptions can be the determining factor between failure and success for a nonprofit venture. As an example, consider the challenges addressed by a home for dependent children located in Orange County, California.

In the early 1980s, Orange County's facility for receiving and holding minors that were placed under protective care by the county's juvenile court system was by all accounts glaringly inadequate. The facility was originally built during the 1950s as a juvenile detention centre and had been converted for housing juvenile victims who because of circumstances beyond their control were temporarily or permanently left without parental care.

The Albert Sitton Home was a series of institutional barracks with an authorized capacity of 45. The facility was housing over 80 children and the census was steadily climbing. To onlookers, it appeared as though children who had already suffered so much personal pain and loss were being placed in a unwholesome situation that would cause more suffering rather than alleviate it.

Contributing to the rising number of children placed in the home was the growth of the county's population and the increasing awareness of child abuse with a concurrent willingness and legal obligation to report it. In addition to abuse victims, the Sitton Home hosted lost and abandoned children, children of parents seriously or fatally injured in accidents, and children of parents who were jailed.

The Sitton Home was designed to provide temporary housing for children ranging in age from 1 month to 18 years old. Children stayed at the home for a period that could last from a few hours to several months. Often relatives were located and other times the children were sent to foster homes. Sitton Home had to have the capability of clothing, feeding, and educating a very broad range of children. In addition, security and a barbed-wire perimeter fence was maintained because some of the children were in danger from abusive parents, and others had a tendency to try to leave the grounds. As a result of the responsibility to provide protection, the facility looked a lot like the juvenile detention centre located adjacent to the home.

The county was under a court order to provide facilities adequate to the demand and appropriate to the nature of those served or face a contempt order and escalating daily fines. In answer to the need, the county, being short of capital funds, convened a 100-member blue ribbon committee of county residents to study the problem.

The chief judge of the juvenile court prevailed on a personal friend to serve as the chairman of the committee. The Blue Ribbon Committee chairman was, at that time, California's most prominent home builder, former Secretary of the Air Force, co-owner of Air California (later purchased by American Airlines) and a man of the highest visibility and stature in Orange County. He was obviously a wealthy man but had no experience in local government or philanthropic fund-raising.

The committee quickly confirmed that there were no county funds to use for expand ing Sitton Home facilities or hiring new staff members without seriously undermining other infrastructure needs. The members felt that the option of seeking money through fund-raising should be explored.

First, the potential donors who were expected to contribute were identified as the key constituency. The relevant behaviors and contexts were essentially the same as for Mardan School; key donors had to feel positively about giving and some of them had to be motivated to canvas their friends to give as well. Choice alternatives external to the house included other possible philanthropic or investment opportunities. Internal alternatives for the home, however, were determined by the committee to be limited to building a new facility.

As one might expect, the ensuing research study uncovered a significant reservoir of sympathy for the children. Potential donors agreed that the children should not only have adequate housing but the best housing and care that could be provided. The obstacle uncovered by the research, however, was their reluctance to provide support for any facility that was administered by the county government. Prospective donors personally distrusted the county government as it was constantly under the public eye for one reason or another. Public opinion, as well as personal experience, had made them quite skeptical about the willingness of county officials to use their money with sufficient care to build a new facility that would meet the needs of the children.

The Sitton Home had extremely high public visibility. It was clearly portrayed and widely understood to be a government facility. To make matters even more difficult, a county probation officer who was given a leadership role on the Blue Ribbon Committee was gaining prominence as a spokesperson for the home.

Her position as a probation officer served to blur the public's perception of the types of children served by the home and the circumstances that brought them under the county's supervision. The public began to raise some questions why a new juvenile care facility for "troubled" children was needed. By raising its voices, the public became part of the constituency that had to be addressed.

In order to conduct a successful fund-raising campaign, it became necessary to manage public perceptions by putting as much distance as possible between the Sitton Home and the county government. Effective management would require taking the right steps to support the desired strategy of separating the home from government. An operating foundation, established to solicit and receive anticipated private support, was activated to become the driving force behind the project.

The foundation was chaired by the Blue Ribbon Committee chairman and the fund-raising campaign itself chaired by another of California's leading home builders. The contact between the operating foundation and the county government was limited to the head of the Child Welfare Department who served on the foundation board along with the wife of one of the county supervisors. Some twenty other board members were prominent private citizens. Management for the building project was not provided by the county government, but put under the control of a board member who was the president of the Mission Viejo Company, developers of a large-planned (20, 000 inhabitants) community. In addition, a complex arrangement was made wherein the county temporarily deeded over the property on which the new facility was being.built to the operating foundation while the buildings were constructed.

Then, as buildings were completed, they were deeded back to the county with the stipulation that they would be operated for the purpose intended for a period of at least 30 years. These steps alleviated the reluctance of potential donors who believed county officials were not competent to be in charge of facility design and construction and felt that the county would use the buildings for some other purpose once they were constructed.

To focus greater public attention on the special nature of the children being served by the home, build on the feeling of community support for the campaign, and ensure the project would not be tainted by a sour public opinion of county government, a considerable amount of effort went into informing public about the composition of the foundation board and the control it would exercise over the project. The plan was successful. The campaign was overfunded. First-rate facilities were constructed and an endowment was established to provide ongoing supplemental support for the home.

Following strategic guidelines helped both the Mardan School and the Albert Sitton Home succeed in their fund-raising activities. In summary, they were able to frame the fund-raising problems that they faced, understand the motivations and beliefs of their key constituencies, and then effectively manage these beliefs to accomplish their fund-raising objectives.

Identifying the key motivations and beliefs held by constituents is critical to developing a customer-based orientation. To accomplish this, organizations must delve into the thoughts and feelings of their constituents to uncover the key reasons associated with the decisions they make concerning their behaviour.

UNDERSTANDING THE PHILANTHROPIC DECISION: THE MEANS-END APPROACH

There are many models of customer decision making. Among the most powerful in predicting and understanding choice is the means-end model. In the means-end framework, physical features or characteristics and their immediate, functional benefits are just the means to an end.

The end people seek is always a powerful psychological or social need, which in turn often is associated with basic, personal values that people hold. Identifying and understanding the role of these psycho-social needs and personal values in decision making leads to predictions of choice that are much more accurate than predictions based only on physical features and functional benefits. Such a perspective removes much of the risk in trying to understand how decisions are made and how people can be taught and persuaded.

A Means-End Model of Philanthropic Donations

Based on the means-end framework, we created a model that describes the decision process of the philanthropic donor. In this model, the organization and its activity are described by philanthropic attributes, which include all perceived tangible qualities of the organization such as the type of service that it provides, its volunteers and paid staff, the level of personal involvement it affords to donors, its organizational structure, and the organization's leadership and management.

These tangible characteristics provide functional consequences to donors, which are the measurable consequences of giving. Functional consequences include benefits such as effectively using the money, fulfilling a sense of obligation for the donor, and helping others in need.

Functional consequences lead to *psychosocial consequences*, which are the emotional states attainable through philanthropic giving. Psychosocial consequences include personal feelings and emotions, such as feeling less stress and worry, feeling accepted by peers, sensing personal growth, and experiencing the thrill of seeing improvement in others. In turn, these emotion-laden needs are associated with stable, enduring personal values or goals that are central to our lives, such as peace of mind, personal security, self-image, accomplishment, and personal happiness. Psychosocial needs pull at the heart strings. When tightly linked to the objective features or characteristics of an organization, a person, a place, or a thing, they become key motivational elements for influencing thought and action.

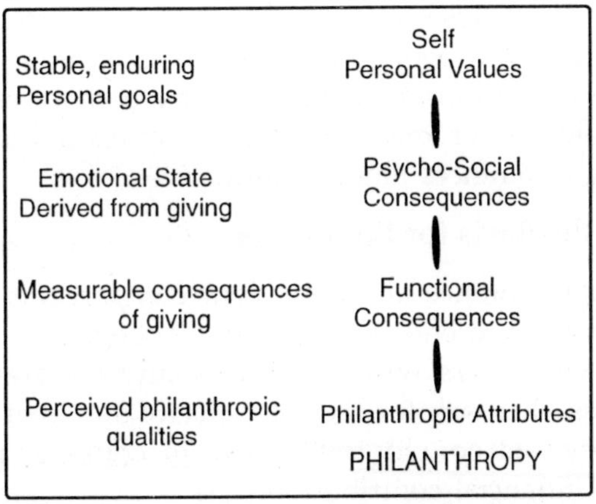

Fig. Philanthropic Decision Making: Prospect Model.

To understand the rational (attribute and functional consequence) and emotional (psychosocial consequence and value) factors that influence constituent's decision making, one must do two things:

- Elicit the distinctions that underpin the choice of one alternative over another in the context of the appropriate situation or frame of reference;
- Determine the reasons why these particular distinctions or choice criteria are important and personally relevant.

Eliciting Distinctions

Eliciting distinctions can be accomplished using one of

several techniques, including triadic sorting, differences by occasions, and preference or behaviour comparisons. In triadic sorting, three alternatives are presented to the prospective donor-respondent, who is then asked to group two of the alternatives together and describe how the two are similar to each other and different from the third. Several triads can be constructed and used in this way.

Differences by occasions is another way to elicit distinctions. Focusing on the situational context of donor behaviour provides a meaningful basis from which the donor can respond. Behaviour does not occur in the abstract; rather, behaviour is always constrained by external factors such as time, location, and people or by externally influenced factors such as societal norms. It is important that both the respondent and the interviewer keep in mind the contextual basis when discussing differences among alternatives.

Eliciting the Basis for Preference

Using preference and behaviour comparisons is a third way to frame the choice situation. To begin, you present prospective donors with a list of many different choice alternatives, then ask for them to specify any alternatives to which they last considered or would consider making a significant financial contribution.

Next you ask them to rank alternatives hierarchically to reflect the relative level of support they would be willing to provide for each option. An exercise based on likelihood of support provided the charity preferences. The responses were elicited from a 75-year-old male who is a CEO and founder of a national chain of restaurants. He was very active in providing both time and money for local and national charities.

Why is a Choice Criterion Personally Relevant?

Once choice criteria have been identified using one of the techniques mentioned or some other method, it is necessary to understand why these particular distinctions are personally relevant or important to people. This can be done by determining how the choice distinctions are linked to important personal motives of the donor prospect using a laddering interview. In its simplest form, laddering aims to uncover why attributes and associated consequences matter or are important to the respondent's physical and emotional well being.

The details of this type of interview have been described in the marketing literature. Laddering involves asking various forms of the question, "Why is that important to you?" Laddering is a structured yet conversational technique adaptable to nearly any type of interview environment, including interpersonal contacts or social gatherings among key fund-raising representatives and potential contributors.

The Decision-Making Map

A decision-making map. Decision-making maps are an aggregation of information collected in laddering interviews of multiple individuals. A map includes the most frequently mentioned ideas or elements, as well as the most common associations or connections between those elements. Each element on the map is a code word that represents a set of similar ideas mentioned by respondents.

Decision-making maps reveal the different types and levels of information that people use to make choices between competing alternatives. The ladders (chains of associated ideas) frequently are based on contextual factors such as the donor's life stage, peer group, ethnic background, reasons for involvement, and past experiences with nonprofit organizations may significantly influence. Therefore, decision-making maps also reflect the influence of these contextual factors on a person's reasons for choosing to contribute.

Quantifying the Map. When a substantial number of ladders are collected from numerous donor-respondents, the aggregate decision-making map can be quantified to reveal the frequency of mentions for individual elements at each level on the map. For instance, the relative importance of the element can be indicated by expressing the number of times that element was mentioned in the ladders as a percent of the total number of mentions for a given level (e.g., psychosocial consequences or attributes). As another example, because ladders are elicited relative to specific organizations, the number of positive mentions for each organization can be contrasted with the number of negative mentions to provide a measure of competitive strengths and weaknesses.

Equities and Disequities

Ladders and decision-making maps can include both positive elements and negative elements (reasons for supporting an organization other than St. John's). Elements with substantial positive balances (seen as much more positive than negative) are considered to be equities (valuable assets), whereas elements with large negative balances are disequities.

Although this type of equity-disequity analysis may not be feasible with fund-raising problems that involve relatively few donors, it might be very useful when many potential contributors, such as the United Way or the American Heart Association. For situations with only a few key donors, one might field a fund-raising feasibility study in which potential donors first describe the giving orientation that fits them best. Then potential donors could discuss the strengths and weaknesses of each donation alternative relative to their giving orientation.

THINKING STRATEGICALLY ABOUT PHILANTHROPIC DECISION MAKING

A consumer-decision map is like a road map that can guide every strategic decision of the nonprofit organization from how fund-raising campaigns are planned and implemented to what the organization does with its funds to how people working for the organization are recruited and retained. For instance, the philanthropy decision-making map in several ways for managers to create meaningful differentiation between alternatives for charitable giving.

For example, one organization might stress the established leadership of their respected board and advisors that allows them to make effective use of money that, in turn, reduces the donors' level of worry and stress. Other organizations might reinforce the sense of obligation people feel based on the nature of an organization's provided service. This feeling of obligation then allows potential donors to give back and help others who face similar circumstances to their own.

Understanding the Equities and Disequities

Understanding the reasons for and against various choice alternatives (the equities and disequities) provides valuable guidance for selecting the most compelling elements to include in a strategy and for identifying the ones to exclude. For example, in the Sitton Home case, "association with local government, " an attribute, was identified as a major barrier to donation behaviour. Their successful strategy hinged on severing the association between government and the Home.

Identifying a Strategic Template

The decision-making map shows that people may use many different types and levels of information to make their donation choices. To position itself effectively, a nonprofit organization must identify the key concepts that are most salient to their target audience and convincingly demonstrate how these elements are connected to personally relevant values and goals of the target donors. This specification of the means-end linkages that connect the differentiating characteristics of an organization with donors' personal motives functions as a basic outline or *strategic template* for managers.

The strategic template is a simplified description of strategic intent — what the organization wants to become. A possible strategic template expressed as an ameoba shape that encompasses the key attributes, functional and psycho-social consequences, and values to be emphasized in the philanthropic strategy. This template represents the strategy of an organization wishing to stress its first-rate leadership and management as instrumental for achieving a hierarchy of benefits (effective use of money) and emotions (secure in decision and no worries) that eventually are associated with a personal value (peace of mind).

The ability of an organization to identify a suitable

strategic template and then match its internal and external behaviour to that template will determine the persuasiveness of its case for donor support and its ability to meet programme needs. However useful for planning purposes, the strategic template is rather lifeless until managers determine how each strategic element will be implemented, particularly in communications with the target audience.

Implementing the Strategic Template

Implementing a strategic template can create an enduring competitive advantage. However, a great deal of work must go into implementing a philanthropic strategy beyond identifying a strategic template.

A major part of the implementation involves how the strategy is to be communicated to donors in a persuasive manner. The communication goal is to form a double bond of rational reasons and emotional rewards across the levels of decision making specified in the strategic template. Managers or directors should constantly ask themselves what they can do to communicate a stronger connection between the concepts that underpin the success of their organization's fund-raising efforts.

Assessing the Strategic Implementation

A fully specified strategic template can also function as an assessment tool. Using the strategic template as the target, managers can determine how well each activity within the organization fits with and contributes to the organization's strategic intent. For example, by identifying activities and tactics that are off strategy, managers can be proactive in shaping the organization and not merely be reactive to events.

Identifying actions that are off strategy can be done either through direct managerial analysis of the specific activities and messages that the organization is communicating to its constituencies. Alternatively, a more rigorous method involves obtaining donor feedback on specific activities or communications. For example, a letter to be sent to potential donors might first be evaluated by a representative group of donors to determine its effectiveness in communicating the key elements of the specified strategy.

Strategic assessment based on the means-end approach may be the single most effective tool for implementing a customer-based approach to doing business. Within the area of consumer marketing, the assessment of a company's behaviour relative to its strategic intent has enhanced product and corporate advertising, consumer promotions, corporate sponsorship activities, new product concept development, retail store operations, training and management of customer service representatives, and recruitment and retention of salespeople. In the context of fund-raising and philanthropy, a donor-based strategic assessment of an organization and its fund-raising activities should have similar success.

BEYOND FINANCIAL ENGINEERING

The misuse of leveraged buy outs in the 1980s is probably best illustrated by Robert Campeau who borrowed nearly 10 billion — that's 10 with nine zeros — from professional, experienced financiers, with no apparent strategically-based business plan to enable repayment. The blatant abuse of the financial system underlying this transaction is evidenced by the roughly £1 billion that went to lawyers, accountants, and investment bankers for the "invaluable services" in closing this megadeal — services that convinced future creditors that Campeau's $10 billion loan was indeed credible.

The explicit trademark of deal making in the 1980s was not really the "art of the deal." Rather, it could be described more aptly as "do the deal, and generate personal fortunes for supplying invaluable services."

Certainly Campeau was hardly alone in being forced to seek refuge in the bankruptcy code. More than half of the mergers and acquisitions that began in the 1980s are in, or appear headed for, the courts. Their flagship brands and subsidiaries have been dragged off to the salvage yards. Assessing each of these deals involves understanding the simple fact that virtually every one of these deals resulted from sophisticated financial engineering — the respected Wall Street science of number generation, classification and thaumaturgical assessment. The moneylenders who lost billions, as well as many of those still employed on Wall Street, probably would agree that rigid analysis of financial statements, cash flows, and projected stock prices is a necessary but not sufficient technique on which to base mergers and acquisitions.

Perhaps the somewhat magical numbers and projections generated from financial engineering made sense to someone. Perhaps it seemed logical and prudent to assume such a staggering debt loador to participate in funding it. However, such actions must rest on the assumption that the assets being acquired are sufficient to support the debt, including the acquisition costs. In this case, those assumptions were based on the analysis of strategic equities (regardless of what terminology might have been used) of the numerous brands being acquired. Those equities in the Campeau example were under both the Federated and Allied banners. Therein lay the problem — there has never been a well-defined, formal definition of equity, much less any accepted method of evaluating it.

The death of financial engineering does not mean that mergers and acquisitions will no longer take place. Rather, it suggests that more realistic methods of analysis should be developed and applied to insure the financial transaction is based on realistic business and market driven assumptions, not mere number crunching. It is clear that total reliance on financial engineering was the fatal flaw.

Although probably a bit melodramatic, it could be said that many of those who lived (quite well, we should note) by these strictly financially based methods also died by these same methods. What is needed are business- and market-based evaluation methods focusing on the strategies that serve as the foundation of the core business. In fact, these market driven methods must underpin all financial analyses. In brief, a paradigm is needed to identify, at a very minimum, the strategic equity of the firms, and in the best of all worlds, to translate and quantify that equity in terms of acceptable financial evaluation methods.

This chapter lays a foundation to address these key issues by providing the details of such a paradigm, beginning with a taxonomy of the concept of strategic equity. Beyond defining equity, we also describe the fundamental consumer-based component in special types of equity. In addition, we give examples of how managers can build equity in a corporate or brand franchise, thereby maximizing long-term profits and shareholder value.

WHAT IS STRATEGIC EQUITY?

Successful acquisitions of the 1980s shared a single, common factor: the combined created real value more than offset the high costs of acquisition. For example, Quaker Oats bought Stokely-Van Camp in 1984 in a deal that included Gatorade, a languishing competitor in the underdeveloped sports-drink market.

Quaker Oats increased advertising, expanded the line of flavors, and refurbished packaging to transform the relatively ho-hum Gatorade on supermarket shelves nationwide. With sales up from £170 million in 1984 to £625 million in 1989, Gatorade demonstrates how the right combination of brands and brand management adds up to dramatic increases in sales, profit, and ultimately, shareholder value.In this case, an unpretentious cereal company knew what the flamboyant Robert Campeau and all of his "invaluable" advisors did not: A key ingredient is missing from the financial engineering approach.

That ingredient is *brand equity*, the value added to a product due to its affiliation with a brand name or trademark. Brand equity gives products such as Morton Salt and Crayola Crayons a virtual monopoly in a market of otherwise undifferentiated commodities. It gives the Courtyard hotel chain higher occupancy because of its association with the Marriott name. It gives Honda lawnmowers a premium price because of Honda's quality reputation for building reliable gasoline engines. The problem, then, is measuring how much of this success is attributable to what, so far, has loosely been termed brand equity — in short, why is brand equity valuable?

WHY IS BRAND EQUITY VALUABLE?

Strong brand names imply a high level of consumer loyalty. Brand loyalty is a behaviour, but it is based on the perceptions of the brand that consumers carry in their minds that, in turn, drive consumer decision making. Positive memories and meaningful associations held in consumers' knowledge structures have staying power and this makes the company that owns well-known, high-quality brands stronger in at least three ways:

- A dominant brand can fend off attacks by serving as a barrier to entry. For example, there is virtually no room for competitors of Arm and Hammer baking soda, Jell-O gelatin, and Vaseline petroleum jelly. This is known as *brand dominance.*
- A good brand image can keep a brand viable through bad times and changes in consumer tastes. GI Joe was profitably resurrected after the anti-war sentiment of the seventies had passed. Budweiser returned as the "King of Beers" when prohibition was repealed in 1933. Tylenol survived a major product-tampering crisis in 1982. Such examples of survivability are known as *brand resilience.*
- Strong brands can serve as platforms from which to launch new products and services. This is the *leveragability advantage* of brand names. For example, licensed products carrying the Disney label number in the hundreds. Bally's best selling Lifecycle machines led to their successful Liferowers. Proctor and Gamble launched Ultra Tide to maintain Tide's position as a superior cleaning agent.

Before evaluating any type of equity attributable to a brand or a company, managers must have a complete understanding of the types of equity that exist in the business environment.

The following taxonomy briefly outlines the types of equity that have been identified and provides examples to illustrate these definitions. This formal taxonomy will then provide the basis for assessing brand equity and will serve as the foundation for consumer input to the equity review and measurement process.

A TAXONOMY OF EQUITY

Strategic Equity

Strategic equity is the value of a company based on its ownership of one or more of the primary equities: brand, distribution, or resource control.

Brand Equity

Brand equity is

- The value, current or potential, that exists because a product or service is in some way affiliated with a brand name, trademark, or other distinguishing brand identity;
- The value of a company that exists because of its ownership of brand names and
- *Cognitive equity*: the value of consumers' memories, either real or imagined, about brands. (There are six specific subtypes of cognitive equity: *bridge, scarcity, borrowed, prestige, promotional,* and *latent*). For example, Waterford crystal is an example of a brand with a high level of cognitive equity. In Waterford's case, the characteristics that consumers associate with the brand are high quality and strong heritage. McDonald's (and kids), Crest (and tooth decay prevention), Coca-Cola (and superior refreshment), Levi Strauss (and ruggedness), and Porsche (and stylish speed) are other examples of brands with high levels of cognitive equity.

Secondary Equities in Brand Equity

Bridge Equity. Bridge equity is the value that is created by brand names attached to a new product or group of products; the original brand name can increase in value through bridging. For example, Jell-O Pudding Pops have successfully bridged the association between Jell-O gelatin and the new frozen dessert snack. Scarcity Equity. This is the value created because a brand has limited availability. For instance, at one time, Coors beer had scarcity equity because of its limited distribution prior to the mid-1970s.

Coors' equity grew by word-of-mouth, creating demand that led to its immediate success when it penetrated new markets in the south and east. More recently, Madonna's 1990 music video had scarcity equity because it had been banned by MTV and other music broadcasting stations. The video restrictions generated dramatic interest due to the unavailability of the product.

Borrowed Equity. This is the value a product gains from similarities it shares with a different brand. Usually the host brand possesses significant brand equity, and the borrowing brand purposely mimics the brand's attributes. The borrowing brand must offer some significant advantage over the host, typically price. For example, Sears profited from borrowed equity because of similarities between its Fox brand and LaCoste's popular Izod shirts. VP Planner software closely resembled the software capabilities of Lotus 123, thereby taking advantage of pre-existing equity created by Lotus in the marketplace. Promotional Equity. This is the value a brand gains from any type of promotional activity for the brand including coupons, advertisements, publicity, and word-of-mouth, or, any positioning activity that creates or builds cognitive equity. Consider that products such as Gillette, Budweiser, Coke, and Pepsi take full advantage of promotional equity through a variety of media, including sponsorships of social and entertainment activities (concert tours and videos) and sporting events.

Latent Equity. This is the value of consumer perceptions having the potential to be linked to a brand. These perceptions are not necessarily a result of product promotion. Or, the value of reactivating consumer memories that do not now exist in a top-of-mind fashion. For instance, Converse shoes can be linked to older male consumers' fond memories of their childhood days due to the brand's virtual dominance of the sport shoe market until the 1970s.

Distribution Equity

Distribution equity is the value of having access to distribution channels that is not a result of cognitive equity or channel power. For instance, Coca-Cola's global distribution channels represent perhaps the most valuable distribution equity in existence today. As a result of this distribution power, Coca-Cola is the best known brand name in the world and dominates international soft-drink markets. Secondary types of distribution equity include: Buyer Proximity and Channel Owner.

Buyer Proximity Equity. This is the value derived from having consumers in proximity to products that are not primarily sought. For example, products or brands in close physical proximity to check-out stand s in grocery stores — like the *National Enquirer*, chocolate candy, and chewing gum — have equity due to their proximal location to the potential buyer. Similarly, bean dip gains sales when it is located adjacent to snack chips in the grocery store.

Channel Owner Equity. This is the value derived from virtual control or ownership of a distribution channel. For instance, Avon has over one million sales people worldwide selling to well over 100 million households directly. There is significant latent value in this sales franchise, which could sell other types of goods ranging from insurance to travel.

Resource Control Equity

Resource control equity is the value that exists because a company owns or controls scarce or limited resources, including intellectual property and patents. Secondary equities include raw material and people. For example, Texas Instruments stock rose sharply in 1989 when competitors were required to pay royalty fees for using TI patents, reflecting TI's control of its intellectual resources.

Raw Material Equity. This is the value of controlling limited resources such as real estate and physical raw material. Consider that DeBeers possesses almost 100% raw material equity of the diamond market.

People Equity. This is the value of personnel assets based

on the uniqueness of their individual or aggregate abilities; or the value of an individual's ability to bring new and creative ideas to the company.

People equity is often found in technologically based companies such as Apple or IBM that hire individuals with unique talents from prestigious companies and schools. The 3M Company, for example, realizes the potential value of its employees and nurtures its people equity by rewarding those who bring new products to market. People equity, then, is also reflected in valuations based on a company's potential to develop new products.

COMBINING TYPES OF EQUITY

The specific equities defined previously represent the basic building blocks of strategic equity. Importantly, these concepts obviously are not totally independent, either in the three major types (brand, distribution, and raw material), or across the various types. For example, the following combinations are commonly seen across the major equity classifications.

Monopolistic Equity

Monopolistic equity is the value that exists because competitors cannot easily enter or effectively compete in a market without significant additional cost and the value that arises from possession of one or more primary equities that prevent significant competition.

For example, Nintendo of America once dominated the home-video market by such a high penetration of households with its computer hardware that its competitors were locked out in the foreseeable future.

Cross-Cultural Equity

Cross-cultural equity is the value that exists because a brand can cross cultural boundaries. Consider that the McDonald's eating experience can be enjoyed by people from vastly different cultural backgrounds, in particular, consumers who desire to emulate the U.S. lifestyle or behaviour. Levi operates in an identical manner with respect to cross-cultural equity, which the company is able to leverage in overseas markets.

The preceding definitions suggest that the concept of strategic equity is nearly universal, encompassing all aspects of strategically grounded value in a corporate environment. Likewise, brand equity encompasses much more than brand - name recognition and buying behaviour. Measuring a brand's value based on perceptions in consumer's minds or the premium customers are willing to pay for the name is a necessary basis and critical to the evaluation process, but it is not completely sufficient.

Applied to acquisition strategy, brand equity can be used to create value in at least two ways: (a) leveraging latent brand equity into new opportunities, and (b) combining brand equity with one or more other components of strategic equity to create additional value. Quaker Oats' acquisition of Stokely-Van Camp, noted earlier, used both methods. First, Quaker Oats leveraged the Gatorade brand itself.

Leveraging a brand requires that the new owner extend the brand into new products or services in such a way that increases the value of the brand franchise. Second, Quaker Oats combined its distribution system with the Gatorade name to move the sports drink into new markets. This example illustrates how different forms of brand equity can be combined synergistically to create a whole that is greater than the sum of its parts.

More recently, Coca-Cola and Nestle announced an international joint venture to market canned coffee and tea drinks. Nestle hoped to combine its well known trademarks with Coke's massive global distribution system in order to bring coffee and tea products to worldwide markets much faster than either company could do alone. In other words, Nestle's brand equity and Coca-Cola's distribution equity were combined to produce additional value (representing both monopolistic and cross-cultural equity) for each firm.

It is important to understand that creating value by combining equities is dependent on owning strong brand names. Interestingly, the resulting equity that could be gained from the joint venture between Coca-Cola and Nestle may well generate additional strategic equities, including equities based on distribution and (new) product. This partnership represents a prototypical example in which the total incremental value to be achieved from leveraging existing strategic equities is significantly greater than the sum of its parts.

BRAND EQUITY ASSESSMENT

Brand equity can be a powerful asset, and those who manage it need insight, not clairvoyance. Financial engineering ignores this elusive asset, so it is not surprising that crystal-ball methods prevail when Wall Street analysts attempt to predict the success of a merger or acquisition. However, with a reliable method for analyzing brand equity, both analysts and managers could correctly plan for and evaluate the merger and acquisition activities that will occur during the 1990s and beyond.

Most importantly, effective brand -equity management would provide a means of adding value to firms that, in turn, would strengthen the overall economy, something Wall Street has been unable to accomplish in recent times.

Currently in the United States, accounting procedures ignore brand equity as an asset unless the firm is acquired for more than book value. The resulting intangible asset of "goodwill" is simply a default category that in no way recognizes the true worth of the brands. Since the 1970s, in lieu of a more valid strategic equity measurement, financial engineering was Wall Street's only method of valuing a firm. Successful acquisitions occurred because gut feelings about marketing issues were correct, not necessarily because the numbers added up.

In an attempt to improve on the evaluation system, several alternatives have been suggested. Wentz suggested;

- Comparing the price of a branded product with the price of an unbranded product in the same category,
- Comparing profits of unbranded products to profits of branded ones,

- Determining how much the product would be worth without the brand name,
- Conducting detailed investigations of factors such as market share, market trends, and advertising in order to arrive at a composite brand worth. Attempts have also been made to show the extent that accumulated advertising, product attributes, product quality, order of entry into the market, and the future potential of the product affect the equity of the brand. However, brand equity is more comprehensive and greater in scope than is indicated by these previous attempts to measure equity. Most importantly, a definitive measurement of the inescapable connection between the consumer and the value of the brand is missing from all previous efforts.

CONSUMER DECISION-MAKING THEORY

Brand equity dominantly lies in the perceptions of the consumer. In fact, marketing reality with respect to brand loyalty is in the minds of consumers. Consumers translate their perceptions into actions that ultimately dictate which products or services succeed and which fail. As a result, before any valuation of brand equity can be developed, it is important to understand how consumers think about products and services, and what aspects of their decision-making processes relate to their personal involvement with the product or service.

The issue, then, is to understand how consumers store information in memory with respect to brand perceptions and the decision-making process. More specifically, how do cognitive associations held in the collective memories of the marketplace motivate brand choice on an individual basis? This difficult research question can be addressed using the means-end perspective offered by the laddering methodology.

Laddering assumes that the consumer perceptual and decision-making process operates on both a rational and an emotive level and includes a range of considerations from product and service attributes (rational) to personal values (emotive). Put simply, the laddering methodology attempts to uncover the associative structure between a product or service and "self, " which then defines the individual decision-making process.

The consumer is seen to maximize desirable outcomes or consequences of consumption with respect to higher level, more personal needs. That is, one's personal values determine the relative utilities for outcomes or consequences of consumption that, in turn, determine the relative utilities or importance weights for product attributes. The relative importance of the attributes, then, serves as the practical basis for product differentiation and ultimately rational choice. For example, the real, top-down, decision-making process for the selection of McDonald's to take the kids for lunch could be translated as:

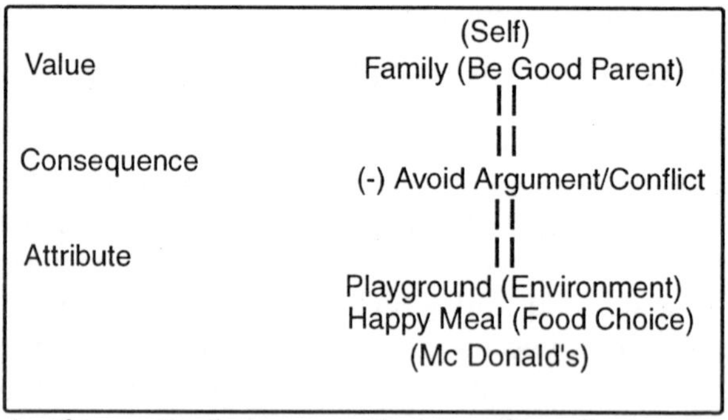

This theoretical perspective implies that consumers purchase products, not so much for their features or attributes, but for the physical and psychological consequences that stem from the attributes during consumption. In the previous example, a desire to minimize stress by avoiding conflict during the meal experience with the kids is guiding and defining the importance of key attributes that then define the selection process of the fast-food restaurant.

The total set of connections between the product attribute and the consumers' value is the personal interpretation that explains why the consumer sees the brand (a fast-food restaurant) to be unique and distinct and, therefore, the brand of choice. The cognitive associations between attributes, consequences, and values (a-c-v) are envisioned as the decision-making memory traces for each consumer. An integral part of the laddering process involves developing summary perspectives for an entire marketplace (a consumer segment), usually with specific brand loyalties as the basis for determining the relevant segments.

An example of what is termed a *Hierarchical Value Map* (HVM) — or more simply, a consumer decision-making map (CDM) — for the fast food category, which represents the dominant perceptual orientations or decision-making ladders for a group of consumers.

A HVM that is constructed using specific user groups, like McDonald's users, provides the framework for developing an analysis of brand equity. That is, once the key decision-making criteria (the salient attributes, consequences, and values) are identified for an entire product class or a set of competitive brands, traditional market research procedures can be used to assign relative importances and belief ratings for the respective options across user groups.

What results is a differential equity index for each decision criteria (across attributes, consequences, and values) for each user group. These scores can then be contrasted to determine the relative equities and disequities of the brand with respect to the competition. This type of cognitive equity analysis explains, for example, why brand -loyal users prefer their product and why the brand -loyal users of competitive brands do not choose other brands (these reasons are the equity of the competition). Clearly, this type of information is invaluable for marketing managers in developing and specifying positioning and communication strategy.

Further, classification of consumers' perceptions of a brand into three types — product, image and personality can provide additional insight into the equity of the brand. Perceptions, as seen in the McDonald's example, are best described by physical attributes or consequences that stem from the functional form of the product or service. For example, McDonald's product perceptions might be "tasty french fries", "fast service", and "clean restrooms". Image perceptions are strongly tied to the abstract, nonfunctional attributes and consequences of a laddering summary or an HVM. For example, McDonalds' image perceptions might include "fun for kids, " "American tradition, " and "helping the community."

Personality perceptions are those that are most strongly associated with human characteristics or traits. In these cases, a character or a person often personifies the brand. For example, McDonalds is personified by Ronald Mc-Donald who embodies the virtues of "fun and entertainment", as well as "caring" — the latter concept derived from sponsoring hospices for seriously ill children and their families.

Understanding how consumers perceive brands with respect this perception classification scheme can provide deeper insight into brandstrengths and weaknesses. In general, strong brands will be grounded in product perceptions (giving consumers clear, rational reasons for buying the product or service).

But, brands will also possess personally relevant image characteristics that both distinguish the brand from competitors and enhance consumers' usage experiences. In essence then, image perceptions can be the value-added result of marketing activities such as advertising and nonprice promotions. Personality perceptions generally serve to strengthen positive emotions consumers may have for the brand and to reinforce image and product perceptions.

A second set of initial research questions to initiate the laddering process can also be used in the study of brand equity. This type of research approach involves simply asking consumers "What comes to mind?" when a specific brand or service is mentioned. In the case of fast-food restaurants, suppose the restaurant asked about was Burger King.

On the HVM derived from the laddering process, we see that "flame broiled, " is a key product attribute that has significant equity with respect to Burger King's "most often" users and "occasional" users. However, in the "top-of-mind" association questioning, the concept of flame broiled did not come up very often. Given that the concept is an important discriminator with respect to consumer choice, and that it is not top-of-mind, strongly suggests "latent equity" that should be leveraged. Research methods such as these provide insights for all types of brand equity, with primary contributions to directly specifying prestige, promotional and latent equity and, equally as important, brand disequities. Secondary inferences from this type of consumer research also yield strategic alternatives or options with respect to bridge and borrowed equity. The development of strategic alternatives or options then permits direct assessment of equities using traditional marketing research techniques.

The impact of these research approaches are primarily in developing marketing and business strategies, which require consumer understanding of the perceptual equities and disequities that exist with respect to the competitive marketing environment. Importantly, the development of new strategic directions that may have been overlooked or underrated gives the analyst specifics to assess in developing a sound strategically based evaluation.

At the very least, the specification of the disequities in this manner yields a strong disaster check to make sure the current business strategies are both on track and devoid of potential weaknesses that may not appear in any other financially based analytic frame.

APPLICATION OF BRAND EQUITY

Consider the example of Converse in the competitive athletic shoe market. In the early 1990s, the market share belonging to Converse lagged well behind that of their primary competitors, including Reebok, Nike, and LA Gear, although at one time, Converse was the market leader in athletic footwear. Using the laddering methodology, an HVM was developed for the athletic shoe market.

Note that it is possible, and often desirable, to describe the HVM with both positive and negative characteristics. For example, the attribute of "been around a long time" is strongly positive for some consumers, whereas for others this attribute is a negative (presumably because it connotes old fashioned or out-of-date).

Following development of the HVM, consumers evaluations of each brand — rated on each of the relevant attributes, consequences, and values — were quantified and compared. The brands rated higher by consumers for specific attributes, consequences, or values dominated the other brands on these decision criteria. One can describe overwhelming dominance as ownership of the decision criteria.

The magnitude of this dominance is a function of both the difference between consumer ratings and the relative importance of the specific attribute, consequence, or value. Top-of-mind frequency can help provide a measure of the relative importance of these characteristics. Comparing brand dominance across all dimensions gives a relative measure of the brand's overall equity against other brands. It is possible, and indeed most likely, that even weak brands may have dominance in certain relevant areas. In terms of strategy, then, Converse might consider three options.

- The first strategic option is to attack from their position of relative strength by emphasizing the positive benefits of their attribute, "been around a long time." Because this attribute currently rates low in relative importance, the strategy would focus on increasing the salience of this dimension. Positive benefits currently exist in some consumers' minds (primarily among older males), so the communication should serve either to remind or persuade customers.
- The second strategic option calls for Converse to create a new benefit of which consumers are not aware, in order to build a strong link between "been around a long time" and a value that Converse could dominate. For example, Converse could create a new functional consequence "my dad used to wear them" to link "been around a long time" with the psychosocial consequence "helps build self-confidence." In this case, the communication execution would teach consumers something new about the product, and at the same time leverage the familial bond.

- The third strategic option involves a mixed strategy of both emphasizing their current strength of "been around a long time" and building additional strengths where competitors are vulnerable. In this case, Converse can strengthen consumers' perception of "good quality" and "the pro's choice of shoes" in order to strengthen perceptions of Converse's ability to "help my performance."

HOW SHOULD BRANDS BE MANAGED

The real financial scorecard for brand management (other than the critical free cash flow) is the net equity gained or lost in a given time period. The value of a firm reflecting shareholder value, is a multiple of the sum of the equities. Following this redefinition of strategic criteria, the equity paradigm has rather strong implications for marketing strategy development and assessment and for evaluating a corporate franchise. Thus, equity management should be the primary criteria for management decision making about brands First, management decisions can and, indeed, should be evaluated by their anticipated impact on each of the components of strategic equity. The merit of a decision will then rest on its ability to improve long-term brand performance and shareholder value.

Such an approach will also insure cross communication between functional areas as managers strive to better understand the overall impact of a decision on the firm. The scorecard for decision making can be a checklist of equities, which can be reviewed for each decision. Second, management, particularly brand managers, should be evaluated and rewarded based on their overall performance for developing and leveraging of the strategic equity of the firm. The formalized decision-making process proposed here could adopt the following sequence:

- The brand manager presents a decision proposal;
- The brand manager and others review and formally assess the potential impact of the decision on a scorecard;

- Higher management or a board of directors assesses the proposal based on the results of the equity review; and
- If the decision is executed, the actual impact of the decision is tracked and subsequently evaluated on the same scorecard.

A hypothetical "Equity Scorecard" that shows the initial equity assessment of the firm, the anticipated impact of a proposed decision, and finally, the results of that decision on the various equities.

Chapter 9

Means-End Theory in Industrial Marketing

INDUSTRIAL AND CONSUMER MARKETS

Many of the examples found in this volume illustrate applications to positioning, advertising, and promotion of frequently purchased branded goods. It is a fact that consumer-goods marketing managers use relatively large market research budgets in support of advertising and promotional efforts to devise and carry out their plans, and they have been methodological pioneers. Business marketers have been later adopters of a number of well-accepted customer marketing tools, including means-end theory.

Why have we industrial-marketing types been slow to catch on? It may be that we have let our own writing on industrial marketing fool us somewhat. We like to point out the differences between the marketing processes used to take frequently purchased branded goods to end-users (marketing Campbell's Soup or Coca Cola) and those used to bring to business or government the things it might require (engineering services bought by a city building a power plant, telecommunications services used by an insurance firm, or diesel fuel used by a fleet of long-haul trucks).

For good reasons, there are some observable differences in these processes. Because consumer-goods marketers do not often meet face-to-face with their customers, formal market research and the use of advertising as a communications vehicle are more prevalent in those markets. Because of the relative complexity of the typical product or product line in business markets, industrial "brand managers" (the title may be different) tend to be older and more experienced than their packaged-goods counterparts. Finally, because the number of accounts or customers is relatively small and geographically concentrated, and the purchase amount per account or transaction is large, direct selling is more often feasible in business markets.

One key difference in consumer and industrial markets is the concept of derived demand. Products such as synthetic fibers are components of such products as carpet, fabric, and tire cord, and the level of demand for those products is partly a function of new car sales. Although certain products such as programmable logic controllers are sold to the literal users of those products, the demand for such devices is in part a function of long-range forecasts of new car sales by those same auto makers, which in turn motivates the firms to invest in plant and equipment.

Although we have ample evidence of the effective use of means-end theory in consumer-goods markets, we have fewer examples of application-to-business markets. In consumer goods, we see the frequent use of the means-end approach in developing (and assessing) impersonal communications such as television advertising, promotional campaigns, and brand -positioning strategies. Although applications to industrial markets are not unknown, they are more rare. We think that is a mistake.

Many differences between consumer and business marketing are largely a matter of degree. For instance, in certain product classes, families engage in committee buying and family members specify products or attributes of products to be bought by another member of the family. Whereas consumer-packaged goods marketers study phenomena such as brand loyalty and switching, business marketers study their analogs: relationships and transactions.

Despite the well-documented importance of the industrial and governmental sectors of the economy and despite some occasional calls for industrial-goods marketers to learn from their opposite numbers in the consumer-goods fields, industrial-goods marketers still lag. That is a shame because understanding the decision-making process of customers in industrial markets is no more or less important than it is in consumer markets.

Salesforce Recruiting—Recruiting for Success

Means-end techniques help you avoid traps. Is your firm engaged in direct selling? If so, among the tasks your managers must master are recruiting and retaining salespeople. We know that all the hundreds of studies of who makes the best salesperson (loud or quiet, introvert or extrovert, flashy or conservative dresser) tell us — well, not much because all sorts of people can and do succeed by some measure in sales; but we also know that a good way to frustrate someone is to establish a set of unrealistic expectations for them, and a good way to get salespeople to quit is to leave them without a base of support when the inevitable setbacks occur.

Here is how one company changed its recruiting pitch based on what it learned about its successful and unsuccessful sellers, which helped link selling the company's products to the self in a meaningful way.

In the mid-1980s, Mary Kay Cosmetics experienced a decline in sales and recruiting that put the firm in jeopardy. To investigate the reasons that people became beauty consultants (sales people), the research team divided their sample universe into sets. One set comprised beauty consultants who were successful and stayed with the company; another included people who were relatively unsuccessful; a third group consisted of people who had left the company.

During a laddering interview, interviewers probed for reasons why all of the beauty consultants joined and for reasons they stayed or left. To understand why they joined, researchers asked respondents to recall the decision context. In doing so, they realized that becoming a beauty consultant was not always a choice between obvious competitors such as rival direct selling organizations or cosmetics firms but sometimes a choice between working 9-to-5 in a retail store or as a secretary in a bank. By asking for the most positive aspects of being a beauty consultant for Mary Kay, as opposed to exercising another career option, managers discovered that there were a number of common themes within each of the subgroups.

Although the linkages between the company and the values people held were many, not all had the same valence for all groups. That is, some were positive only for successful consultants, and some were negative primarily for consultants who left in frustration. An example of the former was a set of linkages dealing with learning (about skin care and cosmetics and about other things such as communication skills and business discipline).

Another was "teaching those skills to others." Both were linked with a feeling of self-worth. By contrast, for consultants who resigned, the linkage between monetary rewards and a feeling of contrabution to family (was strong — and negative.)

When successful beauty consultants spoke about their experience with Mary Kay and how it was different from prior work experiences, they acknowledged financial motives. However, they also indicated that they viewed financial results as less important than the ability to learn, to grow, and to help other people, and the way those outcomes made them feel.

They were motivated by a sense of independence and self-esteem, and even on days when sales were not what they had wanted, they were sustained by other psychosocial gains. In contrast, beauty consultants whose experiences were less positive overall usually had only a financial motive for becoming a sales consultant.

The Mary Kay company used these means-end results to revise its recruiting message to prospective beauty consultants. Besides de-emphasizing money as an end result, the recruiting message also recast financial gain as one of several valued outcomes of the process of learning, growing, and helping other people that could lead to a heightened sense of independence and self-worth. The result? In 1, 200 matched pairs of consultants, the changed recruiting materials produced a 42% increase in recruiting success versus the control group.

Commodity Sales

Sometimes, the traps you can avoid are those you lay for yourself. Does your firm sell products that you and your customers call commodities? Our experience shows that you can differentiate those products. The key is to understand that, if attributes of the product or the extended product are nearly identical across firms, the differentiation needs to take place at the psychosocial level (in means-end theory). Usually, your customers see differences you do not, so ask them.

Consider the case of a major petroleum company selling mid-level distillates (diesel fuel, kerosene, and jet fuel). As the manager expressed it, "This is a points business, not a dollars and cents business. The 'four P' are price, price, price, and price." All of the managers believed it, their salespeople practiced it, and their margins showed it. Yet, when interviewed by members of the research team, their customers' assessment of what was important and why varied greatly. In fact, the interviews uncovered over 25 differentiators of diesel fuel by brand. For fleet buyers and for buyers of jet fuel, price was a dominant attribute.

However, for other customers, a broader set of attributes was important. Among them was price, and it was an important attribute — about 10th on the list, but for most people, price was not a differentiator if it was not completely out of line with the marketplace. Why was price not more important? Because other attributes of the brand — assurance of supply, assurance of consistnecy, speed or response to requests, even courtesy and friendliness — led to more central psychosocial outcomes, and those connections were more highly leverageable than a price that was a little lower than average.

In this case, the attributes that served as differentiators were discovered by starting with a usage amount probe. Researchers asked respondents how frequently they bought each brand of fuel in the past month. For the sake of illustration, suppose a respondent reported stopping for fuel at a Shell station three times, at a Mobil station six times, and at a Texaco station seven times. The differences in those frequencies were used to initiate the laddering probes. The contrasts between purchase frequencies revealed both positive and negative differentiators for each brand. The questions used as probes for this respondent might have included the following:

- Why did you use Mobil more than Shell?
- Why didn't you use Texaco always?
- When you bought Shell, why did you choose it over the other brands?
- What do these three brands have that others lack?

By conducting equity analyses of the category and the brands, team members could in fact find leverageable nonprice equity in their brand.

DEFENSIVE STRATEGY

Understanding the non-price dimensions of competitive advantage is another important application of the means-end approach. A company that supplied protective services (in the form of guards, uniformed or plain clothed, armed or unarmed) to embassies, shopping centers, and businesses found it needed to protect itself from price-cutting competition. Some managers believed that price had become the only dimension of importance.

If that proved to be the case, then they were at a serious disadvantage. Their costs were relatively high because of rigorous recruiting standards and a training process about 100 times longer than the average for such firms. They knew that firms valued other things than price, such as the training, the appearance of the guards, their degree of formality or approachability, and the nature and closeness of supervision, but they did not know how those attributes of their firm were linked to the personal lives of the people who made the decision to retain them.

Understanding the linkages to valued outcomes lets them educate their sales staff to keep them from playing the game by rules that would have put them at a disadvantage. In this case, respondents were generally aware of a small number of competing firms. Therefore, the interviewers began their laddering probes by asking respondents to register their overall satisfaction with their current supplier of protective services: "On a scale from 0 to 100, where 0 means 'awful, couldn't be worse' and 100 means 'perfect, couldn't be better, ' how satisfied are you overall with XYZ company?" The two ends of the scale were deliberately scaled so that even the most satisfied or dissatisfied respondents would not use them. As a result, interviewers could probe for both positive and negative attributes in each case.

- You rated your satisfaction with XYZ a 90. What kept you from rating them higher?.
- What made you rate them so high? (This probe elicits an XYZ positive.)

When respondents mentioned price, interviewers let them vent. Then, they could ask follow-on questions such as the following:

- Suppose they did lower price, and you rated them three points higher. What is the one most important thing XYZ could do to get you to rate them higher still?
- Suppose all firms' prices were identical. Would you still prefer to use XYZ? Why?

POSITIONING

"There ain't no loyalty that two-cents-off won't overcome, " or so it is said. As if to prove the statement, a telecommunications company's commercial customers described their choice of providers as coldly rational. "We write down a needs statement, solicit three bids, assess the capabilities of the firms on relevant dimensions...." That is hardly an environment in which "relationship" as a marketing goal seems achievable. Yet, consider the complex decision-making environment and the limited resources the business user has to direct toward making a choice.

How does one choose among alternative offers of considerable complexity? What is the marginal gain to be made by taking the time and effort to process information about each offer? One way to deal with such cost and complexity is to let the promise of the brand take the place of much complex decision making. That was something this firm's customers were willing to do because the brand had earned their trust. In this case, researchers gained an understanding the components of trust, the signals that indicated that the firm could be trusted. Researchers also found the degree to which different firms were thought to possess those signaling qualities. Probes of decision makers, influencers, and deciders revealed the emotional outcomes of those signal attributes and the ways in which linkages were formed between attribute business consequence personal (emotional) consequence.

Those linkages formed the basis of both *brandstrength* (the ability of the brand to compete in its market) and *brand leverage* (the ability of the brand to grow beyond its current boundaries). By specifying in the positioning statement the linkages to be reinforced, managers, sales staff, and technical staff could see the elements of the marketing mix — advertising, personal selling efforts, and new-product development efforts — as part of an integrated, purposive strategy.

In this, as in many industrial markets, when customers were asked why they preferred provider A to provider B, they responded with summary-level judgments on characteristics such as quality, reliability, and dependability. Such generic answers are not particularly helpful to a marketer trying to understand how to communicate those virtues. Interviewers in this case had to chute downward from such responses, then ladder upward, as the following example illustrates.

- *Interviewer*: Why did you rate ABC Company so high?
- *Respondent*: Dependability. They are very dependable.
- *Interviewer*: How do you know?
- *Respondent*: Because every time they say they will be there, they show up on time.

If the interviewer had asked why dependability was important, a generalized positive might have resulted: "I try to be dependable, others should be, too; I like to deal with dependable companies." By asking for the underlying attribute, a different and more personally meaningful ladder results.

- *Interviewer*: Is it important to you that they show up on time?
- *Respondent*: Sure. I can schedule my appointments and know that I can meet my customers when I promise to. That way, I don't disappoint my customers and look bad.

Often, after probing downward to get the factors or cues that lead to or support a construct such as dependability or quality, the respondent does not return to the original construct but instead goes beyond to a personally relevant consequence. The factors or cues themselves are useful in defining for a service manager the signals by which buyers recognize quality or dependability in a service provider.

INDUSTRIAL STRATEGY FORMULATION AND IMPLEMENTATION: POWER MEANS PREFERENCE, BUT LEVERAGE MEANS GROWTH

Some names have power. That is, within a defined category, they have been able to build purchase preference. Building power is largely a matter of understanding the equities the brand has in the minds of customers and using those equities to reinforce linkages with the self. An example of a (consumer brand name with a lot of power might be Coca-Cola.) Other brands have leverage. They have permission, within the minds of customers in their current product class, to reach beyond their current sphere of business. Brand names with leverage can magnify value in other markets. An example of a brand name with leverage might be Arm and Hammer.

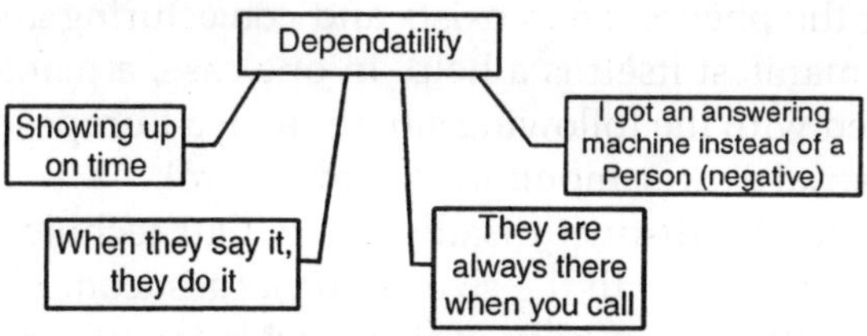

Fig. Cues that Reveal Provider Dependability for one Respondent.

There are ample cases in consumer packaged goods

markets of firms believing that because they had achieved strong brand preference in beverages (or automobiles or typewriters), they could then brand other products such as foods (or sportswear or computers). Their success depended in part on whether they in fact had a brand name that was leverageable and therefore extensible or a name that was merely powerful. We have found analogs among business marketers as well. In some cases, identifying the bases of equity and the reasons for its personal relevance has helped a company understand the level of commitment it had to make to establish leverageability.

One firm selling project management services in a given range of project sizes aspired to capture some of the market for bigger, more complex projects. Through a laddering study, the firm was able to understand how the attributes of the firm and those of its competitors led to personally meaningful outcomes for buyers including the mitigation of psychological risk, the potential for social reward, and achieving certain levels of psychological comfort.

Thus, the firm was able to understand that its primary equities gave it a great deal of power but relatively little leverage. Managers also learned what equities the company had to develop in order to make the firm's name and reputation leverageable or transferable to larger projects.

DISTRIBUTION STRATEGY: JUST KNOWING IT CAN BE DONE CAN MAKE IT POSSIBLE

Good theories are often quite practical. Sometimes, just knowing the phenomenon exists and conjecturing about how it might manifest itself is a help. In one case, a manager was confronted with the following situation, in a European market for industrial power monitoring and control:

We are at a distinct disadvantage. Our technical service staff is about one-tenth the size of our largest competitors. As a company, they have been in this market for 100 years. They have a very large installed base in motors and controls although that is not necessarily the key driver for decisions. We desperately need improved distributor representation.

Distributors think our products are great. But those distfibutors, faced with a decision to carry"us or them, " choose them. I need some way to get these distributors to cast their lot with us. I will tell you, however, that I have sought help from dozens of people, and the answer is unanimous: They are all glad it is my problem and not theirs, because they don' see a feasible solution other than giving away the product.

In this case, the manager and his staff knew the distributors reasonably well, and some had worked for distributors in the past. Therefore, they were able to draw on their own experiences with both firms for insight. All they needed was a framework to articulate the problem as a decision-making problem, and a brief introduction to means-end theory provided that framework. We cast them in the role of respondent distributors and had them role-play, articulating the ways in which they could tell the companies and their products apart in particular sales and service situations.

The actors, playing the part of distributors, tried to put themselves in the distributors' shoes and explain why those differentiators were personally relevant to them. They were able to identify, in this case, plausible positive and negative associations with the two firms, some of which were inherent in the operating methods of the companies. In this case, too, the manager spent some time learning how to ask questions in a way that let him not only uncover needs but link those needs with personally relevant outcomes.

For example, rather than asking about problems with the current supplier, they asked, "What is hard about what you do? "The respondent could then identify a felt need, and the salesperson could ask what benefit would result if that need were met, how the distributor would know the need had been met, and so on, engaging in a kind of laddering process.

With some instruction in the rudiments of constructing a consumer decision-making map, the manager returned to Europe cautiously optimistic. On arriving, he taught his sales staff about means-end theory and gave them materials on laddering methodology. He also told them about the mock interviews he had conducted and gave them his maps, linking performance features of the firms to personally relevant characteristics.

Members of his staff, already trained in asking questions and in problem-solving sales techniques, quickly understood the process and adapted their calling techniques to accommodate the new approach. About a month later, he wrote to tell us of his success at winning over an account worth tens of millions of dollars operating in three countries.

THE SELLING PROCESS

Let us return briefly to the notion of the intersection between communication and decision-making, for it is here in business marketing, as it is in consumer marketing, that the application of means-end theory can have relatively immediate impact.

It is true that advertising budgets in packaged-goods firms are large, and because expenditures that are large draw a lot of scrutiny within companies, it makes sense that consumer-goods marketers would actively search for and embrace techniques to help them pull products through the distribution channels. But direct-selling budgets also are large in almost all business-marketing companies, and much effort is directed at achieving and evaluating selling effectiveness. We see significant opportunities for sales professionals in industrial or business-to-business markets to benefit from a clearer understanding of means-end theory and its application in their work.

Most sales-training programs propose a process or system that codifies the authors' experience in sales. The experience base of Miller and Heiman, explained in such books as *Conceptual Selling*, and the experimental and empirical base that Rackham explained in *Spin Selling*, make contributions that are proven in the field. Their books explain *what* works, or at least, some of what works.

Although we find great insight in their accounts, these books do not explain *why* what works does in fact work. That is, we do not see in these treatments evidence of a general theory of how industrial buyers make decisions. Without such a general theory and understanding, in the end they can only acknowledge that selling, and especially account planning, should be strategic. In contrast, means-end theory provides techniques that help firms establish positioning strategy by specifying the manner in which the characteristics of the brand, service, or firm are to be linked to personally relevant outcomes for a targeted set of buyers.

Using the Sales Force for Strategy Development and Implementation

In the industrial sales force, the single most powerful change agent in an organization is capable of serving as an information source for strategy development and as an instrument for carrying out policy. The sales force can be brought to bear as a weapon of competitive advantage in a few short steps. Salespeople already are talking to the decision makers, and they already know the value of asking questions. What they may not know is how to use directed laddering-type probes — open-ended questions aimed at taking conversations to a higher level of psychological abstraction to gain insight into personal relevance.

In addition, salespeople can be taught how to construct a map — a graphical representation of their findings from their interview notes. Familiarizing the sales personnel with means-end theory and technique would go a long way toward giving them that knowledge.

Let us give an example of how such a process might work. Rackham's *SPIN Selling* differentiates among features (what we call attributes), advantages (functional conseq-uences), and benefits (again, usually functional benefits but ones the customer has asked for specifically, expressed as a need statement).

His or her process could connect to higher level psychosocial implications, but usually it does not. However there is no reason that an interview could not push to higher, more personal consequences:

Seller: and we also have triple-duplex wiring. (A feature in Rackham's taxonomy, an attribute in means-end language.)

Customer: What's that do?

Seller: Keeps you from getting your muffler-bearings crossed.

Customer: I don't have that problem. But I do need to keep the G-4 from impinging on the bearings.

Seller: Why is that? (At this point, the customer has expressed a need; Rackham might suggest making a benefit statement in response. But we are still at the level of the functional consequence, and would like to probe a bit deeper.)

Customer: It's critical; our customers hate when that happens.

Seller: When that happens to one of your customers' machines, what happens in your office?

Customer: Two things. First, they call me, and I don't blame them. and I feel like an idiot because I promised them they didn't have to worry about that

At this point, the probes have reached a low-level psychosocial consequence associated with the attribute mentioned earlier. If it were comfortable to do so, we could continue.

Seller: Why is that important to you?

Customer: Because I am responsible, and because my customers should be able to rely on what I tell them.

Seller: Is that important to you?

Customer: Sure.

Seller: Why?

Customer: Are you crazy?

Seller: (Silence.)

Customer: Okay, I'll tell you. I only have one thing to sell, when it gets down to it: My word. If I don't have that, I don't have anything. Customers have to trust me. and they can. I'm proud of that.

In this case, we have taken this imaginary customer to the values level with repeated application of the basic laddering probes. In many business sales, that is not possible. However, we can usually take people to the psychosocial level and understand something of the emotional drivers underlying their behaviour. Factors such as "gaining recognition, " "I'm important, " "I'm in control, " "I did a good job, " "makes my life easier, " "get more done, " "get in to other things, " "not get hassled" can be important leverage points for communications. As a cautionary note, these laddering probes are inappropriate for meetings larger than one-on-one. The material is a bit sensitive for that.

USING INTERVIEW NOTES FOR INSTITUTIONAL LEARNING

Interview or sales-call notes can be kept in a kind of coding shorth and that represents individual ladders:

	Level
Duplex wiring	(A)
(Not) Cross muffler bearings	(A)
(Not) Impinging on bearings	(FC)
(Not) Make customers mad, call in	(PC)
(Not) Make me feel like an idiot	(PC)
Customers can rely on me	(PC)
Proud of my reputation	(V)

Those notes can then be coded and collapsed into a consumer decision-making map. The results can be analyzed over time for both individual and corporate learning, so that moving sales people from one territory to another does not result in lost history. It also gives your sales staff and management, along with others in the firm, a common language or lexicon with which to discuss your business. That lexicon is not your own internal "company-speak" but the voice of your customers, the most valid language you can use.

Chapter 10

Means-End Chain Theory and Involvement

Since the 1970s, involvement has been introduced as an explanatory or moderating variable in a wide variety of consumer-related research. The construct has shown to mediate such consumer behaviour topics as attitudes, decision making, information processing, advertising effectiveness, cognitive structures, and brand loyalty, to name but a few. The influence of involvement on major aspects of consumer behaviour justifies its central status in contemporary consumer research. Therefore, it is a reasonable research strategy to study the interactions between involvement and concepts newly introduced to the field.

Attention is paid to the relation of involvement with the concept of means-end chains and with the laddering methodology, an area that increasingly is attracting the interest of academic researchers. In this way, this chapter contributes to an increased understanding of both involvement and of means-end chains and laddering. In addition, we hope that this approach revives consumer researchers' interest in involvement.

Despite the fact that the concept has profoundly altered the state of the art in our understanding of consumer behaviour, research on involvement apparently has lost some of its attractiveness, at least in academic circles. One reason for this may be that the plurality of proposed definitions, typologies, and operationalizations have made the concept rather elusive, thereby discouraging academics from undertaking further research. Another, perhaps even more influential reason, may simply be that involvement is no longer a fashionable publishing topic.

Whatever the reasons for the current lack of interest in involvement, important research topics should not be determined by fashion, nor should a body of knowledge acquired through 20 years of research accumulate dust in a dark academic corner. Such neglect is counterproductive for the consumer research discipline.

First, we seek to establish a relation between involvement and means-end chains, primarily through the intervening construct of cognitive structures. Second, we use this relation as a starting point for a series of critical comments and thoughts on the causal implications of involvement on the content and structure of means-end chains.

Third, we hope this discussion stimulates hypothesis formulation and research on the concepts of involvement, cognitive structures, means-end chains, and on the interrelations between them.

MEANS-END CHAIN THEORY

Means-End Chain (MEC) theory proposes a conceptual model for the cognitive organization, structure, and content of product knowledge in memory. The MEC model is consistent with the associative network type of memory structures but some characteristics are specific to means-end chains.

The MEC model distinguishes between three basic components: attributes, consequences, and values. A finer-grained version of the model is obtained by dichotomizing each of the basic levels into two sublevels. Product knowledge can thus be represented at six different levels of abstraction, ranging from the very concrete to the very abstract — concrete and abstract attributes, functional and psychosocial consequences, instrumental and terminal or end values. The different levels are related by causal asymmetric linkages. Thus, attributes may be perceived as producing desired consequences that in turn lead to the achievement of values.

Attributes or product characteristics are the means by which the consumers search to materialize desired goals, values, or ends.

A *means-end chain* is a directed, hierarchically organized structure of interconnected levels of product knowledge of varying abstraction. A product category or brand can be typified by several means-end chains. These chains are not necessarily interrelated, although this often is the case. The entire product schema, in the means-end terminology, referred to as *HVM*, can be thought of as embedded within a larger associative network of product knowledge, including evaluations, affect or emotions, decision rules, product-usage situations, and so forth. Information in such an associative network is retrieved via the mechanism of spreading activation.

Thus, spreading activation drives the generation of means-end chains. This mechanism implies that activation of a value automatically evokes associated constructs, such as consequences and attributes. The stronger the association between two constructs, the higher the probability of activation of one by the other.

Values become salient in memory through the activation of contextual cues such as goals, product use, or decision situations. For instance, different usage or decision situations activate different goal structures and values, which in turn imply different consequences and attributes. In this way, situationally defined means-end chains can be generated within a product class. MEC theory constitutes a powerful approach to study the influence of situational context on cognitions and behaviour by explicating the link between situation and activated knowledge.

The scope of MEC theory exceeds the domain of knowledge representation and organization. MEC theory offers an integrative framework for current perspectives and paradigms in consumer research in two respects. First, the means-end approach integrates insights on a facet of consumers' cognitive structures; namely, the organization of products in coherent groups on the basis of perceived equivalence or categorization. Categorization is considered a fundamental cognitive activity, and contemporary categorization theory is dominated by two seemingly opposing views on the organizing principles of classification. The oldest school of thought posits that resemblance in terms of features or attributes determines the category structure. This approach is commonly referred to as a *taxonomic categorization.*

More recently, another stream of research challenges the first approach for its remoteness from human needs, goals, and values. Adherents of this school claim that classifying objects that serve a common goal constitutes a more natural way of categorizing objects in the environment. Both schools of thought have been advocated for application in consumer behaviour literature.

Interestingly, the taxonomic means-end chain model — describing product knowledge at the attribute, consequence, and value level — appears compatible with both principles for categorization suggested in the cognitive psychology literature. If a consumer groups products together because they possess a set of similar attributes, hence using the information at the most concrete level in the chain, a taxonomical category structure as advanced by Rosch and Mervis is expected to emerge.

Alternatively, the consumer may wish to structure his or her environment according to the perceived instrumentality of products to achieve particular consequences or values. To the extent that the means-end knowledge for products is established in the consumer's mind, this information can readily be retrieved from memory.

The resulting category structure will have more of the "goal-derived" nature as advanced by Barsalou. The central tenet of the MEC theory — that consumers are interested in acquiring products because of their perceived ability to achieve important ends or values — is more consistent with the concept of goal-derived categorization.

Recently, however, it was observed that category representations are rarely invariant but, rather, are contingent on situational constraints, task demands, and contextual cues.

Some empirical evidence supports this issue, demonstrating that consumers are adaptive and that flexible category constructors can readily restructure a taxonomic knowledge basis in terms of goal-derived categories defined by appropriate decision criteria. The model of product-knowledge organization advocated by MEC theory is compatible with such a view on flexible product categorization.

The second point is that MEC theory integrates the two major approaches used to understand and predict consumer behaviour — the cognitively oriented and the motivational approach.

The basic assumption of MEC theory — that products are acquired as a means to achieve certain ends — is not new to the discipline of consumer behaviour. This idea is exemplified in Rosenberg's and Fishbein's theories of attitude formation that constitute the fundamental underpinnings of the multiattribute attitude modeling approach in consumer research. In the Rosenberg model attitudes toward an object are determined by the perceived instrumentality of that object to attain core values times the importance of those values to the individual.

In Fishbein's approach, the *beliefs* (perceived consequences produced by the objects) about an object and their evaluation constitute the building blocks of attitude. Hence, both models imply that favorable attitudes will be developed toward products that offer us the means to attain desirable ends. Although based on similar means-end notions, Fishbein's and Rosenberg's models disagree on the ends consumers seek to achieve and that determine their ultimate attitude toward the product — consequences and values, respectively.

MEC theory contributes to the field of multiattribute attitude modeling by acknowledging that attributes and consequences or values are not independent precursors of attitude or behaviour; rather they are associated in a hierarchical arrangement. In this way, MEC theory formally integrates these two models of attitude formation.

In general, the MEC theory offers a more complete framework for studying and explaining consumer behaviour, which reconciles the seemingly conflicting approaches available. The more cognitively oriented perspectives, supported by a wide range of quantitative techniques, have traditionally focused on the product knowledge part of the chain (attributes and functional consequences). In this view, consumers are thought to perceive products as bundles of attributes from which they derive value.

In this paradigm, attitudes and preferences are explained as a function of product characteristics. The research techniques employed in the cognitive perspective differ in the abstractness of information that is used. Conjoint analysis and perceptual mapping, for example, focus heavily on product knowledge at the concrete attribute level.

On the other hand, the "attributes" in multiattribute attitude models seem to encompass information of a higher level of inclusiveness because these models concentrate on perceived consequences or benefits of the product (cars are judged on reliability, goodness for city driving, or durability; toothpaste is judged on its capability to prevent tooth decay or freshen breath).

The other major paradigm, the motivational approach, focuses on personalities, lifestyles, and motivations to study consumer behaviour. These different types of research are related by their common reliance on values and value systems as the driving force behind consumption behaviour.

Motivations, personalities, interests, and lifestyles can be thought of as different facets or outcomes of the same underlying construct — the core self-structure representing the fundamental goals and values held by the individual. Therefore, this approach posits that the self-schema constitutes the frame of reference for the individuals' consumption behaviour. The cognitive and the motivational perspective share a common restriction. They model consumer behaviour on the basis of a small part of consumers' cognitive structures. The emphasis is on the product knowledge in the cognitive approach, whereas the motivational approach attaches all weight to the self-component of the knowledge structure.

It has been the merit of the MEC theory to point out that

the product is inextricably linked to the self and to take into account both the characteristics of the product and the higher order benefits and values it produces as related and interdependent explanatory variables of consumer behaviour. Hereby, MEC theory formally reconciles existing perspectives on consumer behaviour.

INVOLVEMENT

The number of definitions, operationalizations, domains of application, and correlates of the concept of involvement is abundant. Instead, a definition of involvement in terms of personal or self-relevance can integrate divergent views on involvement. The conceptualization of involvement as the centrality of the product to the self-concept (often called ego-structure) originated in social psychology and found support from many scholars in consumer research. A definition characteristic of this perspective on involvement is offered.

Involvement refers to consumers' perceptions of importance or personal relevance for an object, event, or activity. Consumers who perceive that a product has personally relevant consequences are said to be involved with the product and to have a personal relationship with it.

This definition turns out to be compatible with various treatments of and perspectives on involvement advanced in the literature. Briefly discussed is the suitability of the personal relevance conceptualization of involvement to account for the involvement typology, the distinction between situational and enduring involvement, and the causal schema distinguishing between antecedent states and consequences of involvement. Finally, we note that this perspective holds the promise of reconciling the views on involvement as a multifaceted versus a unidimensional construct.

First, conceptualizing involvement in terms of value-instrumentality can hand le the various types of involvement outlined in the literature: product (product category or brand) involvement, situation involvement, and involvement with a (advertising) message or a communication.

Each of these types of involvement can originate from

perceived personal relevance based on the observed relation of the object, situation or communication with needs, values and interests of the individual.

The typology of involvement is intertwined with the distinction of involvement on the dimension of time. Involvement with a product is commonly assumed to be relatively permanent and enduring, whereas involvement with a situation or message only lasts for a specific time, making it situational specific and transitory.

The time dimension of involvement is incorporated in the definition as well. Enduring involvement is the result of a long-term perceived personal relevance that exists across situations and on an ongoing basis. When personal, relevant knowledge, such as goals and values, is only temporarily activated due to the peculiarities of a situation, the term *situational involvement* is applicable.

Third, the personal relevance conceptualization specifies the components of the implicit causal scheme of involvement. The goals and value systems of consumers constitute the antecedents of involvement. The myriad of sources of involvement indicated in the literature, such as product importance, the amount of interest evoked by the product, motivation, or commitment, are all ultimately linked to thevalues held by the individual.

The internal state of arousal (felt involvement) is determined by the combination of enduring and situational perceived linkages between the product and personal interests, goals, and values. Personal relevance can also account for the process implications advocated by some involvement theorists, such as extensive information searches and complex decision-making. Fourth, the personal relevance perspective allows reconciling the treatment of involvement as a multifaceted versus a unidimensional construct. Proponents of the multidimensional view posit that typifying involvement as a variety of intensity of arousal levels, as is typical for the unitary view, ignores valuable information on the origins of involvement.

Laurent and Kapferer argued that involvement is a profile

shaped by the performance of the product on underlying dimensions or value orientations, such as sign value and perceived risk. Hence, the overall sense of involvement is distributed across the presumed constituent components and is not considered a valuable measure in its own right, which is in sharp contrast to the unitary approach.

The conceptualization of involvement as personal relevance in the Ostrom and Brock fashion, implied that involvement is somehow proportional to the number of values reached. Hence, the overall experience of involvement, which is the measure of concern, is based on the relatedness of products to a series of different values.

The personal relevance conceptualization integrates the benefits of both approaches by attempting to offer an overall measure of involvement intensity and providing the opportunity to examine the profile of value that underlie this overall experience. Central to the personal relevance definition is the acknowledgement that involvement is not a characteristic of the product in itself but is contingent on the personal meaning the consumer assigns to the characteristics of the product. Involvement originates from the interaction between the product schema and the self-schema.

The commonly applied dichotomy between high- and low-involvement products merely denotes that some products are perceived by a large variety of consumers as having high-personal significance to them.

More recently, consensus grows that involvement is, to a large extent, determined by the situational setting. The ultimate level of involvement reached results from the perceived personal relevance of a product to a person in a particular situation. Situational involvement, as opposed to enduring involvement, is a short-term state of arousal, established by a temporary activation of relevant self-knowledge, situation-specific and transitory. In literature, situational involvement is restricted to apply only to the purchase situation and may be interpreted as brand -choice involvement.

The concept of situational involvement further vitiates the

simplicity of the *high-* versus *low-involvement* dichotomy. Products typically referred to as low involving (e. g. batteries, light bulbs, or paper clips) have the potential of acquiring personal relevance in those situations where expected benefits are not realized. For example, as long as the light bulb in one's reading corner performs well, the product is probably not part of daily concern.

However, when it fails, one may become very concerned about getting it replaced as its absence explicates its relatedness to the value system. Not being able to read may be perceived as spoiling the evening, which reduces the satisfaction and pleasure in life. Therefore, a good criterion to distinguish between high and low involvement may be its endurance over time. High involvement can be interpreted as involving on an enduring, ongoing basis. Low involvement often refers to the absence of enduring involvement, which is not identical to stating that there is a lack of connections with the value system.

The definition advanced by Peter and Olson does not explicate the situational facet of involvement, however it does not exclude its occurrence. A more important deficiency is the observed ambiguity at the level of the causes of involvement. Involvement or personal relevance is said to arise out of the ability of the product to help achieve consequences or values of importance to the individual.

A number of questions can be raised on this issue (e.g., do both consequences and values produce a similar amount of involvement; what is the nature of the consequences and values involved; how should the importance of values and consequences to the consumer be measured?). These questions demonstrate that the definition in its current form is not suitable for a straightforward operationalization of involvement in terms of personal relevance.

Zaichowsky's Personal Involvement Inventory, generally considered a milestone in involvement research, recognized the self-relevance conceptualization of involvement as well. However, the unidimensional scale she proposed to measure (enduring) involvement does not constitute a satisfactory operationalization of the personal relevance perspective on the construct.

The scale items seem to reside at the level of psychosocial consequences (e.g., boring vs. interesting, appealing vs. unappealing, beneficial vs. not beneficial) without explicitly establishing the link with the value structure as an origin of involvement.

In conclusion, in spite of the popularity of the value-instrumentality perspective of involvement, a sound operationalization of the concept is lacking in the literature. In addition, most currently available tools heavily focus on the measurement of enduring involvement.

Although involvement is a variable considered to affect major cognitive activities, such as information search and processing and decision making, its influence on cognitive structures is not extensively researched. The general intuitive assumption is that the complexity of the cognitive structure increases at increasing levels of involvement. Lastovicka and Gardner empirically supported this hypothesis by demonstrating significant differences in dimensionality and integration (level of abstraction) between the cognitive structures of high- and low-involved individuals.

They found that the cognitive structures of low-involved individuals can adequately be represented by using fewer dimensions and are less integrative than is the case for highly involved people. It is also acknowledged that the knowledge organization under high involvement is characterized by strong links between salient components.

In addition, some interesting insights on the influence of involvement on cognitive organization can be derived from the expertise and familiarity literature due to the observed correlation between these constructs. High involvement with a product class normally implies that the individual is motivated to devote attention and time to information search and comparison between alternatives.

From this, it logically follows that high-involvement consumers demonstrate expertise in the product class they are interested in. Nevertheless, the correlation will not be perfect as the acquisition of expertise and the level of involvement are time-dependent. Deviations will occur for high-involved consumers just entering the product class and for consumers with high expertise who lost their interest or involvement in the product class.

Except for these cases, it seems plausible to assume that high-involvement and low-involvement cognitive structures can be described by characteristics generally assigned to cognitive structures of experts and novices, respectively. The major findings of this literature can be summarized by stating that experts possess a refined, differentiated, complete, and veridical cognitive structure of a large dimensionality, articulation and a high level of abstraction. Abstraction is the consequence of intensive processing and interpreting and is oftentimes referred as chunking or unitization of information.

THE RELATION BETWEEN THE CONCEPTS OF INVOLVEMENT AND MEANS-END CHAINS

A simple comparison between the concepts of means-end chains and involvement reveals a number of interesting similarities. First, both involvement and means-end chains are assumed to originate from the interaction between the product and the self. Second, both constructs have implications for the cognitive organization of product knowledge in memory. Third, involvement and means-end chains are similar in that they are both to a large extent determined by situational characteristics. Fourth, both constructs are defined primarily at the level of product categories rather than brands.

These similarities point to the plausibility of a relation between means-end chains and involvement. If these constructs are related, then expectations can be formed on the structural and content-related properties of means-end chains for high- or low-involved consumers. Thus, the MEC theory provides a new means to operationalize and measure involvement.

These authors paraphrased their involvement definition from the MEC perspective as: "Means-end chains can help marketers understand consumers' product involment because they show how knowledge about product attributes is related to their knowledge about self". Hence, using means-end chains to operationalize the personal relevance perspective of involvement has promises. This endeavor fills a current gap in the involvement and MEC literature.

This chapter aims at developing (preliminary) ideas on this issue and investigates several ways in which involvement affects the structure and content of means-end chains. The theoretical insights obtained for involvement and means-end chains allow to posit and critically comment on a series of statements on the nature of the relation between both constructs.

The discussion is divided into two major parts, reflecting the distinction between enduring and situational involvement that is thought to be a central concern when implications for content and structure of means-end chains are considered.

The first part comments on the combination of means-end chains and high-enduring involvement. In the second part attention is devoted to the means-end chains characteristics for products that are, in general, only situationally involving. An additional point of concern here is the possibility of differentiating between enduring and situational involvement from the means-end chain perspective.

Enduring Involvement and Means-End Chains

As stated earlier, the observed similarities between means-end chains and involvement justify our endeavors to establish a relation between both constructs. We attempt to elaborate on the nature of this relation at the conceptual level. More specifically, we advance a number of thoughts concerning the effect of the level of involvement on the means-end chains or more generally, on the hierarchical value map (HVM), the consumer holds for a product. Initially, we ignore issues and problems pertaining to operationalization of the measures proposed.

A central assumption in our discussion is that consumers do organize their product knowledge in memory as HVMs. We describe this HVM as consisting of units of information at different levels of abstraction and of linkages between these units. The linkages differ in strength. Some concepts are only weakly related, others are very strongly associated. In addition, we assume that the consumer stores information on the importance or centrality of each of the knowledge components in his or her life. A hypothetical HVM held by a consumer for the product category "computers." In this exemplary HVM the linkages are characterized by numbers denoting the strength of association. Important values, consequences, and attributes are represented by large and bold characters.

The configuration of these HVMs differs across consumers for the same product. If the MEC theory is to constitute a framework to study involvement then the characteristics of the individual HVM should be indicative of the degree of involvement experienced by the consumer. We propose to use them for the computation of an overall involvement score, that is, a measure of the intensity of involvement that is comparable across consumers and across products. Given this goal, we have to identify useful characteristics.

From the examination of the overall appearance of the HVM two potential indices of involvement emerge:the number of means-end chains elicited and the highest level of abstraction reached. In the exemplary HVM, the number of different chains mentioned amounts to seven. The highest level of abstraction reached is the level of terminal values, represented by the values "happiness" and "self-actualization".

These general characteristics may be helpful in quickly dichotomizing between high and low involvement. However, to capture more refined distinctions on the involvement continuum, more detailed information is required. Such information can be derived from the HVM as well. Typically, means-end chains are described at the levels of values, consequences, and attributes. We may develop indices of involvement at each of these levels independently.

Characteristics available at the value level that can be useful to assess involvement are the number of values mentioned, their centrality or importance to the consumer, and their nature (instrumental vs. terminal). We illustrate these characteristics with the help of the HVM. For this (hypothetical) consumer, computers are linked to four values, two of which are instrumental ("cheerful" and "competence") and two of which are terminal ("happiness" and "self-actualization").

Happiness is a value of major importance to this consumer, self-actualization is perceived as being a moderately important value, and cheerfulness and competence are considered of lesser importance, as is indicated by the character size of these values (the larger the size the more important the value is perceived to be). These three indices may be examined for their contribution to the involvement score at the level of attributes and consequences as well.

It has been emphasized previously that the merit of MEC theory primarily lies in its acknowledgement of the existence of linkages between the different components of product and self-knowledge. A good strategy to learn about involvement may therefore be to devote attention to the structure and organization of the means-end chains included in the HVM and to the interrelations between the different levels of abstraction.

In this respect, possible indices for involvement are the strength of association between adjacent levels of abstraction and the degree of elaboration, this is the number of intervening steps between the starting and the ending level of the chain. In the exemplary HVM of figure the attribute "speed of processing" and the consequence "efficiency" are strongly associated, whereas "safe storage of important files" is only weakly related to "feeling secure". The degree of elaboration of the means-end chains varies within the range of four (e.g., the chain connecting "resolution" to "health") to seven (e.g., the chain "resolution" to "self-actualization").

In sum, the HVM provides us with a whole range of information that may prove useful for the computation of an involvement score. We discuss each of these potential indices and the interdependencies between them in the following.

Implications at the Value Level. From the definition

proposed by Peter and Olson it can be inferred that involvement is related to the attainment of consequences and values. The conclusion derived from the observation that values represent a more abstract type of information (information at the value level subsumes consequences) and that high-involved individuals tend to concentrate information at more abstract levels, is that the attainment of values versus the attainment of consequences reflects higher involvement. The same logic justifies the claim that the abstraction of the highest level reached is proportional with involvement intensity.

By definition then, high-enduring involvement is reflected in the attainment of important values. It is therefore convenient and attractive to start the discussion on the indices of involvement in the means-end chains at the level of values. It is also at this level that the main attention in contemporary literature on the issue is focused.

The formalization of involvement proposed by Ostrom and Brock provided initial guidelines to develop hypotheses on how involvement is reflected at the value level of means-end chains. They define involvement as the product of value centrality and value relatedness, summed over all relevant values associated with a product. This can be expressed symbolically as:

Where n number of values considered relevant by the individual, VR_i =value relatedness, or the perceived relatedness of the product to value i of the value structure of the consumer.

VC_i value centrality, the perceived importance or centrality of value i in the consumers core self.

The Ostrom and Brock model offered three interesting propositions. First, it implied that involvement will be related proportionally to the number of values attained. Second, the higher the perceived relatedness of the product to the value structure the higher the involvement with the product will be.

This component of the model is comparable with the notion of perceived instrumentality advance in the Rosenberg multiattribute attitude model. Third, involvement will increase with increasing importance to the consumer of the values attained.

Suggestions similar to those implied by the Ostrom and Brock conceptualization of involvement have already been introduced in the means-end chain literature. Celsi, Olson, and Walker argued that the centrality or the importance of the values attained has to be taken into account ifone wants to measure involvement using means-end chains. In addition, these authors claimed that the number of means-end chain associations established between product and the values is a potential indicator of involvement as well.

The assumption is that personal relevance increases if the product provides multiple benefits that are linked to several goals or values. In essence, the latter argument is conform to the claim that the more values are reached the higher the personal relevance or involvement level should be.

In sum, high involvement seems to be correlated with

- The number of values reached,
- The importance of those values,
- The perceived instrumentality of the product in attaining desired values.

The index for the number of values considers involvement as a cumulative variable. The more values that can be attained by consuming a product, the more closely it is connected to the self and the higher its personal relevance. Nevertheless the argument that multiple relations between a product and values is not a necessary prerequisite for high involvement and that one linkage with a central value in life suffices is sensible as well.

Therefore it is desirable, conform to the Ostrom and Brock approach, to consider the index of quantity in conjunction with the more qualitative dimension of importance or centrality of values attained. The number of values and their importance are compensatory rather than independent building blocks of involvement. Hence, the involvement score in terms of value-attainment assigned to the HVM does not simply equal 4 but has to be modified by the differential weights or importances associated with the values achieved.

The index of perceived importance is currently a theoretical construct only. It is clear that MEC theory would be more complete and benefit from the measurement of the centrality of values.

The information to be extracted at the value level concerns the nature of the values as well. Drawing on the assumption that the degree of abstraction is proportionally related to involvement, it is tempting to posit that the attainment of terminal values deserves a heavier weight in the involvement computation in comparison with instrumental values.

However, we cannot refute the possibility that this higher rank in weights of terminal versus instrumental values is reflected in the importance attached to the values by the individual. Following Rokeach, terminal values constitute the core self of the individual and hence are considered more central or important than instrumental values, which rather refer to preferred modes of conduct to obtain the desired end states.

The analysis of the value level in itself prevails in contemporary research on involvement from the means-end chain perspective. Another pertinent question not dealt with in the literature yet is concerned with how the value level is attained. Indeed, it is an important contribution of MEC theory to explicate how product characteristics are linked to the value structure of the consumer. Therefore, it seems logical to complete the discussion on involvement by integrating the organization and structure of the entire means-end chain. The configuration of the chain as it climbs up to the value level is instrumental for the operationalization of the concept of "perceived instrumentality" advocated to affect involvement in the Ostrom and Brock conceptualization.

The perceived instrumentality of the product in attaining instrumental and terminal values can be determined by two factors. The intensity of the association between the product and the core self, reflected by the strength of association between the adjacent levels connecting the product attributes to the values, can be taken into account. In addition, the directness of the relation can be important. Directness can be defined in terms of the number of intervening constructs. The lesser intervening steps required to establish a relation with values, the more direct the association is. The latter aspect of means-end chains has been referred to as the degree of elaboration. Both aspects of means-end chains, in terms of involvement, will be discussed extensively in the following.

Implications at the Consequences Level. Information on the intensity of involvement of a consumer toward a product can be communicated at the level of consequences. Analogous features as those discussed at the value level apply here. We may try to assess involvement in terms of the number, the nature, and the importance of the consequences mentioned.

Highly involved consumers have usually acquired much product experience over time. Hence, these consumers are well placed to indicate perceived consequences and benefits associated with product purchase and use. Less involved consumers may simply be aware of a few immediate consequences (e.g., cars offer the benefit of getting you anywhere).

These consequences are expected to reside predominantly at the functional consequence level if the hypothesis of low-personal relevance is to be correct. High-enduring involvement seems to imply a more refined discrimination at both the level of functional and psychosocial consequences. The argument on the compensatory power of the importance of a unit of information versus the quantity is equally applicable here. A more accurate measurement of involvement may be obtained by weighting the consequences for their importance to the consumer. Again, the information to be extracted from the nature of the consequences (functional vs. psychosocial) may be intertwined with the importance scores.

Implications at the Attribute Level. Characteristics at the level of attributes can be integrated to refine the assessment of involvement even more. It has been observed in consumer research that high-involvement knowledge structures are characterized by high dimensionality and articulation. Individuals highly involved with a product class will tend to compare and differentiate between product alternatives on a high number of features or dimensions. Due to such extensive processing of information, knowledge will be acquired that enables fine discriminations within each dimension or between the levels of the features.

In means-end chain terminology this implies that highly involved consumers are capable of identifying a large number of concrete attributes. However, cognitive structures of highly involved individuals are also shown to be of a high level of abstraction. Following the unitization theory of Hayes-Roth increased knowledge implies interpretation and processing of concrete information to form more abstract concepts. Information is recoded into chunks or unitary concepts that represent several associated more concrete components. Hence, knowledge elicitation within the attribute level may start at the level of abstract attributes.

Low-involvement consumers, processing information to a lesser extent, are expected to literally store knowledge at the concrete attribute level and retrieve that when probed for characteristics of the product. Hence, a tentative conclusion may be that a more intense discrimination at the level of abstract attributes is observed under high involvement. On the other hand, more knowledgeable persons do not loose the ability to decompose abstract information into constituent parts if the task demands for it. If data gathering for HVM construction is based on the laddering methodology, the subject may be stimulated to produce relatively concrete knowledge.

Our involved computer user example mentions "speed of processing" and "readability of the screen" as important attributes in his or her computer choice. However, when probed for it, this consumer is able to go down the ladder of abstraction and to associate abstract features to concrete properties, namely megabytes internal memory and high-screen resolution.

In summary, HVMs for high- versus low-involved consumers are characterized by a high level of discrimination at the abstract and at the concrete attribute level if they are asked for it. Insights on involvement are thus obtained from the characteristics of the HVM at the three different levels of abstraction. It might be worthwhile to compare and weigh the value of the information at each of these levels in the final computation of the involvement score. The desirability of this approach can be easily illustrated at the attribute level. The sheer number of attributes elicited can be merely indicative of the knowledge inventory stored in memory and, to the extent that the product studied is noted very complex, a moderate degree of motivation may suffice to acquire full information on the product.

One might argue that the number of means-end chains, advanced as a rudimentary index of involvement in the introduction of our discussion, should be strongly related to the number of units of information mentioned at individual levels of abstraction.

The more refined discriminations at the attribute and consequence level are expected to be reflected in the elicitation of larger number of means-end chains for high-involved consumers. Therefore, using the summary index of number of means-end chains is attractive for its apparent property of being a more convenient and manageable criterion to assess involvement while taking into account the information at the different levels of abstraction. Nevertheless, we deem it worthwhile to conduct analyses at the levels of attributes, consequences, and values separately. First, the number of means-end chains criterion is involved with the quantity of information only and ignores qualitative dimensions, such as importance, as discussed earlier.

Second, this index has the potential of hiding valuable information, for example, a subset of the means-end chains extracted may show only minor differences (e.g., they start at a different attribute). By not taking this into account the final involvement score will probably be overestimated. On the other hand, if multiple chains converge to the same value, it can be inferred that the product is strongly connected to that value.

In this case, the number of chains associated with a product communicates more than the knowledge ability of the consumer and seems to function as a proxy of strength of association, which is assumed indicative of involvement. Hence, ignoring this information will probably result in an underassessment of the intensity of involvement experienced by the subject. The majority of chains elicited end at the value of self-actualization. This value assumes a central role in the establishment of a link between computers and the self and is perhaps the main cause for involvement.

Implications in Terms of Interrelations. We point out at several previous occasions that a discussion of involvement from the means-end chain perspective is incomplete if the interrelations between the different knowledge components are not taken into account. In terms of the connections between the levels we devote attention to two characteristics, namely the strength of the connections and the number of connections made.

Previous research on the nature of cognitive structures under conditions of high involvement suggest that strength of association is a valuable index. Indeed, under high involvement, the cognitive structure is demonstrated to be well organized, which is reflected in strong links between salient components. Under low involvement, product knowledge is rarely experienced consciously in daily situations and is only latently present in memory. The links between the different components will be very weak or even not existent.

With respect to the criterion of strength of associations, two important issues emerge. The first is whether the strength of association between all pairs of adjacent levels of abstraction is of equal importance in determining the involvement level. It is obvious that, for instance, the link between concrete and abstract attributes is of minor value for this purpose. We conjecture that a strategy worthwhile to pursue is to assign a higher weight to the link established between the highest level reached in the part of product knowledge and the lowest level mentioned of the self-knowledge.

Otherwise stated, the strength of association between product knowledge and self-knowledge is assumed to be of major importance. Based on empirical data in previous research, we have observed that the self constitutes a relatively permanent knowledge basis where constituents components are to a high extent linked to each other invariantly. In essence, we have shown for a series of products that once the level of psychosocial consequences is reached subsequent levels of abstraction have the same probability of being activated.

The self-knowledge structure constitutes perhaps for most individuals one information chunk of which relevant parts become activated as a whole. To the extent that this is true, it seems advantageous to focus on the strength of association of product knowledge with self-knowledge. A strong link at this level implies that the product in itself is connected tightly to the self and that its contribution to value attainment is not mainly determined by its (maybe small) probability to evoke psychological consequences closely anchored to the value system.

The relevance of this consideration can be demonstrated in the exemplary HVM. We observe that the link between the functional consequence "safe storage of important files" and the psychosocial consequence "feel secure", which establishes the connection between the product (computers) and the self, is rather weak. On the other hand, the value of happiness ultimately attained in this chain is perceived to be of central importance to the consumer. This communicates high involvement if we apply the criterion discussed before that involvement is determined by values attained weighted for their importance.

However, the influence of this characteristic in the final involvement determination is attenuated if one takes into account that the value is mainly evoked within the information chunk activated by the psychosocial consequence "feeling secure, " which is only weakly associated to product knowledge. Conversely, the strong link between "speed of processing" and "efficiency" relating the product to the value "self-actualization" may reflect that the latter value, rated to be of lesser importance than happiness, is the trued underlying cause for involvement. This conjecture is supported by the fact that multiple means-end chains connect computers to this value. A second issue with respect to the integration of the strength of association into the measurement of involvement is the operationalization of the construct. The MEC theory is currently in need of satisfactory (i.e., valid and reliable) way to measure strength of association.

The degree of elaboration of the means-end chain, or the number of connections established between the starting and ending level of the chain, is thought to be another correlate of involvement.

High-involvement cognitive structures are characterized by a clear organization that is reflected by the presence of closely associated salient components. Preliminary evidence for this proposition in terms of means-end chain structures comes from our empirical work on the think-feel product typology. In this study we demonstrated that under high-involvement conditions, the differences between both types of products was accentuated. "Think" products were mainly described by concrete attributes, functional consequences and values, whereas "feel" products were identified at the level of abstract attributes, psychosocial consequences, and values. The description obtained fit perfectly with prior expectations on the salient constituent components of the knowledge structure derived from theory. Apparently, high involvement resulted in the disregard of less important or central knowledge items. Means-end chains under high involvement proved to be shorter.

An alternative perspective that is congruent with the proposition of less elaboration under high involvement is the theory of unitization or chunking. More involved consumers are in general more knowledgeable and tend to combine concrete information into abstract concepts, hence reducing the total quantity of knowledge components. In the illustrative HVM of Fig. 16.1 the link between the components "speed of processing" and "efficiency" subsumes the knowledge that a high-processing speed results in short waiting times implying that more work can be done in the same amount of time leading to the perception of increased efficiency.

Low-involvement consumers, on the other hand, have less

organized cognitive structures. They cannot discriminate very accurately between salient and less salient aspects of knowledge. In addition, the structure implied by the means-end chain formalization is oftentimes not, or only latently present. This requires low-involvement consumers to construct and to carefully climb up the ladder taking all consecutive steps.

Hence, we can expect more elaborated means-end chains for low-involvement consumers relative to the number of levels mentioned. The possibility remains that in terms of total number of steps means-end chains for high-involved individuals are more elaborated than those of low-involved consumers due to their propensity of climbing higher up the levels of the self-knowledge part.

However, it must be noted that the final outcome may be contingent on task requirements. Conover showed that subjects do not necessarily reveal their ability to generalize from more concrete elements of knowledge. If stimulated by the task, they will provide detailed and concrete information. For means-end chains this implies that highly involved individuals may elicit very detailed knowledge structures containing information at each level of abstraction. This may create confusion with the constructed means-end chains of the low involved.

Means-End Chains and Situational Involvement

For clarity of exposition we have deliberately excluded the situational facet of involvement in the previous discussion. If we do, however, introduce situational involvement in the analysis, the implications of involvement for the structure of means-end chains outlined previously may become less relevant and certainly more complex. This is due to the fact that situational involvement in contrast with enduring involvement, is not necessarily related to familiarity and expertise.

Hence, the premises advanced on the basis of the observed relation between (enduring) involvement and the organization of product knowledge in memory are valid to a lesser extent only. Statements with respect to, for example, strength of associations between links and discrimination at the consequences and attribute levels will have to be formulated with more prudence.

It can be argued however that the distinction between situational and enduring involvement is relevant and interesting at the theoretical level only. For managerial purposes and marketing-strategy development it suffices to know how and when the product is involving to the consumer. Analogously, in terms of behaviour the consumer is expected to engage in information search, processing and in complex decision making when there is involvement, whether situation or enduring.

Notwithst and ing this observation, we consider it worthwhile to elaborate on the distinction enduring versus situational involvement because of its relevance to the validity of means-end chains. A criticism often advanced is that the elicitation of chains attaining the value level is an artifact of the methodology applied (most commonly laddering). Such criticisms may derive from equating involvement with enduring involvement and not acknowledging the propensity of means-end chains to reveal situational involvement. Indeed, the nature of the knowledge extraction process of the means-end chain approach encourages the elicitation of situation-dependent information.

The techniques discussed by Gutman and Reynolds to help the individual up the ladder of abstraction explicitly refer to the situational context. Hence, means-end chains of products scoring very low on the traditional involvement scales measuring enduring involvement may attain the value level, which is commonly interpreted as indicating (at least partially) involvement. If the MEC theory is to benefit from its position of providing researchers with a unique framework to study situational involve, it is useful to point out how situational involvement is reflected in the characteristics of means-end chains. We identify some areas that deserve further research to establish differences between enduring an situational involvement.

Situational involvement implies a temporal activation of personally relevant knowledge. The link between product knowledge and the core self becomes salient in particular situational settings only and is therefore assumed to be transient in memory.

If the knowledge required to connect products to the value structure is not or only latently present in memory, a high degree of construction will take place. The subject will have to climb carefully up the ladder of abstraction in order to produce the information required. Therefore, a tentative hypothesis is that means-end chains reflecting situational involvement will be very elaborated.

A second structural difference with the means-end chains of enduringly involved subjects is expected to occur at the levels of product knowledge. In general, consumers will store little knowledge on products such as light bulbs, paper clips, or freezers that are mainly situationally involving. This lack of detailed information and familiarity should be reflected by less discrimination at the levels of attributes and consequences. Once the level of psychosocial consequences is attained, few differences are expected to emerge between means-end chains of situationally and enduringly involved consumers. It has been argued before that the self-knowledge constitutes a fairly permanent chunk of information in memory. Hence, whether activated by the situational aspects or by the product characteristics themselves, the composition of the elicited self-structure will be fairly similar.

In addition, distinctions between enduring and situational involvement in terms of the content of the means-end chains may be searched for. We have scrutinized a wide range of chains for both types of involvement and have the impression that two opposite principles drive the relation between product and self.

If a product is involving on an enduring basis the usage, possession or presence of the product contributes actively to the achievement of a value. This will be reflected in the chain by relations of the form "if, then". On the other hand, if involvement with the product originates from situational aspects, then it seems more appropriate to state that the absence or deficiencies in the product are perceived as reducing the extent in which a value is achieved. The link between product and self is established via an "if not, then" logic or reasoning. An illustrative example may clarify this.

When probed for the product category "hi-fi's", in general more of the high-enduring involvement nature, the subject may construct the following chain:

Attribute: a good stereo sound.'!

Consequence: more pleasant to listen to records of classical music.'!

Value: higher enjoyment in life.

Hence, a characteristic of the product is perceived as being linked directly and actively to the value system. If the hi-fi has a good stereo sound, then the value "enjoyment in life" is achieved to a higher extent.

If, on the other hand, probed for such categories as "light bulbs" typically the means-end chains is formulated by stressing potential negative consequences.

Attribute: (in)sufficient intensity of light.'!

Consequence: (not) able to read.'!

Consequence: (not) satisfied.'!

Value: (no) enjoyment of life.

The chain reflects that a badly performing light bulb ultimately reduces one's enjoyment in life.

The previous statement may overgeneralize: They nevertheless provide useful guidelines for further research on the issue. For example, we expect that high-situational versus high-enduring involvement is reflected by a different focus on benefits sought expressed at the level of consequences in means-end chains, namelythe avoidance of negative consequences and the achievement of positive consequences, respectively.

In all, the discussion on situational involvement explicates once more the need to broaden the conceptualization of involvement from the means-end chain perspective beyond value attainment. In the preceding sections an extended perspective to study involvement is proposed. It was argued that one benefits from examining the pattern of characteristics of the HVM as an integrated whole. The features discussed are oftentimes compensatory rather than independent indicators of involvement.

For example, a HVM described by high-involvement characteristics, such as the attainment of three important values and a strong discrimination at the consequence and attribute level, may still point to moderately or low-felt involvement if the links established between the product knowledge and the self-knowledge are weak.Besides structural principles, content-related aspects of the HVM may be incorporated in the analysis of involvement. This may be of particular interest if the goal is to distinguish between enduring and situational involvement. At present, the exact implications for the HVM of involvement that is primarily situationally induced are less clear.

FUTURE RESEARCH DIRECTIONS

The previous discussion outlines several subjects and directions for future research on the relation between involvement and means-end chains and for the operationalization and measurement of involvement from this perspective.A first avenue to pursue is to examine the scope of the potential indices of involvement identified. Do these characteristics of the HVM independently point to involvement? The major topics of discussion can be formulated a research questions to be investigated empirically:

- Is involvement positively related to the degree of abstraction of the highest level reached in the means-end chains?
- Can we establish a positive relation between involvement and the number of values elicited? Is a significant increase in the accuracy of the assessment of involvement obtained when the importance of values is incorporated as a weighting coefficient?
- Does discrimination at the level of consequences reflect high involvement? Is it desirable to assign more weight to variance observed at the psychosocial

consequence level in the final involvement computation?

- Is involvement reflected by the elicitation of large number of attributes and, if so, do abstract or concrete attributes constitute the main level of concern to determine the intensity of involvement?
- How can the strength of association between adjacent levels be integrated in the involvement computation? Is it meaningful to pursue the strategy of devoting major attention to the link between product and self-knowledge?
- Does the degree of elaboration of the means-end chains communicate how involved one is and, if so, is involvement to be inferred from extensive elaboration or rather from chunking of information? To what extent is this contingent on exogenous and contextual factors?
- To what extent does content analysis contribute to a better assessment of the level of involvement? Should requirements for involvement be met at the consequence level, or at the value and attribute level as well?

In addition to researching each of these issues in itself, there is a need to examine how these indicators can be integrated into a single overall involvement score. Efforts may be devoted to determining the contribution of each index to the involvement score and to identifying an indicator or combination of indicators that constitutes the best proxy for the full-picture assessment of involvement.

Questions pertaining to the manageability and the desirability of such a detailed account of involvement for practical applications may be dealt with. If the computation of the involvement score turns out to be complex and time consuming or if a large proportion of its variance is explained by a few characteristics of the HVM, it is interesting to identify circumstances that justify the effort required to obtain such an accurate assessment of involvement.

These research questions can apply both to enduring and

situational involvement. A comparative analysis of findings in the two domains will shed light on the distinction between situational and enduring involvement in terms of the hierarchical value map configuration. Further, the possibility of integrating the knowledge that situational rather than enduring involvement is concerned into the overall measure, possibly computed by assigning different weights to both types, can be examined.

Although our concern is primarily oriented toward presenting ideas for using the means-end chains perspective to study involvement at the conceptual level, we conclude this section by pointing to a number of measurement issues.

At the measurement level, attention can be directed toward examining whether laddering, the most commonly advocated instrument to measure means-end chains, is indeed a satisfactory technique to gather data for the purpose of involvement analysis. In this respect, it is worth noting that probing the consumer to actively think about the reasons why a particular product is purchased or used probably increase the level of felt involvement.

Moreover, it is inherent to the nature of laddering to induce situational involvement. Therefore, laddering is perhaps a less suitable technique to identify low-enduring involvement; but then again, it was argued earlier that this is not where the true strength of the means-end chain paradigm for involvement determination lies.

Research efforts can also be devoted to issues of operationalization of constructs advances as indices of involvement in the prior discussion. The measurement of the perceived importance of value s and consequences to the consumer and of the strength of association of linkages deserves particular attention.

Useful input on the measurement of the centrality of values and consequences can be derived from the literature. The methods suggested imply reliance on direct and subjective assessment. A possible avenue to proceed could be to let the individual rank order or rate the values attained. This approach is commonly employed in value research at the aggregate level. Alternatively, the subject may be demand ed to rate the entire Rokeach value inventory in terms of perceived importance in his or her own life.

The latter method may be slightly superior in terms of reliability as the subject is offered the opportunity to weigh against one another central values in life. If a consumer associates "happiness" and "true friendship" with a product category, he or she may find it hard to differentiate between the importance of both values.

However, in the context of the entire range of values, he or she may perceive that "happiness" and "friendship" are less important than "taking care of the family" and more central than "social recognition" or "a comfortable life". These observations may help to establish a more reliable importance judgement of the values of interest.

The reliability and validity assessment of measures proposed for importance should be a prime concern given the (presumed) influential role of the construct in involvement determination. Secondly, there is a need for an adequate and reliable measure of association strength. We outline three possible avenues to pursue. The first is to rely on the memory implications of high- versus low-involvement cognitive structures and to utilize latency times in responses as a proxy for association strength.

This measurement approach has the drawback of being very obtrusive and may be detrimental to the sense of comfort of the subject and the spontaneity of the interview. An alternative procedure is to count the frequency with which a particular link is mentioned. The more often the link is referred to during the interview, the higher the strength of association is perceived to be.

A potential criticism on this approach is that frequency of mention may originate from halo-effects. To the extent that the subject has learned that links must be established between consecutive levels of abstraction, he or she may for convenience relate a lower level to the same more abstract level. This is particularly likely to occur between functional consequences and more abstract levels. Note however that frequency of occurrence of a link between two elements is a main variable in the construction of the HVM at the aggregate level and denotes strength of association there.

A third alternative is to demand for subjective estimates of the strength of association between a sequence of components mentioned by the individual. Such direct assessment is best obtained immediately after the elicitation of the means-end chains. There is a real danger that this procedure seriously interrupts the progress of the knowledge extraction.

In essence, creativity will have to be directed toward an operationalization of strength of association that does not impede the elicitation of means-end chains while being valid and reliable.

ADVERTISING AS A BUSINESS ACTIVITY

Ultimate consumers and business purchasers are continually exposed to advertising in one form or another. Whatever the form, the advertiser's message generally appears as a simple presentation. Obscured behind the scenes, however, are a score of important business decisions that have a bearing upon the impact made on the buyer. In many companies, decisions relating to the nature of the role of advertising in the total marketing effort are a crucial aspect of marketing strategy.

Various types of advertising must be considered for different specific purposes; ideas are conceived and advertisements are prepared as a result of careful plans made well in advance of publication; media are selected to convey the prepared message to the prospective recipients; and, for some or all of these decisions, a special institution known as the advertising agency is often employed.

TYPES OF ADVERTISING

The many types of advertising may be classified in a number of ways. Furthermore, the various classes commonly recognized are not mutually exclusive but are often different ways of looking at the same thing. For example, advertising may be classified as *institutional* or *product,* depending upon whether it is aimed primarily at establishing a favorable attitude toward the advertiser or at the development of demand for a given product.

It may be classified, on the basis of the advertiser's status, into *manufacturers', wholesalers', retailers', or cooperative* advertising. Again, advertising may be classified as *consumer, trade, professional,* or *industrial,* in terms of the audience to which it is directed. It may also be classified on the basis of the principal appeal, that is; whether the purpose of such an appeal is to arouse and direct demand toward a specific product or to a given general class of products.

ADVERTISING IN THE MARKETING MIX

When a business firm has identified the market or market segment to which it wishes to make its strongest appeal, it must decide how much of its total promotional effort shall be allocated to various different elements of marketing strategy that may induce prospective customers to buy.

The term *marketing mix* is commonly used to denote the amount of *relative emphasis* placed upon different components of a firm's marketing programme.

Possible components of such a programme for many companies would include advertising, personal selling, pricing, relationships with other institutions in distribution channels, physical availability of product, after sale service, special sales promotional activities, financing of customers, and so on.

Obviously, a firm with limited resources cannot allocate an unusually large *share* of its total marketing effort (funds) to some one component of a marketing mix without making some sacrifice or compromise about the magnitude of the expected contribution of other actual or possible components of the mix.A firm's ability or willingness to devote a substantial share of its marketing mix to advertising is influenced by two sets of factors—one relating to the characteristics of the goods or services being marketed and the other to the characteristics of advertising as they pertain to the particular firm.

FACTORS RELATING TO PRODUCT

Product attributes generally accepted as favorable to heavy emphasis upon advertising in the marketing mix may be listed as follows:

Favorable Primary Demand Situation

Advertising is likely to be effective when there is a substantial opportunity to expand the total market for a product, as illustrated by household air conditioning, motor boats, and hearing-aid devices.

Significant Product Differentiation

When a product offers benefits not readily available from close substitutes, advertising is likely to be especially productive. Differentiation may exist in the physical attributes of a product (e.g., special formula or materials) or in its application or use (e.g., shoe polish packaged for ease of application without getting one's hand s or clothes soiled), or in ease of brand ing (e.g., Sunkist citrus products) or may take other tangible or intangible forms.

Hidden Values

Advertising appeals based upon user satisfaction are often effective to a high degree when the product has some values not readily apparent to a prospective user, as in the case of many mechanical devices and certain types of drugs and medicines.

Emotional basis for Buying

When the purchaser's motives for buying have a strong emotional basis, as illustrated by many health and personal appearance products, advertising can be a strong influence in shifting consumer preferences or in getting new potential users to try a product.

FACTORS RELATING TO ADVERTISING

Certain characteristics of advertising as one form of promotional effort either encourage or discourage heavy emphasis on it, depending upon the situation of the marketing organization. These are as follows:

Nature of Advertising Expenditures

Large-scale advertising requires substantial outlays for current expense. Unlike investments made in plant or store equipment, advertising costs cannot ordinarily be financed through outside sources and amortized over a period of time. Thus, large-scale advertising tends to be limited to big firms with favorable working capital positions.

Low Selectivity

The more limited a firm's distribution or the thinner its market in terms of number of potential customers, the more difficult it is to utilize media in the mass communication field. Many firms encounter serious difficulty in the selection of media which reach an audience that corresponds well with the intended market, either geographically or in terms of customer characteristics.

Inflexibility Through time

Major advertising campaigns involve planning that must take place long in advance of the execution of the advertising programme. This is especially true of network television, magazines, and national campaigns in newspapers. Thus, the firm that must stand ready to adjust quickly to changing market conditions finds that the potential contribution of advertising to its total marketing effort is limited.

ADVERTISING MEDIA

The vehicle or carrier through which an advertising message is conveyed to its intended audience is known as an advertising medium. The prominence of newspapers is explained by the fact that the bulk of local retail store advertising is carried in this medium. Each of the major classes or types of media may be further subdivided; magazines, for example, can be divided into weeklies and monthlies, or into men's, women's, children's, home or "shelter, " general, and so on. From the stand point of the advertiser, the different types of media may be complementary or competitive. Each type has its value, is favored under given conditions, and is subject to certain limitations. Several types are often used simultaneously in well-rounded advertising campaigns, each supplementing the others.

The major classes of media have adjusted dynamically to changing times and each one, through innovation, has become somewhat more readily substitutable for the other. This is illustrated by the increasing availability of high-quality colour illustrations in newspapers; ability of advertisers to buy pages in split-run, regional issues of certain leading magazines; magazine concept of network broadcast media, whereby the high cost of sponsoring programs is shared by a variety of advertisers; and the growth of colour broadcasting in television.

PRODUCT ADVERTISING BY MANUFACTURERS

While the details of manufacturers' advertising programs vary with the kind of product and character of the company, a common function is that of *building acceptance or preference for the advertised product,* and a common pattern of managerial decisions is followed.

First, the advertiser must be certain that the product to be promoted actually satisfies some basic need; otherwise, no amount of advertising can win acceptance for the product. Second, it is necessary to discover the uses or applications of the product, and confine the advertised uses to reasonable ones that satisfy important common needs.

Third is the determination of distinctive characteristics of the product to be used as selling appeals. For advertising to be successful over a period of time, these should be real and recognizable distinctions as viewed from the customer's and not the seller's stand point. Most manufacturers' advertising is characterized by an attempt to give the product a personality or identity which will make it stand out competitively. This requires close coordination between the planning of advertising and package or label design.

Other major management problems relate to the determination of the market for the product, whether general or highly restricted to a segment of the total market; the selection of media which will reach the consumers of the product and possibly also the trade; and the determination of an advertising appropriation that will be adequate to accomplish the objective of the programme.

The appropriation is likely to be large per unit of product if an item is in the introductory stage of development and, hence, is not well known to consumers or distributors; it is likely to be large in total amount, but small per unit of product, if the item is in the competitive stage and similar products are being mass-produced and mass-distributed by a number of companies.

MERCHANDISE ADVERTISING BY RETAILERS

Retailers' Merchandise advertising differs from that of manufacturers' in objective. Whereas the manufacturer usually seeks to build acceptance or preference for his brand of product, the retailer is concerned primarily with *building good will or patronage for his particular store.* Except where exclusive agencies are common, as in the automobile field, retailers' advertisements are characterized more by variety and assortments of Merchandise rather than by individual items. Stress is placed upon patronage motives such as price, selection, location of stores, or services.

In retail advertising there is also more of an attempt *to provoke immediate buying reaction* than is the case with manufacturers' advertising where a long programme may be planned to build or sustain consumer acceptance or preference.

This accounts for very marked concentrations of retail advertising at times when consumer buying urges are most active, as evidenced by heavy grocery advertising on Wednesdays or Thursdays in anticipation of week-end shopping, or unusual quantities of department store advertising at Christmas, Easter, school-opening time, and on other occasions when consumers are most likely to respond to specific advertising appeals.

COOPERATIVE ADVERTISING

Much advertising involves the cooperative participation of a number of individual firms. Such advertising is designated as *horizontal cooperative* when the participants are functionally similar and operate on the same level of distribution. This type is particularly common where the objective is to increase primary demand for a type of product or to influence favorably public attitudes toward an industry.

Illustrative are advertisements by agricultural marketing cooperatives, the cost of which is supported by charges on products marketed by members and by some trade associations. When the participants are organizations on different levels of a distribution channel, the activity is known as *vertical cooperative* advertising.

It exists in a variety of forms including advertisements by manufacturers in which distributors or dealers are listed by name, and retailer advertisements featuring a manufacturer's product, for which an allowance is granted by the manufacturer to reimburse the dealer for some part or perhaps all of the cost of advertising or promoting the manufacturer's product.

The practice of granting advertising allowances to distributors or dealers is especially common among manufacturers utilizing a selective distribution policy, particularly in certain lines of appliances, household equipment, tires, paint, shoes, and men's and women's clothing. It is also prevalent in certain convenience goods lines, notably grocery products, cosmetics and toilet goods.

In the grocery trade, for example, some 75 to 95 per cent of corporate chains, wholesaler sponsored voluntary chains, and retailer cooperative groups report the frequent use of advertising allowances for products in the following groups: canned foods, cooking and salad oils, crackers and cookies, frozen foods, lard and shortening, macaroni products, paper products, soaps and detergents, starches and bleaches, and tea. Many manufacturers grant allowances to finance advertising of their products by dealers in order to guide consumers to local sources of supply, to provide a point-of-purchase tie-in with national advertising, to stimulate the cooperation of dealers, to help gain additional dealers, and to obtain a sort of automatic control over advertising expenditures, inasmuch as advertising allowances are commonly granted to dealers in direct relation to their volume of purchases during specified time periods.

On the other hand, numerous manufacturers abhor cooperative advertising allowances, believing that such allowances provide a drain on their national advertising budget, reduce the quality of copy and layout when advertisements are prepared by dealers, present many nuisance problems relating to bookkeeping and control and in checking of dealer performance in relation to an advertising agreement, and cause many legal complications since under the Robinson-Patman Act, it is required that advertising allowances or special promotional services, when granted to some dealers, must be made available to all on proportionally equal terms.

Regardless of an individual manufacturer's viewpoint, it is difficult for him to avoid the granting of advertising allowances when this is a common competitive practice. From a broader point of view, the practice of granting advertising allowances has a somewhat deleterious effect upon retail advertising, inasmuch as the content of the advertising of many retail stores is determined more by the availability of advertising allowances than by careful judgments about what would constitute timely and interesting buying information for the consumer.

THE ADVERTISING AGENCY

The growth of advertising has been associated with the development of a specialized type of institution known as the advertising agency. The first advertising agents, about the middle of the nineteenth century, were space brokers for media. At that time newspaper editors were anxious to obtain advertising revenue but had no contacts with out-of-town advertisers. The first agents recognized this situation as an opportunity for rendering an economic service.

They purchased or contracted for "white space" from media and contacted advertisers in distant areas, selling the space in units suited to the requirements of advertisers. Gradually the agents began to give advice and assistance to advertisers who were seeking specialized counsel in the preparation of their copy. In time the agents developed new methods and techniques and offered new services. Eventually the advertisers rather than the media became the clients of the agents.

Today the advertising agency is a service organization composed of advertising specialists, and it shares the responsibility for advertising activities with the advertising departments of clients. It is believed that advertising agencies now assist in the creation and direction of more than 90 per cent of all national advertising, more than one-half of sectional advertising, and a considerable amount of local advertising. Between 1948 and 1958 the number of advertising agency establishments increased from 3, 279 to 7, 720. A large per cent of total agency business, however, is accounted for by a limited number of large agencies, most of which are located in New York City.

Services of Agencies

The principal services of modern advertising agencies consist of planning, preparation, and placement of advertising. Planning requires a thorough knowledge of markets, products, distribution channels, and marketing policies. This often involves marketing research, which is carried on by or for the agency. Preparation includes developing a central idea or theme, production of advertisements, production or purchase of art work and printing, hiring radio and television talent and supervising or producing entertainment programs, and preparing broadcast media commercials.

Placement involves selection of media; preparation of advertising schedules; purchase of broadcast time or publication space; shipment of plates, copy, and instructions to media; preparation and mailing of direct advertising; and checking publications or stations to insure that advertisements were run or broadcast properly. Some of the larger agencies also provide a marketing counseling service and go so far as to advise a client on broad management policies for his business. They may assist in product development and package design; secure patents and copyrights; prepare point-of-sale promotional aids for the client's sales force; carry on public relations and publicity work; arrange and plan demonstrations and contests; and prepare training material for dealers' and jobbers' salesmen. In fact, there is almost no type of promotional service which is not provided at least by some agencies.

Why Agencies Are Used

Even the largest advertisers who maintain elaborate advertising departments find that there are several good reasons for using advertising agencies. First, the agency is independent of the advertiser and has an outside objective viewpoint which it can bring to bear on important decisions. Second, the agency has broad experience which results from its work with a number of clients having different products, selling in various markets, using various channels of distribution, and employing numerous types of media.

Third, it must do a satisfactory job in order to hold the account. It is constantly alert to opportunities because it realizes that the advertiser can change agencies easily. If an advertiser developed an advertising department capable of performing all agency services, such a department would be part of the organization and could not be disposed of easily. Fourth, the agency may spread the cost of certain technical services over a number of accounts.

The payroll costs of advertising production specialists and marketing research experts is less than it would be if each advertiser had a staff comparable in skills to that of the agency. A fifth important reason is that all or a large part of the agency's service may not cost the advertiser anything. This is true because agencies obtain a substantial part of their revenue from media commissions which are not available to advertisers who buy space or time direct from media.

Agency Compensation

Advertising agency compensation is largely a carryover from the early days when the principal function of an agency was selling space for media. Most agencies still obtain the greater part of their remuneration from the media, based upon the amount of space or time purchased for clients. The agency purchases publication space or broadcast time direct from the media. With only minor exceptions, it receives a discount usually amounting to 15 per cent of the list price of the space or time purchased.

For example, if the cost of a full page of space in a magazine is listed at $10, 000, the recognized agency is billed for $10, 000 less a 15 per cent discount, or $8, 500. The agency bills its clients for a space cost of $10, 000 and retains the $1, 500 to defray the expense of preparing the copy, placing, and checking the advertisement.

If the advertiser did not use the agency, under existing media price and discount policies, it would probably pay the magazine the full price of $10, 000 and would, furthermore, have to incur the expenses of preparing and placing the advertisement.

Agency commissions from media are often supplemented by service fees paid by clients. The commission is intended to cover the service cost of preparing and placing advertising. It does not provide payment for extensive marketing research work, elaborate art work or engravings prepared outside the agency, talent for radio or television entertainment, preparation of special signs or dealer-helps, or other special services rendered or procured by the agency for the client. For such services it is customary for the agency to levy special charges based on the cost of the services plus some percentage fee agreed upon at the time the relationship is established.

The agency method of commission compensation has often been criticized as illogical, inasmuch as the services of advertising agents are rendered primarily to advertisers rather than to media which pay the commissions. It has also been criticized because the traditional pattern of commission payments became rigidly institutionalized.

Various trade associations of advertising agencies and of advertising media have established criteria to be met by business firms in order for them to be recognized as accredited agencies entitled to receive such commissions. Also, it has been considered an unethical trade practice for agencies to split media commissions or to rebate any part of them to advertiser clients.

The whole agency compensation pattern was called into question in the 1950's when the Department of Justice brought proceedings against various such associations under the Sherman Antitrust Act. Early in 1956 a leading association of advertising agencies and several media associations entered into consent decrees which, among other things, prohibited practices or agreements "fixing, establishing or stabilizing agency commissions or attempting to do so" or "requiring, urging or advising any advertising agency to refrain from rebating or splitting agency commissions. These consent decrees forced a re-examination of the whole pattern of agency compensation and brought forth some experimental attempts between agencies and clients for new approaches to compensation. On the whole, however, the commission basis for agency compensation continues to be the dominant arrangement.

Agency commissions from media have not been an important factor in local or retail advertising. Newspapers and radio and television stations usually have direct contact with local advertisers. Partly because of the news value of local advertisements and partly because the large portion of revenue is obtained locally, newspapers and other local media usually have lower space or time rates for local than for non-local advertisers. Agency discounts do not apply to these lower local rates. This has restricted the use of advertising agencies in local advertising, because they must make a specific charge for the total value of the service rendered to local clients.

ECONOMIC AND SOCIAL ASPECTS OF ADVERTISING

In the preceding pages advertising has been discussed as

an important activity, assumed to be essential to the preponderant majority of business concerns. The broader economic and social aspects of advertising are, however, a subject of considerable controversy. The negative aspects of advertising, or those facets of it which are most readily criticized or scorned, are readily apparent and widely publicized. On the other hand, the contributions and services of advertising are not well understood, even by many marketing and advertising executives.

An appraisal of the economic, social, and public policy implications of advertising is essential for purposes of a functional analysis of marketing, both from a broad or overall viewpoint as well as from the stand point of marketing management, inasmuch as those who plan and carry out advertising programs can do so more effectively by understanding advertising as a part of the social scene.

CONTRIBUTIONS AND SERVICES OF ADVERTISING

The place of advertising in our life is better understood if certain facts relating to the service of advertising to society as a whole are examined objectively. It was suggested that advertising did not become important until large-scale production made certain demand -creation activities necessary. Successful advertising campaigns have in turn *accelerated the movement toward large-scale production* by many manufacturers. As a rule, increase in the scale of form utility production is accompanied by decreasing costs per unit of output.

There are hundreds of examples of reduction in the total cost of production and distribution through successful advertising. It is equally true that advertising and a liberal use of personal selling efforts have been made necessary in order to find a large market in which to sell the increased output resulting from quantity-production methods. *Thus advertising is both a cause and effect of large-scale activity,* with emphasis probably on the latter. In either case, the result is the same. Decreased cost of manufacturing in many cases offsets wholly or in part the cost of demand -creation activities.

Another important service of advertising lies in its *beneficial effect on the standard of living.* One measure of a nation's material progress is a cross-section of the wants of the common people. In other words, advancing civilization is accompanied by increases in the quantity and variety of wants and the means of satisfying them. Advertising has done much to encourage better homes, architecturally, mechanically, and functionally.

Dozens of articles are in use in the average home of today as the result of demand stimulation by advertising. Vacuum sweepers, electric refrigerators, mechanical dishwashers, and modern floor and wall coverings are illustrations. Many advertised articles help to make the modern diet more nutritious, interesting, and enjoyable than formerly.

Since advertising facilitates the profitable exploration and development of markets for new or improved products and uses, *it has tended greatly to encourage innovation and technology.* There is no doubt but that much of the technological progress in the electronic, chemical, and automotive fields recorded in modern times can be attributed to the development of potential demands for the products and uses thus made possible.

The *educational effect of advertising* is likewise important, both directly and indirectly. It is probable that advertisements of dental creams have done more to preserve the teeth of the nation than has the personal advice of thousands of dentists. Correspondence courses which have been of great aid to many people are made possible largely because of advertising. Advertising, insofar as it is truthful, educates by providing information about hundreds of articles which might be otherwise unknown or unaccepted by the average buyer.

The *indirect effect of advertising upon education* is undoubtedly even more potent. Most newspapers or magazines could not be sold at prices that would make them accessible to the masses of our people in the absence of advertising which largely subsidizes them. About two-thirds to three-fourths of the average income of newspapers and magazines comes from advertising. Most radio and television programs would be virtually impossible without sponsorship by advertisers.

Constructive advertising *lessens to a great degree the necessity for buying ability.* In the days of the more simple life it was possible for buyers to be judges of the quality of the articles they purchased, since these were comparatively few in number.

It is now almost impossible for the average buyer to judge with any certainty the quality of the hundreds of articles he buys. But fortunately the use of brands, which is an essential for most advertising, makes it possible to rely on the standard quality of such Merchandise, and identification enables one to avoid repurchase of unsatisfactory brands.

CRITICISMS OF ADVERTISING

Certain considerations tend in part, at least, to offset the social value of the services of advertising. Many criticisms have been made, and some of these are partially sound. Most of the criticisms are, however, at least partly the result of misunderstanding as shown by the following appraisal of some of the most commonly voiced and perhaps also the most important of these criticisms.

"Too Costly." A common criticism is that the cost of advertising is too high and that such high cost adds to the price of the advertised product. This criticism grows out of an inherent characteristic of advertising as an instrument of mass communication, necessitating expenditures of large amounts of money.

It is rather common knowledge, for example, that certain large advertisers spend millions of dollars annually for advertising, that advertising pages in popular magazines are priced in tens of thousands of dollars, and that the cost of producing and broadcasting certain individual television programs may run into hundreds of thousands of dollars. Such amounts appear staggering to the person of ordinary means who forgets that expenditures for advertising are significant only when expressed in relation to some meaningful standard of comparison.

One way of judging the magnitude of advertising expenditures is in relation to total personal consumption expenditures. Advertising expenditures in 1960 amounted to $11.6 billion, but this was only 3.5 per cent of all consumer expenditures for goods and services. Over a long period of years, advertising costs of about 3 per cent to 4 per cent of consumption expenditures have been typical.

This basis of comparison, however, overstates the relative importance of advertising costs. Much advertising is devoted to industrial goods and services and some to goods sold primarily to government. It is, therefore, more meaningful to compare the costs of advertising to the gross national product. Over a period of years, this basis reveals that advertising costs of about 2 per cent are the common situation. Again, advertising cost, when related to the total volume of business transacted, is less than 1 percent.

Another important approach to understanding advertising costs is in terms of units of product. In the case of cigarettes, where all important brands are highly advertised, the great amounts expended for advertising shrink into insignificance when compared to the tremendous number of units of product sold, resulting in costs of only a fraction of a cent per package.

Experience varies from one industry to another. Advertising costs for certain nationally promoted brands of soap, cosmetics, and drugs amount to a significant component of final retail value. These are exceptional examples, however, and the cost of advertising for most companies is quite low when measured per unit of product sold or in relation to total sales volume involved.

The costs of advertising can also be compared with costs incurred for personal selling effort. Advertising expenses of most retail stores are only about 1 or 2 per cent of sales volume, the most notable exceptions being department stores, departmentized specialty stores, and furniture stores where advertising costs often amount to as much as 3 to 5 per cent of sales. In practically all cases this is substantially less than the expense of personal selling incurred by the same stores.

Among manufacturers, advertising costs of about 1 to 3 per cent of sales volume are common experience. While there are some exceptions to such low advertising costs, as explained in the preceding paragraph, the cost of advertising is usually low in comparison to the expense of maintaining a personal selling organization in the field.

If less were spent for advertising, it would be necessary for companies to exert additional personal selling effort in order to maintain their position, and *total selling costs* would undoubtedly be considerably higher. The experience of the business community has been that advertising, when properly performed, is a *relatively* inexpensive form of selling effort and that it makes personal selling more efficient, since it paves the way for the salesman.

In the last analysis, the question of how much is spent for advertising is not particularly significant. It is much more important to inquire about *how much we get for what we spend.* A student of the subject should be more interested in the *values that are added by advertising* in relation to expenditures therefore than in costs.

Many critics of advertising have blissfully assumed as a criterion of pure or perfect competition the existence of a state of complete and accurate knowledge, shared equally by all buyers and sellers in the market. At the same time, such critics often fail to state or appreciate that the task of providing such an ideal state of knowledge would involve social costs perhaps hundreds or thousands of times total annual expenditures for advertising if, indeed, it could ever be achieved at all.

Emphasizes Minor Differences

Another criticism is that advertising has tended to develop and emphasize minor differences in the construction or formulae of advertised goods in order to have "something to advertise." It is much easier to call forth additional effective demand for a product if it is new or appears to be so than when it is just another brand of the same general type as dozens already on the market.

For example, it is probably true that there are many brands of advertised toothpaste which are not essentially different and which perform the same functions as previously established brands. It has, therefore, been necessary to emphasize minor chemical differences or new features in packages which are not always worth while. The effect of this is, in part, to reduce the scale of operations of the factories already producing toothpaste with the possibility of increased production costs. To the extent that this is true, the featuring of new brands, not essentially better than those already on the market, may be economically and consequently socially unjustifiable.

But advertising of new brands does not necessarily divert demand from older manufacturers. In many cases additional advertising has the effect of increasing the total consumption of the article under consideration. This additional consumption may or may not occur at the expense of other articles formerly purchased. When a new make of air-conditioning equipment is placed on the market, its advertising may increase somewhat the total sale of such equipment. In part it will divert to the new manufacturer sales which might otherwise have gone to existing suppliers. The effect may be to divert funds to the purchase of air-conditioning equipment which might have gone for clothing, alcoholic beverages, entertainment, insurance, or to savings accounts. In such a case, the social service of advertising must be judged by the relative social values of the alternative purchases.

Planned Obsolescence

A somewhat related criticism is that advertising makes possible and encourages planned obsolescence. To evaluate this criticism, it is necessary to distinguish what is generally meant by planned obsolescence from other types of product obsolescence. There is, on the one hand, *obsolescence of function,* which has to do with the outmoding of a product by the introduction of another that performs the same function in a better way, as illustrated by automatic home laundry equipment to replace old-fashioned wringer-type washers.

Nearly everyone welcomes and praises the obsolescence of this type and regards it as progress. On the other hand, there is *obsolescence of quality,* or deliberate under engineering of a product, so that it will wear out quickly or be used up rapidly thus, in a sense, creating and enlarging, its own replacement demand. No sensible person can condone this type of obsolescence if the manufacturer can for the same money or for very little more provide a product that would yield more lasting benefit.

Neither the obsolescence of function nor the obsolescence of under engineering of products are usually the issue when planned obsolescence is the question at debate. Such discussions usually have to do with what has been termed the *obsolescence of desirability*, for it is this type which, to the greatest degree, is made possible and greatly facilitated by advertising. In one appraisal of the subject by a well-known advertising trade publication, this type of obsolescence was defined as "yearly or other regular superficial changes in products, styling or prestige selling appeals to persuade the public to purchase new items before the old are worn out." This criticism is most frequently directed at the durable goods industries, notably automobiles and household appliances, where annual model changes are the general practice, but it also is commonly aimed at the fashion apparel industry as well.

Proponents of planned obsolescence and its antagonists to some extent are engaged in a moral debate. Planned obsolescence would be morally indefensible if advertising of regular superficial changes in products brought about increased public emphasis upon material or conspicuous consumption at the expense of the attainment of higher social goals. It is certainly not clear that this is the case.

The lesson of history is that the attainment of a high level of material well-being precedes rather than replaces the achievement of higher ranked social goals (e.g., better schools, medical care, or public recreation facilities). Moreover, public response to the marketing strategy of planned obsolescence indicates that advertising of new models is a basic appeal to a rather pervasive desire for "newness" throughout our culture. In other words, advertising reflects rather than creates the social significance widely attached to innovation and change. This viewpoint is fortified by the fact that certain products are marketed on a basis where the main appeal is the absence of annual model changes, with the claim of little or no obsolescence, owing to changes in product which are confined to functional improvement.

While nearly everyone abhors to some extent at least some aspects of planned obsolescence, even its critics see certain benefits which partially compensate for alleged wastes or abuses. Critics often seem to imply that consumers actually discard functioning products simply because they want to own a newer (but not necessarily an improved) product. Actually, second-hand automobiles, appliances, and even useful articles of clothing enter another market themselves, thus becoming worth while product acquisitions of consumers who cannot afford or who do not wish to make the monetary outlay for new items.

Moreover, there is some merit to the argument that planned obsolescence is partially a matter of planned product improvement handled on a regularly scheduled basis. Certainly it is quite frequently the case that one model of a given make of automobile is not greatly different from the preceding model. If the annual models of any make of car are compared over a long period of years, however, a much different conclusion is reached. Such a comparison brings into evidence a continuous parade of product improvement. The automobile of the early 1920's differs from the car of today by the sum of hundreds of relatively minor year-to-year advertised differences.

Solely Competitive

Another criticism is that advertising is solely competitive and that the net result is to divert demand from one good product to another which is equally good but not superior. There can be little question as to the truth of this assertion insofar as much advertising is concerned. The potential market demand determines to a considerable degree whether or not advertising has the criticized effect. In the foregoing illustration concerning air conditioning, it was assumed that the potential demand for air-conditioning equipment is great and that a part of the effect of the advertising was to develop additional primary demand. Had the illustration referred to bread, the effect would have been vastly different. Advertising of brands of bread has relatively little effect in increasing the demand for bread as a whole, since the primary demand for bread is well developed and is considered to be relatively stable. But who is to say that the market for bread is limited solely to the level of purchases of present users or whether it may be expansible in the sense of being only part of a larger market for starchy foods.

If one describes the market for this product in terms of its present and potential uses or satisfactions rather than in terms of its generic characteristics, the possibility of increasing primary demand appears to be more reasonable. Much advertising, nevertheless, is largely of a competitive nature wherein the selective buying or patronage appeals for a specific good or service have the effect of increasing or enhancing the market position of the advertiser rather than of increasing primary demand, even though the latter may be, to some extent, a by-product.

This is, however, one of the characteristics of a competitive society. Most students of the problem recognize that much competitive effort could be eliminated were it desirable to establish a more paternalistic or dictatorial form of government. Under such circumstances it might be possible to control and even to eliminate advertising that is solely competitive. But such control would be at the expense of free competition, and freedom of competition is generally believed to be so desirable as to justify some of its inherent wastes as a necessary price for its maintenance.

Inefficiency

Another alleged weakness of advertising as conducted at present in this country is its inefficiency. To be sure, some advertising is inefficient, and doubtless all advertising is less efficient than it could be. Even among large users of advertising, jokes are sometimes made about the efficiency of advertising. Sometime about 1910 George Washington Hill, famous president of the American Tobacco Company and an outst and ing innovator in advertising methods and approaches, is reputed to have said, "I am convinced that 50 per cent of our advertising is sheer waste, but I can never find out which half."

To this date, this statement is a popular quotation in advertising industry meetings and often appears in press comments about the subject.

It must be understood that advertising is a relatively new art. It is not yet a science, although scientific methods of procedure are being rapidly developed. Many valuable methods and principles have been and are being evolved as the result of the contributions of psychologists and sociologists. Such study has led to improved typography, more appealing copy, and improved layout. The more widespread practice of testing trial advertisements has eliminated considerable waste resulting from poorly conceived advertising programs. Media are now selected with more skill as a result of extensive research regarding characteristics of the circulation or audience of specific and general classes of media.

Motivation research has yielded a better knowledge of consumer buying behaviour and has enabled advertisers to harmonize selling appeals with buying motives, with the effect of minimizing waste or inefficiency in the use of advertising appropriations. Other improvements in technique are constantly being developed which will no doubt lessen some of the crudities of the past.

Progress in the application of more scientific procedures has indeed reached a point where many critics are more concerned about the efficiency rather than the inefficiency of advertising. This would certainly seem to be the view of some writers who regard advertising as an objectionable, manipulative art which causes people to do things they would not otherwise do, or which they should not do, if judged by the personal value standards of the critic.

Misleading and False

An often-heard criticism of advertising is that many advertisements are misleading or definitely false. There is no doubt that this is true. Numerous advertisers have cleverly created a misleading impression even though every statement in their message, when separately considered, is literally truthful; others have quoted carefully selected findings of authoritative research studies out of context and in such a way that the quotations are construed as a product endorsement.

Still others have artfully contrived to divert the reader's attention from the true nature of the terms of an offer by emphasizing headlines which give a false impression; additional advertisers have devised sensational tests which make a convincing sales argument but which have no relationship to the consumer's satisfaction from the use of the article.

It is nevertheless significant that the Federal Trade Commission in its examination of hundreds of thousands of magazine, newspaper, and broadcast advertisements finds that only a very small percentage contains statements that appear to be misleading or false to a degree which justifies possible action by the Commission. No responsible citizen can condone misleading or false advertising, but to condemn all of advertising because of the objectionable practices of a deceptive minority is ridiculous. The answer, rather, is to focus attention on the control of abuses.

CONTROL OF ADVERTISING

Popular credence in the printed word endows advertising with great potential power. At the same time, advertising is more or less centralized and is, therefore, susceptible to control. These factors no doubt explain in part the widespread control of advertising on the one hand and the complete absence, with but rare exceptions, of control over the broader area of personal selling on the other.

Control of advertising has been directed principally to the elimination of falsehood, fraud, and deceptive practices and the prevention of advertising of harmful products. More recently, partly in response to consumer pressure, attempts have been made to eliminate or minimize "bad taste" in advertising and to make advertising more informative and therefore more useful in making choices. Efforts at these various controls have been shared by many types of agencies and organizations.

Federal Trade Commission and Advertising.

Foremost in the control of advertising is the Federal Trade Commission which was created in 1914 by the Federal Trade Commission Act and was charged, among other things, with the responsibility of determining and preventing unfair methods of competition. One form of unfair competition is misleading advertising intended to deceive the public to the detriment or injury of competitors. The power of the Commission was greatly expanded by the passage of the Wheeler-Lea Act in 1938. This law amended the original Federal Trade Commission Act in three important respects. First, it broadened the Commission's jurisdiction to include practices that injure the public but which may not involve or injure a competitor. Prior to this amendment, action could be brought only upon complaint of a competitor who was presumably injured by an allegedly unfair practice. Now, the Commission may take action of its own accord if public injury can be shown.

The second major change pertained to the enforcement of orders issued by the Commission. The process of enforcement was regularized and shortened by making cease and desist orders of the Commission effective after 60 days unless appeals are made to the federal district courts. Furthermore, it was provided that the Commission may bring action in the federal district courts in the case of violations of such orders, and substantial penalties of $5, 000 were provided for each proved violation. It has been claimed that this penalty is not sufficiently severe because a violation may involve a considerable period of time. Some unethical advertisers doing a large volume of business found that such an amount is a small price to pay for the privilege of violation. For this reason, it has been advocated that the penalty be increased or made more severe so that a fine of $5, 000 or more may be imposed for *each day* of violation.

The most important of the three principal changes made by the Wheeler-Lea Act is that which pertains to the *advertising other than labeling of foods and drugs.* It definitely prohibits false advertising of food, drugs, cosmetics, and therapeutic devices. Certain infractions involving these items are rendered criminal when injurious to health or when involving intent to deceive or defraud, and are punishable by both fine and imprisonment.

Temporary injunctions are provided to stop these practices pending issuance of a complaint and determination of the charges. The law also permits factory inspections and forces submittal of these commodities, when required, for testing purposes; if found harmful, their sale may be prohibited. One of the effects of this law has been greater confidence in advertising by virtue of the protection afforded. Another result is greater emphasis on specific and more informative statements in advertisements. A third result has been a re-examination of products for characteristics that could be advertised under the law. This has led to research and product improvement.

Control by Other Federal Agencies

A number of other federal agencies have some control over advertising. One of great importance is the Pure Food and Drug Administration which operates under the authority of the Food, Drug and Cosmetic Act of 1938, which was an amendment to the Pure Food and Drug Act of 1906. Under the newer law, cosmetics and therapeutic devices were brought under control in addition to food and drugs; misbranding and misleading advertising of the specified products are banned; seizure of adulterated or contaminated foods is permitted; labels must warn of habit-forming drugs; factory inspections are permitted; and no drug can be placed on the market until after it has been tested to determine whether it is harmful. The various prohibitions may be enforced by injunction. Labeling must include the address of the manufacturer, packer, or distributor as well as facts concerning the quantity of the contents, major ingredients, and warnings against misuse of drugs. The Pure Food and Drug Administration works closely with the Federal Trade Commission. With respect to the selling function, the former agency is concerned primarily with packaging and brand ing. Although it watches for deceptive advertising, it usually hand s over questionable cases of advertising to the Federal Trade Commission for action.

The Alcohol and Tax Division of the Treasury Department exercises powerful control over the advertising of alcoholic products. Under federal licensing regulations, this agency may require approval of all advertising and labeling of intoxicating beverages. It is very strict in the regulation of misleading advertising and has definite requirements as to the use of names for beverages and specification of exact age, type, and alcoholic content. The Post Office Department also exerts some control. Federal laws forbid the use of the mails for fraudulent purposes. While cases are relatively rare, there have been instances where the use of the mails has been forbidden to organizations that cooperated in fraudulent advertising.

State and Local Control of Advertising.

A considerable degree of control is exercised over advertising in intrastate commerce. This has become effective through the widespread enactment of the so-called Printers' Ink Model Statute which was drawn up by the advertising trade publication of that name in 1911. The purpose of this legislation was to extend the "Truth in Advertising" movement to trade not susceptible to control by federal legislation.

It aims, in general, at preventing in an advertisement "any assertion, representation or statement of fact which is untrue, deceptive, or misleading, " by declaring such a statement a misdemeanor. This law has been enacted in 27 states and the District of Columbia, and 17 additional states have enacted adaptations of it. Only six states have no law of this kind. In addition, many cities have ordinances relating to the use of deceptive or fraudulent local advertising.

Index